THE SOVIET FAR EAST

THE SOVIET
FAR EAST

E. STUART KIRBY, B.Sc.Econ., Ph.D.

Professor of Economics
University of Aston in Birmingham

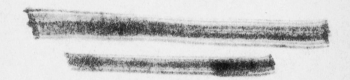

St Martin's Press

First published 1971 by
THE MACMILLAN PRESS LTD
London and Basingstoke
Associated companies in New York Toronto
Dublin Melbourne Johannesburg and Madras

Library of Congress catalog card no. 70–175931

SBN 333 12955 5

Printed in Great Britain by
R. AND R. CLARK LTD
Edinburgh

For
RUTH

Contents

List of Maps ix

List of Tables xi

Introduction xiii
Scope and method of the book

1 THE CHARACTER OF THE SOVIET FAR EAST 1
Distance. Climate and environment. The vicissitudes of planning. Natural obstacles. Population. The temperament of the Siberians. The armed frontier

2 POPULATION AND LIVELIHOOD 15
The distribution of population. Labour shortage. Migration, mobility and incentive. Privileges and inducements. Housing and amenities

3 ECONOMIC DEVELOPMENT 27
Transport and trade. Fuel and power. Other minerals. Industries. Agriculture. Forestry. Fisheries

4 TRANS-BAIKAL: THE MONGOLIAN THRESHOLD 79
Pacific watershed. Chita Province. The industries of Chita. Eastward development. Underpopulation and underdevelopment. Agriculture and transport. The central sub-region. The central south. The Argun' district, facing China. Shilka: mines and cereals. The north and the east: the outlands and the full frontier

5 AMURIA: FIRST FACE TO CHINA 97
Rich lands on China's border. The upper Amur. Food and minerals. The northern interior

6 KHABAROVSK: THE MEETING OF THE WATERS 113
Jewish Autonomous Area: far from Zion. Khabarovsk: the central city. China's easternmost frontier: the lower Ussuri. City of the Young Pioneers. Maritime Khabarovsk. The northern wastes. A new door to the westward

7   THE MARITIME PROVINCE: PACIFIC SEABOARD   137

The upper Ussuri forestry area. The fertile lakeland. The
Golden Horn. Industry and mining. Fisheries, food and elixirs.
The north-eastern Maritimes

8   YAKUTIA: MAIN HINTERLAND   168

The life of the northland. Population and occupations. Food,
trade and transport. Central Yakutsk. The north-eastern limit
of farming. Western Yakutia: the Siberian Kimberley. Mining
in the south. Yakutia to the eastward

9   MAGADAN: THE FAR NORTH-EAST   192

The Provincial capital. The Kolyma goldfields. Chukotia: the
farthest east. The central north of Magadan Province. Anadyr':
prospects of gold and oil

10   SAKHALIN: THE ISLAND BEYOND JAPAN   212

Resources. Conditions. Development in the south. Coal and
timber in the west. The undeveloped centre. The northern
oilfields

11   KAMCHATKA AND THE KURILES: PACIFIC
SCREEN   230

The isles of mist. The great peninsula. Fisheries. Inland activities. The metropolitan south-east. The central basin. The
rough south-west. The north-eastern tundra. Outwards to the
Pacific

12   SUMMARY AND CONCLUSIONS   249

Notes   255

Bibliography   258

Index   261

Maps

1   Major economic planning regions of the U.S.S.R.   7

2   Rural population density   15

3   Agricultural zones   56

4   Sown area   60

5   Fisheries areas   72

6   Trans-Baikal and South Yakutia   81

7   Amuria, Khabarovsk, the Maritimes and Sakhalin   99

8   The North and North-East   169

9   Kamchatka and the Kuriles   231

Tables

1.1 Population of the S.F.E.   11

3.1 S.F.E.'s trade with other Soviet Regions   29

3.2 Composition of trade with other Soviet Regions   30

3.3 Trade of the S.F.E. with Eastern and Western Russia   31

3.4 Pattern of freight in the S.F.E.   32

3.5 Sea-freight pattern of the S.F.E.   33

3.6 Rail-freight pattern of the S.F.E.   34

3.7 Use of fuels in the U.S.S.R.   38

3.8 Coal production in the S.F.E.   39

3.9 Soviet coal production   42

3.10 Sakhalin oil production   43

3.11 Production of electric power   44

3.12 Production of iron ore   45

3.13 Distribution of industry in the S.F.E. by Provinces   50

3.14 Light industry in the S.F.E.   53

3.15 Livestock in the S.F.E.   62

3.16 Fisheries bases in the S.F.E.   71

3.17 Distribution of the total Soviet fisheries catch, North Pacific   73

3.18 Composition of the S.F.E. fisheries catch   74

5.1 Industry in Amur Province   102

5.2 Sub-regions of Amur Province   103

6.1   Location of activities, Khabarovsk Province   118

6.2   Types of industrial activity in Khabarovsk
        Province   119

7.1   Levels of agriculture in the S.F.E.   139

8.1   Exports of the Yakut Republic   181

9.1   Occupations in Magadan Province   195

11.1 Industries of Kamchatka   235

11.2 Fisheries, Kamchatka Province   235

11.3 Agrarian activities in Kamchatka   240

Introduction

SCOPE AND METHOD OF THE BOOK

THE vast territories of the U.S.S.R. comprise about one-sixth of the land surface of the globe. Some three-quarters of this area is in Asia, reaching all across the northern half of that continent to the Pacific Ocean. This gigantic domain – which spans a quarter of the earth's circumference and is larger than all North America, with natural conditions broadly resembling those of Canada – has correspondingly enormous natural resources with prodigious economic and political potential.

The difficulties of developing this area are also tremendous; but the task is being extensively and purposefully attempted, the effort constantly enlarging in scale, deepening in skill and experience. By the 1940s the economic and strategic centre of gravity of the Soviet Union had already shifted markedly eastward beyong the Urals. Not only was the Soviet position in Central Asia consolidated but effort and investment concentrated notably on industrialisation in Siberia.

This eastward shift stood the Soviet Union in good stead in the Great Patriotic War of 1941-5 against the German invadere; it may indeed have saved the country at that time, this reservs capacity having been a practical condition of victory. The movement continues; looking ahead, the possibility must clearly be considered that ultimately this may be one of the great economic areas of the world. Perhaps the balance of world power may in the next epoch come to be centred in this great 'heartland of Eurasia', one of the last great 'challenge' areas of the world.

The question is not only that of a reassessment of the potentials of this area as against other supra-powerful bases in the world such as North America, Europe and Japan. For the major consequence is the rise of a new and most portentous confrontation between the Soviet Union and the rest of Asia, which is already growing massive and acute, particularly vis-à-vis China; the two giant Communist states are obviously now in sharp antagonism to each other, crying anathema, excommunication and war.

The Sino-Soviet rivalry can hardly be deemed merely superficial. Blood has literally been shed in the last few years, in border clashes. This is, metaphorically, on the tips of the icebergs; underneath there are massive forces moving in strong currents through chill waters at murky depths. The ideological struggle has evoked torrents of bitter and lurid abuse by each side of the other; both have uttered unforgivable words, irrevocable denunciations, insults that can never be swallowed or digested, short of a change of government in either country, an extreme ideological and strategic surrender by one or the other.

Not merely national pride is at stake, though that is a very powerful force – especially with the Chinese, in whom the concept of cultural superiority is deep and wide. Their own name for their nation is the Central Country; from their long history of a high culture, with indefinite and ever-changing frontiers surrounded by hordes of barbarians who have persistently wronged and humiliated China (the Russian 'Big Noses' having been, and continuing to be, prominent among these), the Chinese maintain this proud attitude of 'face'. The *défi* is now extended into the plane of contention for leadership of Communism and its World Revolution, beginning with influence over the 'Third World' of Asia, Africa and South America. Russia and China are in a conflict the bitterness of which recalls the great religious schisms of previous ages in the world's history.

Still deeper, more primitive or primary motivations underlie the matter. 800 million Chinese, rising soon to over 1000 million, are in dire need of *Lebensraum*; in the direct sense of more land for settlement of huge numbers, or the less direct sense of access to natural resources which would sustain China's industrialisation. One of the simplest and most immediate directions in which the Chinese may look for space and materials – in view of the complications and impracticalities of spreading into South-East Asia, or far overseas to (say) Australia or Canada – is the whole area called Siberia, largely unpopulated and with huge untapped resources. This area they may well consider their 'own back yard', in view of its proximity and relative accessibility, and also because in historical fact large tracts of it were once within the Chinese domains and allegedly inhabited or used by Chinese long before the Russians appeared there.

A recent book vividly assesses the prospect of *The Coming War between Russia and China*.[1] Such a war in some form must now seem a distinct possibility. In any case there is an extreme and acute state of conflict, in every sphere from pure theory to border-battles: in the most-used phrases of Chairman Mao, an evident state of polarised 'struggle', involving 'contradictions' which are absolute or 'antagonistic', not merely relative and 'non-hostile'.

The following pages give a full account of the Soviet Far East, i.e. the Far Eastern portion of the U.S.S.R. called in Russian *Dal'nii Vostok*. This is only one of four physical sectors on which the Sino-Soviet clash might be resolved. It involves the border-lands – spacious, rich and promising from the Chinese point of view – just over the frontiers of Manchuria, a major area of recent Chinese settlement and development, where the conditions on the two sides of the border are similar, plus a northern area beyond, which is climatically much bleaker, but as large as Western Europe. The pressure of Korea, at the south-eastern apex, must also be noted.

Moving westwards along the protracted frontier, there next intervenes another buffer state, long the scene of muffled but intense rivalry and intrigue between China and Russia – the People's Republic of Mongolia, or 'Outer' Mongolia. This state is largely under Russian influence whereas 'Inner Mongolia', to the southward, has for ages been more completely a zone of Chinese penetration and influence. The Mongols appear here as a 'buffer people', as well as a buffer state, between the Russians and the Chinese. Mongols dwell also within the Soviet Union, where they have their own Autonomous Soviet Republic, the Buryat Republic, in the Region of the Transbaikal. Russia's frontier with China's Manchuria, along the Ussuri, Amur and Argun' rivers, is about 3000 km long; its frontiers with the Mongolian Republic nearly as extensive (about 2700 km).

Thirdly, still further west, there is the large area of Chinese Turkestan, called in Chinese Hsinkiang, meaning 'the new dominion', with a large Central Asian and Muslim population;

another confrontation between the races, cultures and policies, thrusting into the Middle Asian south of the U.S.S.R. an area with its own special complexities and portents, of quite a different character to Siberia. In this region there are formidable natural barriers, great mountains and deserts, unlike the open forest-steppe of the Far Eastern frontier. China's North-West Frontier area (as we may call Hsinkiang, on the analogy of usage in India) involves a border nearly as long as the others (some 2350 km), but under quite different conditions.[2]

The fourth geo-strategic dimension, in the event of actual Sino-Soviet war, is that the issue might be settled stratospherically high above these land-fronts, by exchanges of long-distance missiles striking at the interior centres of the one country and the other. The present Russian superiority in this respect is obvious, but the Chinese are making very significant efforts. In April 1970 the Chinese put their first space-satellite into orbit. Emitting the jaunty Chinese tune ,'The East is Red', it passed over both the United States and Vladivostok[3] – a name which especially affronts the Chinese, as its Russian etymology suggests 'possessing the Orient'. The jest, popular in Russia, that this was achieved by the entire Chinese population standing on each others' shoulders and pushing together, is of course a crude witticism, but it seems metaphorically not altogether inept.

This launching implies a developing Chinese rocket-capacity to place all Siberia within reach of intermediate-range missiles. It must certainly increase the pressure of Soviet 'hawks' who urge pre-emptive action by the U.S.S.R., striking in good time and first at China's nuclear and missile capacity, centred apparently in Hsinkiang. More or less simultaneously it would be possible for the Soviets to 'take out' industrial and other bases elsewhere in China. Mao, however, believes absolutely in his guerrilla strategy: the peasant multitudes will 'encircle' and storm, by overwhelming numbers, the 'cities' or the technologically more advanced countries. He has clearly expressed his calculation that in a nuclear holocaust China with its many hundreds of millions would emerge as the dominantly populous surviving nation.[4]

Before, during and after any hypothetical Russian strikes, large numbers of Chinese, greatly outnumbering the local

Russian population, might well flow into the Soviet Far East, where the areas of Vladivostok, Khabarovsk and the upper Amur are notably vulnerable to such a large human tide. On this front also, Moscow strategists must surely ponder the advisability of pre-emptive action ahead of the Chinese, to pin them back into China proper beyond the Great Wall; mindful that the Soviet Army, in 1945, overcame the war-strained Japanese, occupied Manchuria within a few days (and, within weeks, stripped it of industrial equipment). The alternative might well be a state of confusion in the Russian Far East resembling that which prevailed in 1918-23 before the Soviet Revolution finally conquered in that area.

This book does not analyse all these strategic possibilities. It attempts a full account of the Soviet Far East, the area on the Russian side of China's North-East Frontier: an area about which the Western world knows even less than it does about China, though this region has intrinsic importance in world development and, in the perspective sketched above, being already one of the world's major confrontation-zones, may at any time suddenly become its newest battlefield.

Not that the Soviet Far East can be studied in isolation as a self-contained unit. The planned development of the U.S.S.R. proceeds in an absolutely integral way, nationwide for the whole Soviet Union; the Soviet Far East is greatly linked with the next major Soviet Region to its westward, Eastern Siberia, and onwards in a working net with Central Asia, Western Siberia, the Ural Region and European Russia. The following pages, while summarising all the available information about the Soviet Far East – with special reference to a comparative spate of published information in the mid-1960s in the Soviet Union, after decades (and even centuries) of secrecy, though by the late 1960s the flow of information was again diminishing – must therefore treat it as distinctly part of pan-Russian developments and policies.

In the 1930s one writer aptly described Manchuria as 'the Cockpit of Asia'.[5] That was the time of Japan's onslaught on China. Now the contestants are Russia and China, and the arena extends critically to Russia's furthest, most exposed and least developed flank – the Pacific seaboard and its hinterland. There is a considerable literature in English and other world languages on China and the borderlands on its side, also on Siberia more generally, but practically none on the Soviet Far East as such. The present work attempts to fill that gap.

Some practical points may be noted. A bibliography, maps, index and gazetteer are provided. Footnotes are used only for sources and references; all substantive material is in the text-pages. Metric measures have been used throughout, but 'billion' is used in the American way (1,000,000,000). 'Soviet Far East' is abbreviated 'S.F.E.' in this book; it refers generally to the whole area east of Lake Baikal. 'The Region' refers, however, to the U.S.S.R.'s Major Economic Planning Region of the Far East, which excludes the Buryat Republic, Chita Province and (in recent years) the Yakut Republic. In Russia as in other countries, 'Siberia' is used loosely for the whole area east of the Ural mountains and north of Central Asia; this is divided, how-ever, into the Major Economic Planning Regions of the Ural, Western Siberia, Eastern Siberia and the S.F.E. The term 'region' is also used, by the Russians as by others, in several ways: for climatic, geographical or economic regions, etc. But by the Russians it is used in yet another way: their *rayon* is also a 'district', a unit of local government. The Russian adminis-trative nomenclature is further ignored in this book by render-ing both *krai* and *oblast'* as 'Province'; the Maritimes (Primor'ye, 'the seaboard') and Khabarovsk are *krai*, Chita, Amur, Maga-dan, Kamchatka and Sakhalin (which includes, since 1945, the Kuriles) are *oblasti*. Similarly 'District' or 'Area' are used here for the Jewish Autonomous *oblast'* of Khabarovsk Province and the Koryak National *okrug* of Kamchatka, none of these terms being material to real issues.

Direct transliteration is used, with 'e' usually to be pro-nounced 'ye' as in 'yet', sometimes 'yo', though accepted English usages like Soviet, Komsomol, Moscow, are retained.

Equally simplistic are the separation of potatoes from (other) 'vegetables', the inclusion of whaling with 'fishing', of other agrarian pursuits with 'agriculture', etc., following the local and general usages.

The aim is a practical and realistic description, in all the dimensions – not merely the econometric but also the natural, historical and human perspectives of this important area and its people. The method is as follows: the first three chapters survey the macro-problems of the S.F.E.; Chapters 4 to 7 portray the Provinces in detail; there follows a brief summary, textual notes and a bibliography. Finally there is a full index, which also serves as a gazetteer, the places named being grid-referenced on the maps in this book.

CHAPTER 1

The Character of the Soviet Far East

DISTANCE

'SIBERIA' conveys to the mind of the whole world vastness, loneliness, hardship, unendurable cold, with great wealth perhaps in such things as gold and furs, but inaccessible, except at dreadful human cost. These perspectives apply no more and no less than they do to the very comparable areas of Canada, Alaska, Lapland. Distance is certainly the first dimension; from Murmansk to the Bering Strait along the Arctic Circle is roughly 12,000 kilometres, from westernmost Alaska to the east coast of Newfoundland about 9000, while Canada's greatest expanse from north to south is some 6400. From Vladivostok to Uelen on the Bering Strait is 4280 km in linear distance, 4800 by sea; from Vladivostok to Moscow by rail 9200. These are approximately twice and three times the west to east and south to north dimensions of Russia-in-Europe (Kaliningrad–Sverdlovsk 2500, Sebastopol–Murmansk about 3000).

It is well known that the Soviet Union has developed greatly eastwards, tending to shift its 'centre of gravity', from the industrial and strategic points of view especially, distinctly beyond the Urals. Industrialisation has reached the area of Irkutsk on Lake Baikal, but there is little in the S.F.E., and the nearest major or 'complex' industrial base for the S.F.E. (other than Japan or China) is the area of Cheremkhovo or the Kuznetsk Basin, which is over 4000 km from Vladivostok and well over 3000 from Khabarovsk. In this and every other aspect the S.F.E. depends vitally on transport, in particular the great Trans-Siberian Railway, which is both its artery and its backbone. The layout, depending on the main railway which traverses the gentler southern part of the country, while forests, rich minerals and tundra lie out to the vast northward, is broadly reminiscent

of Canada – more strictly, of Canada before the modern highway era, since Siberia has hardly any modern highways; also
of the perspective that Siberia and the S.F.E. must contain
similar potentials of economic and general development. This
is the greatest untapped store of natural resources in the world,
its major remaining Development Area.

The overwhelming consequence is that transport costs are
extremely high. Inter-regional division of labour, territorial
specialisation, is inhibited. The S.F.E. is dependent on supplies
from great distances, and has to hold a high ratio of inventories
to current production. Reliance on local production is encouraged – or almost inevitable. This is a 'high friction' economy,
'driving in low gear', 'the productivity return is high, but
the locational return is low'; such are the comments of the
Soviet Academy of Sciences.[1]

If the Region were linked economically with the Pacific and
Asia, particularly Japan and China, the picture would be quite
different. But the Soviets, at this eastern end especially, have
eschewed any major dealings with capitalist states (since about
1930 at least, when the New Economic Policy and the granting
of concessions to foreign operators for mining and other enterprises, which lasted longer in the S.F.E. than in the rest of
Russia, came to an end). The expressed reason is that such
dealings would expose the U.S.S.R. to dependence on world
prices, the notorious instability of capitalism; doubtless other
kinds of 'contamination' were also feared. (In the aspect of
prices, the context[2] also hints that Soviet production could not
compete with world-market prices.) Nevertheless, a major
scheme of Japanese collaboration in the economic development
of the S.F.E. and Eastern Siberia is being elaborated. Meanwhile, trade and other relations with Communist China have
greatly declined since the breach between the two countries
about 1960; on this background, the U.S.S.R. turns to economic relations with Japan, considering also Japan's prodigious
advance in industry and technology, besides increasing its trade
(and naval activity) in the rest of Asia.

CLIMATE AND ENVIRONMENT

The second factor to be considered is the hardness of the environment. The coldness of Siberia is proverbial. The temperatures range down to world records in winter, though -30 to $-40°C$ are more typical. In the brief summers the temperature rises to 20–25° or more above zero. It must be stressed that the winter cold is more bearable than is widely supposed, because of the extreme dryness of the air. Again, high cost is the most obvious economic consequence, with additional building and heating requirements, the difficulty and slowness of all operations in winter.

The summer lasts only from eight to ten weeks in Chukotia (the Far North-East), ten to twelve in Kamchatka, sixteen to eighteen in the Aldan–Okhotsk area, twenty to twenty-six in the Amur basin and the Maritimes, twenty to twenty-two in Sakhalin and twenty-four to twenty-eight in the Kuriles. But the thaw is mostly very partial; over much the greater part of the area the soil is always frozen, often to great depths (600 metres in the north). This is the permafrost – which, in places, has been there for centuries – patchy and unstable, but generally in process of secular 'degradation'. Extending as far south as the frontier in Chita Province and a little north of the Amur in Khabarovsk Province, permafrost underlies a good half of the S.F.E. It greatly complicates all building and civil engineering works, raising all construction costs by a good 30 per cent. As forests are cut, towns extended, dams built, permafrost is expanding under them, rather than contracting; or the alternation of thawing and hardening is accentuated, hence the instability of structures.

All the seas of the S.F.E. are frozen for part of the winter; even at Vladivostok and Nakhodka, some use of icebreakers is necessary. The iciness has minor compensations; vast 'tracts' on open land and many waterways can be used for sled or vehicle transport while they are hard, in the north mine shafts and adits are cut without pitprops, the cost of making rough roads is halved in winter. But King Frost is far more cursed than blessed.

In the summer, the sharpest curses are perhaps for the mosquitos, leeches and other insect pests. Then there is the monsoon; 60 per cent of the precipitation in the S.F.E. is in the warmer half of the year, bringing disastrous floods. All the riverine areas of the Region are extremely marshy, always either icy or waterlogged. This affects the frontier zone especially. In the Amur Province alone, 48,000 sq km are subject to floods. The incidence is especially in summer and autumn, but for snow-fed rivers also in spring. In the sixty-three years 1896 to 1958 there were 'unusually prolonged' floods in forty-three years. 'There is no definite periodicity' and the damage is always severe. 1928 was one very bad year, when the whole southern part of the S.F.E. was affected by the inundation of the Amur basin; yet the Amur Province alone, in 1953, suffered economic damage from floods eight times greater than the total losses in the S.F.E. in 1928. And in 1958 flood-losses in the Amur, Maritime and Khabarovsk Provinces were no less than thirty times greater than those of 1928.[3]

Paradoxically, in this land of extremes and uncertainties, the farmed areas are also affected by intermittent droughts, caused by the next unfavourable factor to be listed, the changing winds. Long-term records show dry winds, reducing the moisture in plants and roots to between 27 and 63 per cent below the required amount, for periods of six to nine days in April, six to eight in May, two to four in September and three to six in October. Water conservancy works have done little to offset these difficulties; they have been found to raise the winter temperatures only one or two degrees, lower the summer ones one or two degrees, raise the relative humidity some 5 per cent and increase the annual precipitation only insignificantly.

In the coastal Provinces storm winds are the greater menace. In Kamchatka and the Kuriles they reach velocities of 40 metres per second, diminishing in the mainland interior to between 2 and 4 metres a second. It has been calculated that 646 billion kW of power could be generated by harnessing the winds; unsuccessful experiments were made in Kamchatka about 1960, when storms destroyed the generators, but efforts continue.

The rivers provide some facility for transport – but practically all run the wrong way, into the empty northlands (only the Amur system runs west to east, in its upper and middle stretches, but then turns north). All of them freeze in winter, the small ones down to their beds. The Kolyma and Anadyr' are ice-covered for seven to eight months in the year, the Kamchatka rivers for five and a half to six, the Aldan–Okhotsk watershed for seven to seven and a half, the northern part of the Amur basin for five and a half to six, its southern part for four. At the beginning and end of the icing they are encumbered by floes; in autumn for three to four weeks in the case of the northern rivers, only one to one and a half weeks in the southern parts, in spring for about one month in both the north and the south. Sakhalin is tempered by its island position; its rivers freeze for only two and a half months, often not thickly, and the spring floe does not last more than two weeks.

The flood problem is far more complex than just a question of the summer rains. There are thousands of lakes, surrounded by tundra or swampy forest (taiga), moss beds or sedgy marshes, sometimes turf; a chronic state of waterlogging almost everywhere. The subsoil waters have roughly the same levels as the rivers. On the lowland, the whole is a 'self-regulating' system, unless and until the total moisture becomes excessive and the system is overloaded, when water spreads everywhere; while, under the higher slopes and terraces, water is held above the river-levels – often in the form of unstable permafrost, or pocketed in ice-formations – emerging torrentially at times. Even outside the permafrost belt, in the Maritimes for example, there is flooding due to the soil being impermeable, or to the jamming of ice floes, floating timber, etc.

Kamchatka and the Kuriles are highly volcanic; Sakhalin, the Maritime, Khabarovsk and Amur Provinces mildly so. This occasions such amenities as hot springs or spa resorts (forty in the Maritimes), but renders Kamchatka, Sakhalin and the Kuriles liable to earthquakes and tidal waves. Shocks of 6 to 12 points on the seismic scale are recorded. This is another factor raising construction costs locally – by 4 per cent in force 7 areas, 8 per cent in force 8 localities and 12 per cent where force 9 is allowed for, though different allowances are made for various structures, rather than by geographic zones.

THE VICISSITUDES OF PLANNING

Thus Nature imposes seven plagues on Siberia – distance and isolation, cold, pests, floods, droughts, winds and earthquakes. Against these must of course be set the present and potential wealth of the Region, apart from considerations of strategic value, national prestige or sentiment. The Soviet Union is making enormous, sometimes impressive, efforts to offset or abolish all these adversities, to develop the amenities of modern living in the northlands. Electricity is the magic word. Besides transforming industrial and domestic conditions, it is envisaged as applicable to agriculture, both through mechanisation and by heating not only greenhouses but the soil itself.

Yet, in respect of distance and isolation, Soviet policy has accentuated rather than combated the difficulty. It has subjected this Region to its policy of autarchic Soviet economic development, isolating it from interchanges with Pacific countries, particularly the neighbouring Asian lands which would seem most important and natural to its eventual development. The sole exceptions are first a brief honeymoon with Communist China during the 1950s, ending in a bitter estrangement, and second the recent opening of economic talks with Japan.

Soviet policy has also accentuated the effect of distance. Not only the S.F.E. and all Siberia, but most of European Russia also – the entire expanse from White Russia on the Polish border and the Baltic States to the Pacific within telescope-sight of the United States (near Alaska) and Japan (in the southern Kuriles) – forms one great political unit. This is the R.S.F.S.R. (Russian Soviet Federated Socialist Republic). Political and administrative centralisation is extreme, the machinery prodigiously bureaucratic. All sorts of decisions for and about the S.F.E., of immediate as well as long-term significance, are taken in Moscow, the capital of this super-Republic that embraces more than three-quarters of the U.S.S.R. – a place distant about one-third of the circumference of the globe at its latitude from Russia's Farthest East. It is, in terms merely of distance, as if Singapore and Cape Town were ruled from London; or the District of Columbia removed, not merely to Alaska, but beyond Hawaii. Incidentally this illustrates the falsity of the impression that the Soviets have abolished the name 'Russia'; this is the Russian Federation.

Consequently there is an unceasing flow of complaints from the S.F.E. about the ineptitudes of remote planning and remote control; its slowness and lack of dynamism (in an area which should by now, in the view of local patriots – which Siberians

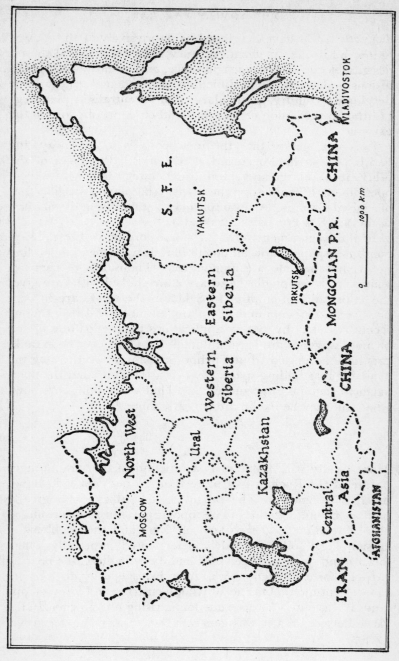

Map 1   Major economic planning regions of the U.S.S.R.

distinctly are – have developed as impressively as the United States did in the nineteenth century); the decisions taken and designs selected in extreme ignorance, or disregard of local conditions and needs. Such difficulties are endemic in any large developing country, particularly under centralised planning; but the Soviet Union carries this kind of 'contradiction' to the extreme.

It is not merely that the metropolis is so far away, the R.S.F.S.R. so heterogeneous. Each of the Provinces of the S.F.E. itself is large and complicated enough to generate these operational difficulties, on the managerial plane as well as that of general planning. An example may be taken from the smallest of the S.F.E.'s Provinces – Sakhalin.

In the Region generally in 1966, according to the railwaymen's newspaper, 'non-fulfilment of railway-waggon unloading norms has become a commonplace. Thousands of cars are waiting to be emptied, the wharves are choked with cargo, yet the ships sail half-empty.' In Sakhalin the tracks are in very poor condition; maintenance plans are not fulfilled, let alone reconstruction. 'Every day applications for the loading of 500 or more waggons are left unfulfilled. . . . [Yet] over 6000 tank-cars have accumulated at Yuzhno-Sakhalinsk, overflowing the available marshalling-space. . . . It is astounding that the management remains unperturbed. . . . That's how things are now; what will they be like in a few years' time?'[4]

NATURAL OBSTACLES

More locally still, isolation is a function of the mountainous nature of the Region. Not more than 20 per cent is lowland, much of it marshy. The ranges, cold and exposed, greatly hamper communications. The topography must be considered also in relation to the pattern of rivers and the problems of erosion. The soils are widely deteriorated, especially where forest stands have not been well maintained; there, the bearing capacity for constructions was given in 1966 as 2·5 to 3 kg per square centimetre. On the alluvial, lacustrian and forest-steppe lands it was only 1 kg on sandy loam, rising to 4 on clay. In the Zeya–Bureya area it was generally 1·5 to 2, rising on gravel to 3·5.

There are 17,000 rivers in the Region, ranging in length from 10 to nearly 5000 km but mostly short, chiefly on the foothills (hence torrential), only four, the Amur, Kolyma, Anadyr' and Zeya, exceeding 1000 km. The depth of water is about three times the average of rivers at the same latitude in European Russia. In the mountains the flow represents 80 or 90 per cent of the annual precipitation, on the plains 30 or 40 per cent. The whole Amur is mainly rainwater-fed (75-80 per cent), to a less extent snow-fed (15-20 per cent) and augmented from subsoil waters (5-8 per cent); whereas further north snow-water predominates (50-60 per cent), rain contributes 30-40 per cent and ground-water 10 per cent. The seasonal consequences in terms of flooding, the damage to the great number of bridges and conservancy works that are necessary may easily be deduced.

Rivers and mountains suggest hydroelectric power. The potential of the Amur basin is given as nearly 50 million kW. But this could only be developed in collaboration with China; the experts of the two countries made a major survey together in the earlier 1950s, but the breach followed and present negotiations are only on navigation, boundary demarcations, etc. Only one large project is in hand, on the Zeya river in Soviet Amuria. Any such on the lower reaches would seriously affect the fisheries. Industrial pollution is just beginning to threaten the S.F.E.: at two places only, as regards water pollution, namely in connection with chemical-paper plants at Komsomolsk on the Amur and at the southern end of Lake Baikal. Urban smog is a slight problem; curiously, it exists in the north, where palls of smoke and moisture hang above the settlements in the still Arctic air.

No chemical fertilisers are produced in the S.F.E. The soils are not of high grade, except in the 'black earth-like' pockets of the Zeya–Bureya and Lake Khanka areas; and there are difficulties of choice. Local specifications are exacting, especially in the forest-steppelands where chemicals could be best applied; most of the soils are deficient in phosphorus, nitrates are in many cases only useful on a phosphate base, potassium is rather ineffective.

The sea is another dimension of the Region. The waters are cold, but full of fish and other marine foods; some exotics con-

tinue to be taken for the Oriental markets. Octopus fishing
began off Sakhalin in 1967. Sea transport is not well developed,
because of the unpopulated state of the coasts and the physical
difficulties. There is ice, in crust, pack and floes. The west coast
of Kamchatka has many sandbars. In many other places,
notably the Amur estuary, ships have to lie off and be lightered
at heavy charges. There are the storms, tidal waves and winds,
already mentioned. In the Japan Sea fogs prevail for one day
in three in spring and summer, necessitating extra radar
equipment. They are effects of the cold currents, which help
navigation to the northward, but slow southward passages.
There are very high tides in places. This is another potential
source of power which has been studied, on the basis of experiments on the White Sea in European Russia, with reference
especially to the 13-metre tide-lift in the northern Okhotsk Sea,
where a potential of 20 million kW is estimated, with hypothetical stations in the Shelekhov and Penzhinsk gulfs putting
out 170 billion and 47 billion kWh a year respectively.

POPULATION

The world knows Siberia, next, as a vast prison. Over centuries,
convicts and political prisoners or exiles have been sent there,
and forced labour has been a key means of developing it. Under
the Tsars, conditions for the 'politicals' were almost genteel.
Lenin's place of Siberian exile, for example, was a decent house.
Those of the convicts were not so bestial as the concentration
camps established in the Stalin era. Chekhov's book on his visit
to Sakhalin in 1890 defines conditions less utterly degrading
than those of Stalin's Siberian and Far Eastern camps. (On the
latter, see Conquest, 1968.) Stalin's camps in the Kolyma goldfields and elsewhere were closed about 1956, shortly after his
death; but milder forms of banishment persist.

Loneliness would seem to be the general condition, since the
overall average density of population in the S.F.E. is less than
1·5 persons per square kilometre. However, a startlingly large
proportion live in towns or townships, some in large cities
(200,000-400,000 people). No less than 75 per cent of the
population is now 'urban' (this expression including some small

townships). The sparseness of population in the outlands is accordingly marked – though, while some fishers, trappers, prospectors for minerals and rare plants, or others, still operate essentially in loneliness, even these activities have been collectivised, in the Soviet way of life.

Table 1.1   Population of the S.F.E.

	Total (millions)	Of which Urban (millions)	(per cent)
1897 (census)	0·37	0·08	(27 per cent)
1911 (est.)	0·87	0·25	(29 per cent)
1926 (census)	1·26	0·34	(27 per cent)
1939 (census)	2·56	1·27	(50 per cent)
1959 (census)	4·35	3·03	(70 per cent)
1964 (est.)	4·68	3·46	(74 per cent)

The natural rate of increase is high (about 2·2 per cent per annum, cf. about 1·7 per cent for the U.S.S.R. as a whole). The population is predominantly young, the sexes fairly equally balanced, though many of the young people work only for a time in the Region. The population, too, is extraordinarily mobile between employments, to the extent of instability. This is avowedly a frontier land, only beginning to tap its vast resources.

THE TEMPERAMENT OF THE SIBERIANS

Despite all the difficulties – or perhaps in response to the challenges – the morale of the Soviet Siberians and Far Easterners is apparently high. It has had some literary and artistic expression. During the Second World War, when the spread of industries to Eastern Siberia contributed greatly to the Russian stand, Siberian and Far Eastern regiments played a notable part. The pride of these people in their way of life and their land, their frank and realistic manner, are conveyed even to the most casual traveller, who may also happily encounter their remarkable hospitality. Very marked also – tell it not in Gath – is their ingrained individualism or love of personality. These people are characteristically adventurous immigrants, finders of 'space to live' (room for the mind, as well as the

elbows) in these wide landscapes; or trappers, hunters, marks-
men, skiers, fishers, prospectors, handymen. Prisoners released
from Stalin's eastern camps elected, in many cases, to remain
in the Region rather than return to western Russia and the
remembrances of even older sufferings.

The guerrilla tradition is strong, locally the supreme tradition
of the Revolution, the long Civil War and foreign intervention
which caused particular confusion and damage in this Region.
They are determined not to repeat that ordeal; if it is forced
upon them again, as they take the Chinese vociferations to
imply, they appear extraordinarily confident that the Soviet
Partisans, alongside their Red Army with its modern equipment, can make short work of the Chinese hordes.

THE ARMED FRONTIER

This Region confronts – to use a current and appropriate term
– both the present and the future with some confidence. In the
long run its prodigious resources must ensure spectacular economic and technical development; the wealth is so great that
even an inept handling can only slow down and postpone that
development. Immediately, the confrontation is with Mao's
China, in which this is a main part of the long frontier. It is
necessary to bear in mind the whole extent and depth of the
Sino-Soviet quarrel. This is by far the longest international
boundary in the world. It is now also the most heavily armed.
It is divided into three sections. The first faces Hsinkiang,
where the Chinese have located a main part of their nuclear
and rocket developments. This sector of the frontier is mostly
very mountainous (10,000-25,000 ft); it will be recalled, however, that Chinese Liberation Forces have crossed similar obstacles into India.

Next to the east is the People's Republic of Mongolia (M.P.R.),
allied with the Soviet Union and co-operating with it politically,
militarily, economically and generally. The national (Mongol)
and Buddhist heritages are variously strong in that sector. The
terrain is broadly flat desert, still partly the domain of nomadic
pursuits, though settled agriculture is much more widespread
in the M.P.R. than is generally realised in the West. To its

southward and eastward, where Inner Mongolia is under
Chinese suzerainty, Chinese immigration and other pressures
are resented by the Mongols.

The heirs to Jenghis Khan – such expansionist formulae are
strong and recurrent among the Mongols – reside partly in the
Soviet Union (Buryatia, with some 160,000 Mongols, but about
four times that number of Russians), partly in the M.P.R.
(population about one million, practically all Mongols) and in
some large but less defined numbers within China. The pressures of both Sinification and Russification may be resented,
but clearly material and technological benefits, with more concessions to the independent spirit of the Mongols, sway that
people towards the Soviet Union. For example, the M.P.R.,
which is anxious to enhance its international standing and
statehood, is a member of the Comecon, unlike People's China,
North Korea and North Vietnam who have not been made
members.

East of the M.P.R., all along the Amur and Ussuri rivers to
Vladivostok, is the frontier of the S.F.E., China's North-East
Frontier. Here, in the Amur, Khabarovsk and Maritime Provinces are areas claimed by China as having been taken from
that country by duress and chicanery. This is the empty quarter
to which the immense and growing Chinese population may
mainly look.

It is notable that each of these three sections of the frontier
rivals in length the celebrated 'Iron Curtain' of Europe around
Greece, Yugoslavia, Austria and West Germany. There are
even some curious geopolitical similarities. In each case one end
of the line abuts on the Near Eastern and Islamic world; in the
middle are divided peoples – the Mongols and the Germans;
at the other end of the line the Soviet Union reaches the ocean
and the vicinity of major industrial areas, Western Europe and
Japan. Moreover, the main weight of Soviet armour appears
clearly to have been mustered along the Sino-Soviet border.
In the latter part of 1970 the Soviet order of battle was believed
to be as follows: '28 divisions in Mongolia and the Far East
military district, 34 divisions in the southern and southern-
central Asian military districts'. This compares with 20 in
Germany, 6 or 7 in Czechoslovakia, 2 in Poland and 4 in
Hungary. There are 148 Soviet divisions altogether, or nearly

2 million men. Thus over 40 per cent are facing China directly; and some part of the remaining centrally based 22 per cent are presumably east of the Urals.[5] The above figures include ground forces only. The Chinese have presumably massed some equivalent weight on their side of the line; but (despite having recently put up a satellite and exploded their tenth nuclear device) the Chinese must feel relatively very vulnerable in the air, in the stratosphere and at sea.

The U.S.S.R. is deemed to have 10,200 combat aircraft, 1300 inter-continental ballistic missiles, 70 nuclear submarines (25 in the Far East), 300 conventional submarines (80 in the Far East), 170 missile-carrying ships (with a larger proportion in the Far East – 86) and merchant shipping totalling nearly 14 million tons.[6] The Director of the Japanese Defence Agency stated in 1965 that at that time the Soviet Union had 3000 military aircraft in the S.F.E.[7] To all this, China has little riposte in ultra-modern weapons; in the event of hostilities China's industrial capacity, at least, could presumably be promptly eliminated, leaving some millions of people armed largely with scorched red booklets. Such is the character of the S.F.E. – and its portentous position in this fissile world. The following chapters consider various practical aspects in increasing detail.

CHAPTER 2

Population and Livelihood

THE DISTRIBUTION OF POPULATION

THE population of the S.F.E. is not large. The terms are relative: 4,347,000 people in 1959, over 5 millions now, is a considerable number. Four nations in Europe, two in Africa, one
in Oceania, even two in Asia, have less (Denmark, Finland,

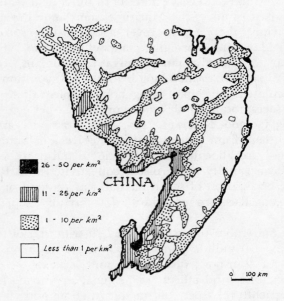

Map 2   Rural population density

Eire, Norway, Libya, Zambia, New Zealand, Israel, Lebanon).
The population is small in relation to the area; the average
density is not more than 1·5 persons per square kilometre,
overall. However, being 75 per cent urban, it is more 'mobilised'
from the military and economic points of view than would
appear at first sight. Though the outlands are indeed 'empty'
even there it is a question of numerous small groups. The density
varies greatly; it is over 9 per sq. km in the Southern Maritimes,
over 7 in southern Sakhalin, just over 2 in the Amur Province,
only 1·5 in Khabarovsk Province, but 4·7 in its Jewish Autonomous Area. For all the rest the figure is only in the range of
0·1 to 0·5.

The population is evidently small in relation to that of China,
which has 50 millions in nearby Manchuria alone. In that
connection the Russianness of the S.F.E. population is note-
worthy. It is marked everywhere, both numerically and qualitatively; most of all in the Maritime and Amur Provinces. In
those Provinces there are, however, also Ukrainians and, in the
Southern Maritimes especially, compact groups of White Russians, Tartars, Mordvinians, Chuvash, Estonians, Latvians;
many of these were formed long before the Revolution and are
well assimilated. The small indigenous peoples, about a dozen
tribes or races, totalled only 43,800 or about 1 per cent in 1959,
against 3,530,700 Russians, 429,500 Ukrainians and some
700,000 others from places west of the Region. Some of the
'aborigines' are allocated large 'National' Districts, but their
life has been rapidly modernised, collectivised and Russified.
After the occupation of south Sakhalin at the end of the war
some 400,000 Russians moved into that territory, replacing the
Japanese.

In the mid-1960s the occupational distribution of the work
force, some 1·6 million persons, showed the high proportions
required for transport, distribution and services. 31 per cent
were in factories and offices, 15 per cent in transport, 15 per
cent in agriculture, 7 per cent in construction, and 26 per cent
in distribution, trade and services. 3-4 per cent are in education
and the arts. These may be included in services above, miners
may be included in 'factories' and foresters in 'agriculture'; the
Soviet statements are not given in complete detail. The administration is certainly large, including the political apparatus.

There are various paramilitary organisations as well as the regular forces and police. In March 1965 the Khabarovsk *Young Communist* newspaper praised the special Youth Organisations which had been formed to help the frontier guards. Political education is naturally stressed; in 1969 there were seven hundred 'Leninist lecturers' constantly at work in the Maritime Province alone, according to its Head of Agitprop Department.[1] Thus the State apparatus may well account for the residue of 6 per cent which can be deduced from the above figures. The proportion of people directly engaged in manufacturing, especially, is low, and most of the factory work in the S.F.E. consists of processing operations rather than manufacturing; the natural conditions compel a large part of the labour to be expended in mere maintenance and repair work.

LABOUR SHORTAGE

The most vital requirement for the S.F.E. and Siberia is to raise the total population and to increase and improve the effective work force. A huge immigration from European Russia is the overall aim, necessarily a long-term one; but the immediate, compelling requirement is to increase the labour force; directly and primarily in terms of sheer numbers, but especially the supply of semi-skilled and skilled workers who are scarce, and highly skilled workers who are very scarce; that is, to raise the average levels of skills. Per 1000 workers the proportion with 'middle or higher' qualifications was, in 1967, 102 for the R.S.F.S.R. as a whole, as high as 107 in Western Siberia, but 97 in Eastern Siberia and 96 in the S.F.E.[2] It is also imperative to reduce the fluidity and increase the stability and permanence of the work force, for a very high proportion has consisted and still consists of persons (especially young persons) who come to the S.F.E. for only a short period, while older people move out, or retire elsewhere. Moreover, this kind of transitoriness has in recent years been superimposed on an underlying tidal ebb: the drift, all over the Soviet Union, of people away from the bleaker parts of the country to the more pleasant and fertile areas, usually the southern parts. This is quite understandable and is the trend in many other countries. While Siberia was

losing, in 1959-67, a quarter of a million people (net), the population of the Northern Caucasus rose through immigration (as
much from European Russia as from elsewhere) by half a million.

It is widely asserted that Siberia in general, including the
Far East, has suffered a net decline of population for many
years now. From what has just been said, it might well appear
to be so, but the census figures do show an increase since the
natural rate of growth is high. The question is complex and it
seems that the S.F.E. has not suffered from these tendencies so
badly, or in exactly the same combination, as other areas.
Reference in most of the statements quoted is to 'Siberia',
which should properly mean the Planning Regions of West
Siberia and East Siberia, but may loosely be extended to the
whole country east of the Urals, except Central Asia. Conditions
change from one period to another. Monetary and other incentives, reduced drastically after Stalin's death, have recently
been restored. Some of those who left Siberia proper went, not
to European Russia, but to the S.F.E. Within the S.F.E., there
is southward movement; the Trans-Siberian railway belt distinctly possesses comparative advantages.

In the much shorter run, reliance is avowedly on rationalising
the use of the present work force, or a moderately growing work
force, by improving the structure, pattern and location of industry in the Region, improving the utilisation and productivity
of labour and making fuller use of it, especially of any unem-
ployed or underemployed persons. One immediate aspiration,
constantly voiced, is to make more use of the female population
and other dependants. For example, the Academy of Sciences
stresses that towns in the process of formation (such as Nakhodka,
Ussurisk and Artem) have from 14 per cent to 25 per cent of
their inhabitants not gainfully occupied; these are, for the most
part, the 'second members of families', whom it is imperative to
draw into productive work. A manager is quoted as saying 'the
sole outlay would be for buses; the wives of the power-station
workers have their housing provided by the plant.'[3]

MIGRATION, MOBILITY AND INCENTIVE

The last words show where the rub is, for each of the necessary policies – mass immigration, improvement of skills, or inducing workers to stick to their jobs and their wives to take up employment – depends on the provision of all sorts of infrastructural facilities to make this possible, plus powerful incentives to make it attractive. It is not merely a question of making buses available, but of adequate housing, education, civic facilities, recreation, health services, crèches and the like, plus adequate pay. The position may be most vividly illustrated by presenting a number of examples, selected at random, as follows. The labour-shortage is general, affecting agriculture and services as well as factory-industry, though Soviet utterances tend to feature the latter.

The overall population problem is much discussed. It was officially avowed that 'over the five years 1959-63, a quarter of a million more people left Siberia than arrived there'.[4] In Chita Province, in 1966, 5000 new rural settlers arrived, but 12,000 left. 'In 1968 alone, one and a half million people left Siberia', reported a leading national newspaper;[5] but this presumably refers to 'Siberia' in the widest sense. In 1969 the leading economic journal reported on the background of the labour shortage as follows. In the S.F.E. local agriculture supplies only 30 per cent of the local needs; in some parts, the ratio for vegetables is only 20 per cent, for fruit 10-15 per cent. Owing to the bad condition of agriculture and the net emigration, the Collective farms of Western Siberia are only 70 per cent manned. But those of the Far East are even worse off; the average work load per worker is about double the all-Union average. Enterprises in the Far East are often working at 30 per cent below their capacity, and the seasonal variations are very marked. This article gave the net annual outflow of people from 'Siberia' (again, probably exclusive of the S.F.E.) as 700,000 – though the gigantic sum of 300 billion roubles has been spent on fostering the settlement of people beyond the Urals.[6]

PRIVILEGES AND INDUCEMENTS

In the twenties and thirties and later, voluntary settlers received material inducements, which were very large by Soviet standards. These 'Stalin privileges' were withdrawn in 1956. Cer-

tainly, in the early 1960s, the loss of differential income was
sharply felt in the S.F.E., though 'objective' conditions were
improving there; and in 1964 it was noted by a national
scientific congress that 'in recent years our Far East as a whole
was characterised by a negative migration balance'.[7] Sakhalin
was given as an example: it showed a net emigration in 1955-7
which was temporarily outweighed by the natural growth, but
from 1957 there was a net decline.

This topic has not been so prominent in the S.F.E. recently:
some say because of official discouragement of statements on the
matter, others because, in that Region at least, population
growth has resumed. At all times there have been other official
statements contradicting such revelations as the foregoing and
asserting big plans for future immigration. In 1967, for example,
a leading national economic newspaper asserted that 'between
1939 and 1961, the population of Eastern Siberia increased by
2·2 millions; by 1980, it is intended to have 12·7 millions, more
than five times the pre-war population. The same tempo is
intended for the S.F.E.'[8] Such optimistic strains are of course
sounded especially in connection with the quite frequent,
though sporadic, 'drives' to enlist immigrants. One medium is
that of sentimental journalism. The *Young Communist* newspaper,
in 1962, discussing the difficulties of settlers in Chita Province,
made much of propagandist correspondence under the title 'I
Love Life', drawing 5000 letters from people wishing to emi-
grate, especially to Chita Province.[9] Many examples of this sort
could be given, including women's-magazine stories of 'how
she got her man – in the Far East'.

When the heads come to be counted at the recruiting stations,
rather than the heartbeats in the *feuilletons*, it appears that the
recruitment of Young Communist League members for service
in the S.F.E. has not been pressed with consistent energy. The
first national 'Rally' to call for 'construction shock-brigaders'
for this was in Krasnoyarsk in 1963. Eight hundred took part
from eighteen Provinces between the Urals and the Pacific. At
that time there were in the Soviet Union altogether 130 All-
Union Komsomol Construction Projects, but only 34 of these
took part in this rally. It was six years before another such *slyot*
was convened, meeting in Novokuznetsk in June 1969 with a
thousand delegates representing 'all 42' of that category of

projects. It was noted that the difficulties were poor housing, low pay and too much manual labour for the volunteers. The Central Committee of the Party had, however, formulated plans for the development of Siberia and the S.F.E. during the 1930s which would require sending people there literally in millions.[10]

Meanwhile, pending immigration (but constituting an important part of the background) the burning question was the excessive mobility of the labour already in the Region, and the very bad atmosphere in the work-places, in such respects as the 'low social quality' of some of the workers. The Academy of Sciences pronounced formally in 1967 that 'the increased mobility of labour is characteristic, and has a negative influence on the development of production'.[11] Under the Seven-Year Plan (1959-65) over 40 per cent of industrial investment was to be east of the Urals. Under the latest Five-Year Plan (1965-70) industry was to grow in the same area twice as fast as the national average. The requirements of inputs of labour, as well as capital, 'by the millions' – through massive immigration – were equally stressed. Such efforts seem largely to have failed, in a setting of chronic and worsening shortage and impermanency of labour.

The new Tyumen' oilfield in Western Siberia, for example, was 'starred' as one of the greatest and most exciting resource developments of modern times. The correspondent of a leading newspaper found that in the main complex there, in the year 1967 alone, 13,000 workers gave up their jobs; 17,000 more were recruited. The latter were very mixed, including

> solid family men, men fleeing from maintenance orders or other legal writs, young and old, enthusiasts and sceptics, those seeking more money, those seeking a better place, those arriving under their own steam and those sent by the authorities. . . . The turnover is enormous. The graph of mobility – alarmingly – is not creeping down, it is rising sharply. In 1966 more than half the workers at the Tyumen' Main Combine gave notice, in 1966 this had risen to 72 per cent . . . experienced workers are often replaced by inexperienced ones. Many, on barely acquiring a professional qualification, rush to the staff office to hand in their resignations. There is loss upon loss, and an acute shortage of qualified personnel.[12]

Even the best elements in the proletariat are less amenable than they used to be. Workers nowadays resist direction to new enterprises – and other forms of 'Commandism'. A well-known example was the refusal of the workers on the great Bratsk hydroelectric station in Eastern Siberia to be transferred, when it was completed, to chemical plants.[13]

If the 'spirit' of the ordinary workers was unsatisfactorily negative, pessimistic or 'defeatist' attitudes could be displayed even in the upper ranks of the Soviet technocracy. The view that remote areas such as the Far North-East, owing to the difficulties of any balanced economic development in the natural conditions, should see only *Raubwirtschaft* for a long time to come, has been held even by some members of the Academy of Sciences and incurred official admonition. The heads of the North-East Gold Combine and Geological Board wrote in 1968: 'the concept of a diversified all-round harmonious development of the North-East is opposed by another: to develop solely mining, or to develop other branches only on a subsidiary, temporary basis. They say agriculture is not necessary, nor is machine building or local industry. Extract the rich deposits of ore by the quickest method – and get out of this cold, God-forsaken place!'[14]

Nevertheless, among the younger people especially, the outer tundra areas actually seemed more attractive, more appealing to their spirit of adventure – at least, for not too long a stay – than the more comfortable southern centres of the Region. Magadan provides an interesting example. Since its development in the Stalin era had centred so largely on the concentration camps, everything was disoriented when these were closed. It was several years before the official propaganda could present a rosy picture; in fact, this began on a large scale only about 1963 (*Sovietskaya Rossiya*, for example, featured in July of that year a series of highly euphoric letters by a woman building engineer to her mother). The First Secretary of the Provincial Communist Party wrote in 1963 that most of the camps had been liquidated in 1956. Even in 1955, volunteers began to come: 800 young workers who had finished trade school and about a thousand specialists. In 1956, from Moscow alone, 7500 persons arrived. 'In 1959, people were sent from Kuibyshev, Minsk and other towns. Thereafter there was a stream of enthusiasts', but labour is still short; and 'the stabilisation of cadres is slowing down at present' (i.e. the turnover was becoming higher). The gold prospects were opening up, the prospects of people were not.[15]

From about the mid-1960s the 'privileges' or material inducements were effectively restored and augmented. In 1965 the establishment of recruiting centres to engage demobilised soldiers and workers in general for agriculture in the S.F.E. was announced by the Maritimes Party newspaper. The recruits would receive the following inducements: house-building credit 2000 roubles in Kolkhozes, 2400 in Sovkhozes, 280 roubles to buy a cow, consumers' co-operatives to sell flour at very low prices to a limit of 150 kg for the head of a family and 50 kg for each other member, exemption from agricultural taxation for five years.[16] These are very large sums for a Soviet peasant. An unskilled worker in the U.S.S.R. may typically have 60-100 roubles a month – and no significant 'fringe' benefits.

The decree of the Council of Ministers of 16 December 1967 provided elaborate bonus schemes for workers in 'the Far North and places on the same footing as the Far North', including bonuses of 35 per cent of wages – doubled after two or three years' stay – and 'privileges' in housing space, facilities for families, etc. New settlers in Siberia and the S.F.E. received, from the beginning of 1968: free travel for families, plus a free baggage allowance of two tons, a cash grant of 150 roubles to the head of the family, 50 roubles to every other member, 4000 roubles credit on arrival, for house-building, 400 roubles for purchase of livestock, exemption from farm taxation for two years. Industrial immigrants receive similar grants, substituting tools for livestock, etc.[17]

It was stated in 1969 that wages in the Far North were 80 per cent higher than in Central Russia, with an additional bonus of '10 per cent for every six months worked, plus a grant of 200 roubles for every complete year worked in the Urals, Siberia or the Far East, plus 30-40 per cent on completion of projects.'[18] The basic unskilled wage rates seem, however, to be only 150-160 per month. Against which it is noted that girls working as clerks or storekeepers in the Kuriles receive 280-300 roubles a month (gross?). In the Little Khingan (Obluch'e) tin mines in 1968 a miner's average wage was 185 roubles, but

drifter-men made up to 300-350; moreover premia represented
an additional 100-300 roubles and there were good provisions
in such facilities as crèches.[19]

HOUSING AND AMENITIES

The building industry in the S.F.E. is weaker than that of most
Soviet Regions. In terms of capital input, for example, in the
earlier 1960s, it took 725 million roubles a year, a larger sum
than many Regions of West Russia, but only about half East
Siberia's and a third of the Ural Region's. There is constant
complaint of acute 'disproportionalities', meaning lack of, or
inferior, structures or dwellings. Fishing bases, factories, etc.,
have in many cases been erected incompletely, or ahead of the
provision of housing and ancillary buildings. There is no regional planning in the modern town planner's sense. The
allocation of capital funds quoted above represents 2·3 per cent
of the all-U.S.S.R. total, but the actual outlays in the S.F.E.
represented 3·13 per cent of the grand total. This reflects especially the high ratio of outlay on repairs, as distinct from
capital-construction. There were over 750 building enterprises
in the Region, nearly all small.

Cement production (around 2 million tons a year, usually
insufficient for the Region's needs, nevertheless some is exported) is slightly above the R.S.F.S.R. average per head of
population; other building materials (except glass) generally
below. Builders in European Russia are able to use two or three
times as much ferro-concrete, per unit of construction, as their
comrades in the S.F.E., who must rely correspondingly on
wood, bricks, slate, etc. A great effort is being made to develop
the production of new materials and prefabricated items.

The housing situation may also be illustrated by giving a few
random examples. In 1962 the press[20] cited cases of new factories
in the Maritimes being completed without housing, occasioning
losses of production totalling 100 million roubles, though the
capital equipment was available. It revealed how bad the existing housing was in the Amur Province: 88·8 per cent of
houses lacked water supply, 90·2 per cent had no sewage dis-
posal, 93·1 per cent no bathroom, 83·7 per cent no central

heating. All such reports are interlarded with comments on other aspects of the situation. The source just quoted continues, for example, with the following. The S.F.E. lumber industry was short of seven hundred engineers; only twenty or thirty immigrated every year. There were comments on the bad quality of immigrants generally; some of them were 'adventurers'. In a Magadan factory, for example, many of the new workers were drunkards; in a mine in the same Province which received fifty-five immigrants, sixteen left within one month and twenty proved to be too weak in health for work. Since the Government had reduced engineers' earnings by 20 per cent since 1956, there were many protests, including assertions that some workers earned more than foremen and therefore refused promotion. The lack of fresh food was serious, especially on ships.

A boiler works under construction in Khabarovsk was making poor progress in 1968; the workers' housing conditions were 'very bad'. Vladivostok had planned housing construction totalling 18,000 sq. metres over three years, but the actual outcome was only 5000. The national press gave the number of houses ready to receive settlers in Chita, Amur, Khabarovsk and the Maritime Provinces at the beginning of 1968 as 7200. For the construction of the thermal electric station at Vladivostok, as of 1968, 'an additional amount of machinery was transferred' (more than planned) and the work force was augmented by 250; the pace of building living quarters for the workers was accelerated, but not sufficiently.[21]

The unplanned way in which such a town as Petropavlovsk in Kamchatka grew up is noted with due regret. 'Buildings were merely placed where convenient', wrote *Pravda* ingenuously in 1969. The town has over 2 million sq. metres of dwelling-area, or more than 20 per inhabitant (a princely space in the U.S.S.R.). However, though Kamchatka abounds in building materials, they are 'very, very dear. We pay fifty to eighty roubles for the transport of every ton. Building is indeed problem number one for the whole of the North and Far East. . . .' The Provincial union Kamchatstroi has a house-building capacity of 35,000 sq. metres, a small building-block plant and a metal-fittings factory. Another ferro-concrete plant is to be established at Petropavlovsk in 1970 or 1971 with a capacity of up to 40,000 cubic metres of ferro-concrete blocks, but still another is needed, with a capacity of 70,000-100,000. The Kamchatka fishing fleet – now taking 700,000 tons of fish, increasing its catch year by year and expecting to reach one million tons soon – requires half a million square metres of housing space for its crews, which cannot be provided; the Ministry must help.[22]

Under the title 'How they plan . . . discomfort' the *Young Communist* daily reported in mid-1969 the complaints of the leaders of an all-Union Young Communist construction project of the greatest importance – the new Primorsk electric station and the Luchegorsk coalfield centre south of Bikin in the Maritimes. The local Government allocated one and a half million roubles for the provision of a relay line from Spassk to Luchegorsk, but planned no family housing, only provision for bachelors – which totalled 28,000 sq. m. Economies were made by not providing any television or other amenities; and each worker received only 5·4 metres of dwelling space on the average, instead of the 9 called for in the plan. Inferably, the work force was 5185; the difficulties of accommodating such a number on an entirely new development are obvious.[23]

The foregoing has outlined especially the human and social basis of the Region's life; in the next chapter the economic framework is described, in terms of the main activities.

CHAPTER 3

Economic Development

The perspectives of distance and climate were emphasised in Chapter 1. The following are some further implications. Consider, first, the grip of frost. The Angara river at Irkutsk never freezes. It is fast flowing (60,500 cusecs), regulated by Lake Baikal. The land around the Angara freezes; so does everything else to the eastward, even to the shore-waters of the S.F.E. Lake Baikal freezes from December to May, the Amur river at Blagoveshchensk for about five months in the year, the sea between Sakhalin and the mainland is ice-bound in winter. The Northern Sea route through the Arctic Ocean all round the north coast is kept open for a mere two and a half months in summer solely by the use of powerful icebreakers, including the famous nuclear-powered vessel *Lenin*.[1]

Then there are the distances. Per head of the whole population in the U.S.S.R. in 1964, the transport of goods worked out at 9100 ton-kilometres; in the S.F.E., counting transport within the Region alone it was 13,500, or nearly 50 per cent higher. The *average* freight-consignment distance in the U.S.S.R. as a whole is about 1500 km. For the S.F.E. it is over 6000 km. Freights to and from other Soviet Regions take 6 per cent of the gross product of the S.F.E. The freight on one ton of diesel oil, for example, from Omsk to the Far East represents double the cost of the oil itself. Transport costs add 40 per cent to the price of rolled steel brought from Magnitogorsk, over 50 per cent to that of grain fetched from Kazakhstan. Three or four transfers are often necessary en route, frequent 'breaking bulk'. For instance, in 1966 one ton of freight from Belogorsk near Blagoveshchensk via Sovietskaya Gavan' to Arkagala in Magadan cost 55 roubles (nearly $60 or £25 at the official par) of which 13 per cent was for loadings and unloadings en route. The port facilities are inadequate almost everywhere, with a main reliance on lighterage costing 3 or 4 roubles a ton, besides delay and losses.

The S.F.E.'s low ratio of self-sufficiency in almost everything has been noted. Nevertheless transport difficulties oblige the metropolitan authorities to exhort and press the S.F.E. to reduce its drawings on the rest of the country. For example, on 21 March 1969 the newspapers published a proclamation enjoining everyone in the Region to use local materials and products. Macro-economic difficulties in European Russia can affect the S.F.E. seriously. An instance was in 1963, when the Soviet Union was importing grain and the Government admitted that mechanisation was causing unemployment in European Russia. There was difficulty in supplying consumers in the S.F.E. Goods trains took twenty days; for Magadan, Kamchatka and Sakhalin five or six transhipments were required. Meat was generally shipped in whole carcases, only 65-70 per cent edible meat. One third of the rail and ship capacity was thus wasted. The decentralisation of wholesale trade had worsened the situation in the past year: 'many trading organisations began to avoid making contracts with buyers in the Far East'. The Maritime Province, for example, received 1·1 million roubles less of tobacco in 1962 than in 1961, half a million (roubles' worth, or pairs?) less of hosiery, 90,000 fewer gramophone records, and was otherwise seriously affected.[2]

Besides crises or policy changes, there is a constant stream of complaints about the ineptitudes of planning and inefficiency. To cite one example: in 1967, 350,000 tons more freight arrived in Vladivostok and Nakhodka by rail than had been anticipated; this had to be kept standing in waggons. 'Damage at the junction is still going on.'[3]

The S.F.E. has greatly increased its trade with other Regions of the U.S.S.R., raising its exports to them, but remaining heavily dependent on imports from them. (Note the construction of Table 3.1; it takes the S.F.E.'s total exports to other Regions in 1940 as an index base of 100. The figures are to the nearest five percentage points; it is not possible to distinguish all destinations with complete accuracy, but Table 3.1 shows the broad pattern.)

Table 3.1   S.F.E.'s trade with other Soviet Regions

	Total	East Siberia	West Siberia	Central Asia	Ural	European Russia
Exports to:						
1940	100	65	0	0	0	35
1950	155	100	55	0	35	65
1960	535	200	65	65	70	135
1963	705	185	135	100	100	185
Imports from:						
1940	500	200	100	30	45	135
1950	500	125	75	70	115	135
1960	885	270	270	70	150	125
1963	1250	530	260	60	180	230

Figures on the same base are unfortunately not available for later years, but this series shows how the dependence on long hauls increased with development. The S.F.E.'s exports multiplied about sevenfold. Exports to European Russia increased in similar proportion, and exports to the three other distant Regions were developed, each to the dimensions of the S.F.E.'s *total* exports in 1940, while the exports to the nearer Region, Eastern Siberia, increased only threefold. Imports increased only to two and a half times those of 1940, and imports from European Russia in lesser proportion, but a considerable import from the Ural and Central Asia developed; the overall deficit balance greatly increased at the end of the period.

The composition of the inter-Regional trade was broadly as shown in Table 3.2 – in rough indications, to the nearest five percentage points. The table, summarising various Soviet statements, indicates the pattern, though the large 'miscellaneous' category greatly predominates.

63 per cent of the Region's imports are bulk cargoes: oil (60 per cent of the Region's oil requirements being imported), grain (60 per cent imported), ferrous metals (80 per cent imported), salt (100 per cent imported). The other imports are machinery, hardware, mineral fertilisers (not yet brought in bulk) and sugar. This (37 per cent) is a high proportion of non-bulk freights; Eastern Siberia has 40 per cent and Kazakhstan also 37 per cent, but the Moscow area has 27 per cent, the Volga 20 per cent, northern Ural 21 per cent, the Don and the Dnieper 15 per cent. Trade with the Eastern Regions (Siberia,

Table 3.2 Composition of trade with other Soviet Regions (approximate percentages)

	Total				East Siberia				West Siberia				Central Asia				Ural				European Russia			
	1940	1950	1960	1963	1940	1950	1960	1963	1940	1950	1960	1963	1940	1950	1960	1963	1940	1950	1960	1963	1940	1950	1960	1963
Imports from:																								
Coal	15	15	10	10	30	60	30	40	–	–	15	30	–	–	–	–	–	–	–	–	–	–	–	10
Metals	10	10	10	10	–	–	–	–	–	–	10	10	–	–	–	–	–	–	25	20	–	–	–	–
Timber	5	–	–	–	20	–	–	–	–	–	–	–	–	–	–	–	–	–	–	–	–	–	–	–
Cement	5	–	–	–	–	–	–	–	–	–	–	–	–	–	–	–	–	–	–	–	–	–	–	–
Cereals	15	15	10	10	20	–	20	15	45	45	15	5	–	–	–	–	–	–	–	–	–	–	–	–
Miscellaneous	50	60	70	70	30	40	50	45	55	55	60	55	100	100	100	100	100	100	75	80	100	100	100	90
	100	100	100	100	100	100	100	100	100	100	100	100	100	100	100	100	100	100	100	100	100	100	100	100
Exports to:																								
Coal	35	30	5	–	50	65	20	20	–	–	–	–	–	–	–	–	–	–	–	–	–	–	–	–
Metals	–	–	5	–	–	–	–	–	–	–	–	–	–	–	–	–	–	–	–	–	–	–	–	–
Timber	–	–	20	25	–	–	15	–	–	–	40	35	–	–	50	50	–	–	–	–	–	–	–	–
Cement	–	20	15	5	50	35	25	20	–	–	–	–	–	–	–	–	–	–	–	–	–	–	–	–
Fish	–	–	15	10	–	–	–	10	–	–	–	10	–	–	–	–	–	–	–	25	–	–	–	30
Miscellaneous	65	50	40	60	–	–	40	50	100	100	60	55	100	100	50	50	100	100	100	75	100	100	100	70
	100	100	100	100	100	100	100	100	100	100	100	100	100	100	100	100	100	100	100	100	100	100	100	100

Ural and Central Asia) has increased much more than trade with European Russia.

Table 3.3   Trade of the S.F.E. with Eastern and Western Russia

	Imports from other Regions			Exports to other Regions		
	Index	Eastern Regions	European Russia	Index	Eastern Regions	European Russia
		(%)	(%)		(%)	(%)
1940	100	67	33	100	64	36
1950	100	69	31	170	73	27
1960	175	83	17	455	83	17
1962	210	84	16	425	78	22
1963	240	82	18	493	78	22

Notably, bulk cargoes from European Russia have declined (28 per cent in 1940, rising to 33 per cent in 1950, but down to 20 per cent in 1962). European Russia supplies the 'expensive' imports of the S.F.E.; it is revealing of the poverty of Soviet life that 'expensive' items include not only machinery but textiles, other consumer goods and some fruits (food, jams and even sugar). From the Eastern Regions the S.F.E. obtained mainly coal, oil, grain and metals (together, 75 per cent of the imports in 1963 from the Eastern Regions).

The S.F.E.'s exports consist of forest products (22 per cent), fish (10 per cent), cement (6 per cent), Raichikhinsk coal (2 per cent); and a mixed group of paper, metals, even some heavy oil for use in metal industries, makes up another 20 per cent. In the above period, the intensive development of Eastern Siberia had a marked influence. Immediately afterwards, the near-cessation of trade with China accentuated some trends. For example, the S.F.E. sent 234,000 tons of cement to Siberia in 1940, 900,000 in 1961, but only 384,000 a year or two later, owing to the break with China. The increasing demands for pitprops and other timber in West Siberia and Central Asia stimulated the rise in timber exports from the S.F.E. from 92,000 tons in 1950 to 1,413,000 in 1963.

It is difficult to distinguish accurately the element of foreign trade (proper, with other countries, or transit trade with them) in all this. The Soviet materials are secretive on this, the

Chinese and North Korean figures undisclosed, those of other countries on different bases. Timber is the largest export prospect, in relation especially to Japan, whose total imports had multiplied twentyfold since about 1952; those from the U.S.S.R. were 1,763,000 cubic metres in 1963. The main items of export interest are, however, planks and veneers, in which the processing capacity is still weak; and the main locations the Amur mouth and the Sikhote–Alin' range, where there are other difficulties. The Amur mouth is barred by sandbanks; a ship canal is projected through Lake Kizi to Tabo Bay, shortening the passage by 500 km, and extending the ice-free period by six weeks. The Sikhote–Alin' uplands are simply inaccessible, until the projected extension is made of the railway from Varfolomeyevka to Tetyukhe. The absolute preponderance of the southern part of the Region is great: it has 75 per cent of the intra-Regional freights and 90 per cent of the inter-Regional freights.

Per thousand square kilometres of area, the Region has only 1·8 km of railway line (one-third of the U.S.S.R. average). Per head of population, however, the S.F.E. has about double the national average of rail-track and about the national average of roadway. In addition to the main railways (5600 km) some narrow-gauge lines are important, principally for forestry. The freight-pattern in 1963 is shown in Table 3.4.

Table 3.4   Pattern of freight in the S.F.E.
(percentages, 1963)

	Volume of freightage	Freight turnover	Inter-Regional	Transit	Intra-Regional
Rail	23	58	87	100	17
Sea	4	35	13	–	3
River	2	3	–	–	2
Pipeline	1	1	–	–	1
Automobile	70	3	–	–	77
	100	100	100	100	100

The railways are worked far below the national average; cargo load in 1963 totalled 13·7 million ton-km per km of track, whereas the optima were given as 40-40 for diesel traction and 60-70 for electric. Freight costs are 50 per cent over the national average, five times those of the best railways in the U.S.S.R. (such as the Omsk line). Moreover the costs vary enormously within the Region. They are extremely high in Sakhalin, almost five times the mainland's; from Volochayevka to Komsomolsk and Sovietskaya Gavan', 30 to 40 per cent above those of the Siberian main line.

The sea link is vital to the outlying territories in the Pacific. The S.F.E. had 13 per cent of the Soviet Union's sea freight in 1963.

Table 3.5   Sea-freight pattern of the S.F.E. (in 1963)

Type of shipping	Volume of freightage (%)	Cargo turnover (%)
Small coastal	79	48
Export	19	40
Large coastal	2	12
	100	100

The small coastal shipping is concentrated largely between the southern mainland and Sakhalin, Kamchatka and Magadan; 21 per cent of the cargoes in this category are from the southern mainland to Sakhalin, 14 per cent from the mainland to Kamchatka, 13 per cent from the mainland to Magadan. 16 per cent has been between Sakhalin and Kamchatka and Magadan, lately declining as Magadan has taken less coal from Sakhalin. The rest of the small coastal shipping is almost entirely on the extremely local scale, i.e. within the Provinces.

The large coastal shipping represents the sea link with European Russia, whither it bears chiefly fish and concentrates of light metals. The traffic to European Russia greatly exceeds the return movement, which consists of oil and general cargoes; via Suez it was distinctly cheaper than rail, around Africa less distinctly so. Meanwhile rail costs have been somewhat reduced to become more competitive for the south of the Region, though the Arctic sea route (despite the shortness of its open season) must be maintained as it is vital for the northern territories.

It is possible to identify the shape, though not the absolute

Table 3.6 Rail-freight pattern of the S.F.E.
(in 1963)

Note: The total reaching the western end of the Region from Eastern Siberia (i.e. imports reaching Magdagachi from Nyever) = 100

Between:	Eastward							Westward						
	Total	Coal	Timber	Ferrous	Building materials (mineral)	Cereals	Others	Total	Coal	Timber	Ferrous	Building materials (mineral)	Cereals	Others
Magdagachi/Tu	100	25	0	0	0	15	60	50	4	8	4	4	4	25
Tu/Belogorsk	100	25	0	0	0	15	60	50	17	8	4	8	0	13
Belogorsk/ Raichikhinsk	92	17	0	8	4	15	50	55	25	8	4	8	0	8
Raichikhinsk/ Izvestkovskaya	133	50	0	4	0	15	58	50	4	17	4	8	0	17
Izvestkovskaya/ Khabarovsk	125	50	0	4	4	15	50	42	0	8	4	8	0	20
Khabarovsk/ Spassk	75	17	8	4	4	8	38	42	4	4	8	8	4	13
Spassk/ Ussurisk	92	8	17	8	8	8	42	50	17	0	4	0	4	25
Ussurisk/ Vladivostok	92	17	17	8	17	8	33	50	21	0	4	8	4	13

quantities of the flow of railway freight through the Region (Table 3.6).

These are approximate figures – absolute figures are not published; the above has been deduced from Soviet publications which appear essentially accurate and consistent. In the eastward traffic, note the flow of grain, also consumer goods and oil (included in 'others') especially as far as Khabarovsk, the input of metals and coal especially at the Raichikhinsk coalfield and Khabarovsk, but again when the southern Maritimes are reached, where the carriage of timber also rises. In the westward flow, the nodalities are similar, but from the vicinity of Raichikhinsk (where there are large demands for pitprops, etc.) timber flows westward. This has been described informally by a local economist as 'too much of a two-way economy, sending the same things eastward and the same things back westward. Traffic jams in the middle. A long supply line, bulging in the middle.'

The rail freight from Komsomolsk to Khabarovsk, on the same base, was 25, composed of ferrous metal 6, timber 8, building materials 4, others 7. The freight from Khabarovsk to Komsomolsk represented 42, with coal 18, 5 or 6 each of ferrous metals, timber, and cereals, others 7. Rail freight from Vanino (Sovietskaya Gavan') to Komsomolsk represents on the same scale about 4 units of 'others', while some 7 of timber (shipped from South Sakhalin) and 10 of 'others' go in the opposite direction, to Vanino; two-thirds of the latter, the miscellaneous goods, are passed on by sea to South Sakhalin. North Sakhalin sends to Komsomolsk on the scale of 18 in the same comparison, including oil by pipeline and other commodities by ship.

From Vladivostok by sea, miscellaneous goods ('others') went out eastwards to the index of about 20, of which about 8 were landed in South Sakhalin and 12 continued eastwards. South Sakhalin itself shipped almost the same amount eastwards, so that the eastward shipment continued on the scale of 20 (all in the category of 'others' – representing the provisioning of the outposts), 7 or 8 each going to Magadan and Kamchatka, 4 to the Farthest East and North-East. These areas shipped to Vladivostok valuable items such as furs, but in terms of tonnage their only significant entry was about 4 of timber, mainly from Kamchatka. Finally, from north to south within Sakhalin

passed in 1963 some 10 units of freight southward, equally
divided between coal, timber and others, while the northward
traffic on the island was about 5 units, all in the category of
'others'.

The foreign trade, apart from China (now slight), North
Korea, Cuba and North Vietnam, mainly concerns Japan.
Timber goes from Nakhodka, Vanino and the Amur mouth,
coal from Sakhalin, crude oil from Moskal'vo and oil products
from Vladivostok. The imports are sugar, fruits, salt, cement,
machinery and metal wares.

River transport represented in 1965 only 2·3 per cent of all
the freightage and 3·1 per cent of all the cargo handled in the
S.F.E. There are 6000 km of navigable river in the Region, but
nearly all this (95 per cent) is in the Amur basin; the inter-
Regional river transport is only 10 per cent of all transport.
Mostly only very local hauls are made by river, with such loads
as building materials, coal and oil. In 1940 the share of building
materials in the Amur traffic was 7 per cent, but in 1963 it had
risen to 40 per cent. The general average distance for river hauls,
now only 40-60 km, fell 40 per cent in that period. The upper
and middle Amur is little used, because the shore facilities are
deficient, transfer is expensive, the navigation season short; and
latterly there have been difficulties and hostilities with the
Chinese. In 1960 the cost per ton-kilometre was 4 per cent less
by rail than by river; this margin appears since to have increased. The use of the rivers is surprisingly low, for both freight
and passengers, though there are modern vessels on regular
routes between Blagoveshchensk and Komsomolsk, on the
Amur.

The importance of motor transport is obvious, but roads are
largely lacking; the average truck trip is only about 20 km in
the Amur Province, only about 10 in Khabarovsk and the
Maritimes. In Magadan, however, there is the unique highway
all the way through eastern Yakutia, the Kolyma goldfields are
fairly heavily served and the average trip rises to 40 km. The
sections of better road in the south (Svobodny–Ekimchan, the
western end of the Yakutia–Magadan highway near Skovorodino and the road in the Maritimes from Varfolomeyevka to
Kavalerovo and Tetyukhe) do not carry a great deal. The
actual mileage of roads in the S.F.E. in 1966 was over 33,100

km, of which 12,500 were of National or Provincial grade, the rest only village or departmental, mostly passable only in winter or in dry periods in summer. Properly surfaced or asphalted roads represented only 1200 km, a mere 4 per cent of the total. The rest are used only in the hard winter – but then intensively, with long columns of trucks which temporarily reduce transport costs by 25 per cent. There is some new road construction, even in the Arctic, but in the south the need is still to secure and improve the existing network. Passenger travel by bus trebled in the Maritimes in the first half of the 1960s.

Last but not least, the aeroplane has made an increasingly spectacular presence in the S.F.E. and Siberia. In 1962 passenger-departures originating in the main airports totalled about 400,000; departures for Moscow alone reached 100,000. Passenger journeys within the Region were nearly one million. The Aeroflot S.F.E. network was as follows in 1970, pivoting on Khabarovsk:

Khabarovsk–Moscow
Khabarovsk–Birobidzhan
Khabarovsk–Blagoveshchensk–Svobodny
Svobodny–Shimanovsk
Svobodny–Ekimchan
Svobodny–Novo-Kievka–Maiski–Gluboki
Maiski–Oktyabrski–Zeya–Bomnak
Khabarovsk–Novokurovka-Pobeda and Kukan–Sredni
    Urgal–Umal'ta–Sofiisk
Khabarovsk–Troitskoye–Komosomolsk
Komosomolsk–Poliny Osipenko–Kherpuchi
Komosomolsk–Mariinsk–Bogorodskoye–Nikolaevsk
Nikolaevsk–Okha
Nikolaevsk–Tutur–Chumikan–Nel'kan–Kurun Uryakh
Nikolaevsk–Okhotsk–Magadan–Kamenskoe–Anadyr
Khabarovsk–Yuzhno–Sakhalinsk
Khabarovsk–Shakhtersk
Khabarovsk–Petropavlovsk
Yuzhno–Sakhalinsk–Shakhtersk–Nogliki–Okha
Petropavlovsk–Sobolevo
Petropavlovsk–Mil'kovo–Kozyrevsk–Magadan
Petropavlovsk–Ust' Kamchatsk–Palana
Ust' Kamchatsk–Gilichiki–Kamenskoe

FUEL AND POWER

The U.S.S.R. as a whole is much more dependent than other industrial countries on coal, though very recently its use is declining, while that of petrol and natural gas is rising; the one-time importance of such primitive fuels as firewood and peat has declined (Table 3.7).

Table 3.7   Use of fuels in the U.S.S.R.
(output of all fuels reduced to thermal units)
(per cent)

	1940	1945	1950	1955	1958	1960	1965
Coal	59	62	66	65	59	54	43
Petrol	19	15	17	21	26	31	36
Natural Gas	2	2	2	2	6	8	16
Firewood	14	15	9	7	5	4	3
Peat	6	5	5	4	3	3	2
Oil shale	0	0	0	1	1	1	1

100

Up to one-third of the coal consumption is low-grade brown coal – double the pre-war proportion. These features are especially marked in the S.F.E., where over 70 per cent of the fuel consumption (in thermal units) is in the form of coal. Unless natural gas and hydroelectric power can be drawn on more rapidly and extensively than has been expected, or new oil strikes occur, the S.F.E.'s dependence on coal is not expected to be reduced to below 60 per cent. The supposed hydroelectric potential (at 47·6 million kW) is over 14 per cent of the whole Soviet Union's, but very difficult to develop. The S.F.E. is said to contain 160 billion tons of coal, easier to develop, so that the concentration on coal will almost inevitably continue. The Region exports a little coal (some 300,000 tons a year), and imports a little from the Baikal area, a transaction the authorities dislike as uneconomic, but cannot eliminate. Half the coal output of the S.F.E. is taken from open cuts. In 1963, 66 per cent of the production was lignite, 34 per cent hard coal; 70% of the lignite was from open cuts. The requirement for 1980 is for production to be at least doubled, mainly from open workings.

The reserves of the Suchan hard-coal basin near Vladivostok are limited, the geology inconvenient. The Artem lignite basin nearby is nearing exhaustion. The Bikin field, further north in the same Province, should become its main centre; its large electric station and industrial base, Luchegorsk, has recently been established. The Maritime Province imported half a million tons of coal in 1963, from Sakhalin and Raichikhinsk in the Amur Province. About half the Maritimes' own production came from Artem and a quarter was the higher-grade Suchan coal. It is hoped that Bikin, plus other developments, will cover this Province's own needs and provide some surplus for export.

The Bureya reserves are about 25 billion tons, but inconveniently located and unlikely to be strongly developed in any near future. The Ogodzha field on the upper Selemdzha yielded in the mid-1960s only about 80,000 tons a year, all from opencasts; this was the cheapest coal in the Region, though not of high quality. Amur Province (Raichikhinsk) should be able to cover its own needs and most of those of Khabarovsk Province for a very long future.

Sakhalin has some 20 billion tons of coal reserves, mainly good underground coal (including coking coal) accessible by adits from sixteen mines on the west coast; and lignite has been significantly developed at Vakhrushevo on the other coast. About 75 per cent of the output is utilised on the island, the rest sent mainly to Magadan (200,000-300,000 tons a year) and Kamchatka (350,000-400,000), which greatly depend on this; also some is exported and some is for bunkering. The high cost of Sakhalin coal has impelled its use mainly within the island; the mainland has begun to reduce its purchases from Sakhalin,

Table 3.8   Coal production in the S.F.E.
('000 tons)

| | 1940 | 1959 | 1961 | 1963 | | | |
				Total	Coal	Lignite	Opencast
Maritimes	3,711	6,245	6,567	6,800	2,900	3,900	288
Khabarovsk	15	773	965	1,087	1,087	–	–
Amur	2,776	8,136	8,900	9,593	–	9,593	9,593
Magadan	126	1,126	913	1,322	1,238	84	319
Sakhalin	589	4,400	4,324	4,400	2,673	1,727	673
Total	7,217	20,734	21,675	23,212	7,898	15,314	11,283

and Kamchatka and Magadan would like to do so. Magadan
has its own Arkagala coalfield in the Kolyma goldmining area,
the output of which is mostly used locally by the power station,
though some goes to the Yakut Republic.

Electricity is generated in the S.F.E. on a highly localised
basis, from coal and oil. The practical possibilities of hydroelectric development are largely in the Amur basin, where some
fifty stations are theoretically envisaged, producing about 75
billion kWh a year; but half this basin is in China, the whole
of it is afflicted by devastating floods, there is no local market
for a large amount of electricity, moreover there are conjoint
difficulties of irrigation or river transport being likely to be
interrupted by major schemes. Work is well in hand on a large
station near the town of Zeya. Other sites for future development are Zheludinsk on the Bureya, the Amur near Kuznetzovo
(35 km south of Ushumun station) and later Khingan, Blagoveshchensk, Dagmar on the Selemdzha, Dal'dykansk on the
Bureya and Ulakinksk on the upper Ussuri.

The production of oil is limited to the extreme north-east of
Sakhalin, really a small field. Thirteen units were working in
1963, eight of oil, four of gas and oil, one of gas. Geologically,
much more oil should be findable, in the south of Sakhalin as
well as the north. The need to develop this is urgent; Sakhalin
provided in the mid-1960s only about 40 per cent of the S.F.E.'s
oil requirements, which are greatly growing. All this must be
considered against the background of the Soviet fuel position
as a whole.

Shabad (1969) gives a penetrating summary. There was a
disproportionate concentration on coal, into the 1950s, while
the Western world was switching to oil and gas. Initially this
was because the coal reserves were better known than those of
other fuels and there had been prior development of transport
towards them. Even after new oil and gas reserves had been
identified, the planners were slow to develop them; not merely
through ineptitude but also deliberately to decentralise development in the sprawling country for strategic reasons and
to reduce the tremendous haulage distances. Thus industrialisation moved into the Urals, Western Siberia and Eastern
Siberia from coalfield to coalfield.

In 1950, 30 per cent of all rail-freight in the U.S.S.R. (178·2 billion ton-km out of a total of 602·3) consisted of coal; the traction was 95 per cent by steam engines, using much coal en route. In 1930 the tonnage of coal produced was 2·5 times the tonnage of crude oil; by 1950 this ratio had risen to 6·8. This trend was, however, reversed in the 1950s, as major discoveries of oil and gas were made, while the iron and steel industry developed a large capacity to manufacture and install pipe-lines. Moreover the defence needs changed; as the age of missiles came, older concepts of decentralisation were modified. Finally the economic criteria became more sophisticated; it was after all better to transport some high-cost fuels over long distances, with improving techniques, rather than rely on locally produced low-grade fuels which now appeared to show inferior cost-benefit ratios.

By 1965 the ratio of coal production to oil production had returned to its 1930 level, 2·4:1. Meanwhile the scale of opera-tions had risen enormously. The total freight carried trebled, to 1950 billion ton-km; the production of coal had almost doubled, but it now represented only 20 per cent of the freight (at 397 billion ton-km). Meanwhile the railways had gone over to diesel and electric traction; only 15·5 per cent was steam-drawn by 1965.

Most of these trends were especially marked in the S.F.E., the large but scattered coal reserves of which are little devel-oped. In the more industrialised parts of the country, the use of peat and of the more costly underground deposits of brown coal was reduced. Even there, however, brown coal and oil shale were still much used, if easily available locally on open cuts or by strip mining, especially for small local power stations in the scattered settlements. Such is especially the case in the S.F.E., where soft coal greatly predominates.

The main industrial base of the S.F.E. is thus far back to the west, in the Kuznetsk Basin (Kuzbas), i.e. south of the line from Tomsk to Krasnoyarsk. The Kuzbas produced nearly 23 million tons of coal in 1940, nearly 100 million in 1965; it ships coal to all parts of Siberia and is still the basic source, for this half of the Soviet Union, of coking coal and high-grade coals. The eastward extension of this, from the bituminous coalfield at Chernogorsk and the brown coal deposits of Nazarovo and Irsha-Borodino, is the bituminous field of Cheremkhovo, around

Table 3.9 Soviet coal production
(million metric tons)

	U.S.S.R.		of which: KUZBAS			EASTERN SIBERIA			S.F.E.	
	total	(index)		(index)	% of U.S.S.R.		(index)	% of U.S.S.R.	(index)	% of U.S.S.R.
1940	166	(100)	22	(100)	13	9	(100)	5	(100)	4
1945	149	(90)	29	(132)	20	8	(89)	5	(100)	5
1950	261	(157)	38	(173)	14	18	(200)	7	(200)	5
1955	301	(181)	58	(264)	19	27	(300)	9	(245)	6
1958	496	(299)	75	(341)	15	36	(400)	7	(300)	4
1960	513	(309)	84	(382)	16	37	(400)	12	(310)	4
1965	587	(348)	96	(436)	17	47	(522)	14	(410)	5

which there is a substantial industrial complex in the Angara–Bratsk–Irkutsk area. The S.F.E. shows a remarkable rate of growth, but is outstripped by the Kuzbas and Eastern Siberia; and the S.F.E.'s coal is almost entirely lower-grade (Table 3.9).

None of the S.F.E. coalfields is the scene of any major or 'complex' industrial development. The most notable workings are

Province	Higher-grade coals	Brown coals
Chita	Bukachacha	Gusinoozersk, Chita, Kharanor
Yakutia	Chul'man, Sangar	
Magadan	Arkagala, Zyryanka, Beringovski	
Amur	Srednii Urgal	Raichikhinsk
Sakhalin	Uglegorsk	
Maritimes	Suchan	Artem

Nearly all of these are difficult of access and costly in transport.

The S.F.E.'s only oilfield, nearer than the Middle Ob' and Tyumen' fields half-way from Lake Baikal to Moscow and the Caspian fields half-way to Africa, is in northern Sakhalin. The distant fields just named are, however, connected by pipeline to a completed refinery at Omsk and another at Angarsk near Irkutsk. The Tyumen' field began to produce in 1969 at about one million tons of crude. Sakhalin shows a rising, but not massive output; the bulk of the S.F.E.'s oil requirements must therefore be brought from vast distances to the westward (Table 3.10).

Table 3.10   Sakhalin oil production
(million metric tons)

	Sakhalin	U.S.S.R. total		Sakhalin	U.S.S.R. total
1940	0·5	31·1	1958	1·0	113·2
1945	0·8	19·4	1960	1·6	147·9
1950	0·6	37·9	1965	2·4	242·9

The perspective is thus of Sakhalin producing about 1 per cent of the U.S.S.R.'s total oil supply. This is, however, very useful to the S.F.E. The pipeline from Sakhalin to the refinery at Komsomolsk has just been duplicated.

In electric power, the S.F.E. increased its output some thirteenfold since 1940, against the whole Soviet Union's tenfold, but still accounts for less than 2 per cent of the national total and is outstripped by Eastern Siberia, which raised its output sixtyfold and rose from a similar share of the national total to 8 per cent, even finally exceeding Western Siberia, in 1965, in the production of electricity (Table 3.11).

Table 3.11   Production of electric power
(billion kWh)

	U.S.S.R. total	of which Far East	Eastern Siberia
1940	48	0·7	0·7
1950	91	2	2
1955	170	3	5
1960	292	5	16
1965	507	9	43

The Region nevertheless looks technically far ahead. In the remote north-east of the Siberian land-mass, an atomic power plant has been constructed in the Bilibino goldfields. This is small, but may be a prototype for very remote areas. Soviet development of nuclear power for peaceful uses can be summarised as follows. The first unit, established in the Urals just east of Sverdlovsk in 1964, was a graphite-moderated steam-heating plant, reaching 200,000 kW capacity in 1968. Another, water-cooled and moderated, plant was established in 1964 near Voronezh on the Don, reaching a capacity of 585,000 kW in 1969, to be raised to 1·5 million kW in the 1970s; it was decided that this should be the general model for future two-unit stations of 880,000 kW capacity. The construction of two such stations in fuel-poor areas has begun: one in the Kola Peninsula near Murmansk, the other far to the south near Erivan. The construction of Bilibino (48,000 kW, boiling-water graphite-moderated) began in the late 1960s, as did another station of 350,000 kW to the north-east of the Caspian Sea.

OTHER MINERALS

The perspectives for the development of iron and steel industries are essentially similar. Siberia and the S.F.E. contain vast resources of iron ore, other metals and alloys, still very little exploited. The same pattern is displayed as with coal, development starting with the most accessible deposits and moving further afield as these become exhausted; also some decentralisation as a matter of deliberate policy in the Stalin era, but entering a new phase from the 1950s when the technological situation changed. The S.F.E. still has no considerable output of iron; even the recent massive development in the Kuzbas represents only about 5 per cent of total Soviet output (Table 3.12).

Table 3.12   Production of iron ore
(million metric tons of usable ore)

	1940	1945	1950	1955	1958	1960	1965
U.S.S.R. total	29·9	15·9	39·7	71·9	88·8	105·9	153·4
of which Kuzbas	0·5	0·8	2·2	3·6	5·0	6·0	7·5

To which should be added the output of Zheleznogorsk, some 480 km north of Irkutsk, beginning with another 0·8 in 1965. Curiously enough, the S.F.E. has two technically advanced steel centres, with no pig-iron output: one of old standing at Petrovsk at the western end of Chita Province, the other, new in the Second World War, at Komsomolsk on the Amur.

In alloys and non-ferrous metals, however, the S.F.E. makes large contributions. None of these are used locally, all are transported thousands of kilometres, after minimal treatment on the spot, to distant industrial centres. By far the most of the Soviet Union's gold comes from the S.F.E. – the output is secret – making an incalculable contribution to the gross national product and the international position of the U.S.S.R. Large diamond fields (of domestic and industrial significance, rather than for export) have recently been developed in Yakutia. The Region is the country's main provider of tin; it makes impor-

SFE C

tant contributions of molybdenum, tungsten and the range of rare metals.

In all these, as in other minerals, the broad pattern has been initial exploitation of easily accessible deposits, decentralisation of primary production, centralisation of processing in the more industrialised areas, new industrial centres however being established further and further eastward, now reaching Lake Baikal. This has been followed in very recent years by a deep change in the technical situation: improving techniques lower the threshold of easy access and the margin of unprofitability, while the advent of the nuclear and rocket age creates new demands.

Many new surveys and new workings ensue, while old ones are reassessed and reprocessed, particularly for rare metals. In the Kuzbas, a significant ferro-alloy plant is part of the large metallic complex of Novokuznetsk, and molybdenum is produced at Sarsk. Molybdenum and wolfram are mined at Zakamensk south of Irkutsk. The old mining areas of Chita Province are of particular importance for the rare metals vital to rocketry, stratospheric operations, thermonuclear apparatus, etc. For this reason alone, Chita Province is a particularly vital area for the Soviet Union to develop – and to hold against Chinese incursion at all costs.

For the same reasons as were adduced above in respect of coal and 'technological metals', the foci of other kinds of mining activities moved, from the mid-1950s, towards the Far East and Far North-East of the U.S.S.R. Mica, an important material for all kinds of electrical equipment, was found and developed increasingly in the hinterland, particularly in the Yakut Republic. In that area the output is of phlogopite (magnesium mica), used for up-to-date electrical equipment, displacing the muscovite or common white mica. A remote deposit of mercury at Plamenny (68° 25′ N, 177° E) began to be productively worked in 1967. Some fluorspar workings should also be noted. There is much quarrying of limestone and other materials, principally for building.

The above gives only a general and partial impression of the pattern of minerals. The information available is not complete, and the deficiencies should be borne in mind as well as the assets. Alumina and bauxite do not figure in the S.F.E., though they are considerably developed in Eastern and Western Siberia, the Ural and Kazakhstan; possibly for that very reason, good new aluminium plants are available at, for instance, Bratsk and Shelekhov (Irkutsk). Alumina deposits certainly exist in the S.F.E.; the reason they are not much utilised is obviously, apart from questions of accessibility, that aluminium production requires much more electricity than the S.F.E. can yet provide. The future of most of these items must be much greater than their present level of activity. The S.F.E. is one of the world's greatest potential areas of mineral production of every kind. One metal should perhaps be specially mentioned as a main candidate for proximate development, namely copper. One copper deposit is reputedly as large as the deposits of Central Africa. It lies in the Udokan mountains in northern Chita. Though highly inaccessible at present – a good 2500 km as the crow flies from the nearest specialist smelter (Glubokoye in Kazakhstan) and over 300 km of difficult country from the Trans-Siberian railway at Mogocha – it was nevertheless mentioned by the Soviet authorities in 1970 as a potential area for technical co-operation of Western or Japanese firms.

The above does not include the most valuable and special mineral contribution of the S.F.E., at present and probably in the future, namely gold. Gold is very actively produced, with a tendency to develop continuously further north-eastwards. Unfortunately the output of gold and the trends and problems of its mining are matters of the highest secrecy in the Soviet Union. Certainly the S.F.E. yields large quantities of gold to the Soviet State, principally from the Kolyma and Indigirka fields in the north-east, but also from many other places developed in the Stalin era by concentration-camp methods, since the mid-1950s by more up-to-date Soviet methods. It was stated in 1969 that 35 per cent of the gold mined in Magadan Province comes from deposits opened in the past five or six years. The workers are young; in many places 60 per cent are under the age of thirty.[4] The extent to which the focus of gold mining has shifted to Kolyma and Chukotia was emphasised by statements that more than 80 per cent of the expenditure on prospecting for gold is now in those areas, where more than half the output would be from underground deposits.

INDUSTRIES

The pattern of manufactures is deducible from the perspectives already stated. There is a strong compulsion to develop the export of high-value-for-bulk commodities (furs, gold, machinery, instruments); but a contradictory urgent need to furnish the requirements of the Region itself, which is very short of cattle-feed, fish meal, meat products, flour, plywood, cardboard, packing cases, crates, vats, corks, chemicals, tinplate and other metalware, besides consumer goods of all kinds, of which there is a dire lack. Port facilities, on which the whole North-East is especially dependent, also cry out for investment. Leading sectors, metal factories in Komsomolsk, cable works in Khabarovsk and others, have far outstripped the provision of the complementary activities, without which they cannot operate with full rationality. In Western economic terms, there is hardly any development of external economies, quite apart from internal economies of scale; and the leading industries of the S.F.E. are the world's most extraordinary example of location at tremendous distances from *both* the sources of raw materials and the markets.

The Region sends to the rest of the Soviet Union some good engineering-industry products which cannot be used locally, while importing from the rest of the Soviet Union equally high-grade items in the same categories which it produces insufficiently or not at all. While the leading plants of the Region, such as Amurlitmash, Energomash and Amurkabel', export to other Regions various kinds of machinery, including some sophisticated items, it must import machinery of types which it needs itself, in such categories as building and roadmaking machinery and equipment for the fisheries. The latter greatly exceeds the former; thus in 1963 the S.F.E. exported products of the machine-building industry to the value of 120 million roubles, but imported such items to the extent of nearly 370 million.

For the rest, the industrial activities within the Region are still of the nature of repair and maintenance work, processing and minor extensions of primary activities. In the Soviet formulation, industrially it has no 'complex' development, it 'lacks an upper storey'. The small and numerous local workshops are dispersed widely over the vast territory, 'buttoned up' in 'seclusion' (*zamknutost'*). The small and scattered electric stations have been very inefficient and costly, running either on small local deposits of low-grade coal or on oil fuel expensively imported from great distances; only recently have grids been developed or even a single hydroelectric project concretely envisaged.

Much of the industrial activity is directly or indirectly subsidised. In 1966 it was avowed that many enterprises were unprofitable, supported by State subsidies totalling 150 million roubles a year. Details were given concerning coal, oil and building materials. For each ton of coal produced by the Urgal' administration a subsidy of 2·44 roubles is given; in the Maritimes even more, so that subventions to coal mining in the S.F.E. totalled 20 million roubles a year. The cost of Sakhalin oil was some multiple of the national average. A ton of cement cost 16·72 roubles; cf. a national average of 10·20. State subsidies in building materials included 4·18 roubles per thousand bricks, 3·82 per ton of lime.

In the mid-1960s fisheries, with 22 per cent, were the biggest contributor to the Region's gross product, followed by machine building 20 per cent, food other than fish 14 per cent and forestry 13 per cent. The remaining 31 per cent, including the manufactures, consisted of small and heterogeneous items (Table 3.13).

This is on the usual Soviet basis of 'material output'. It exaggerates the contribution of the northern Provinces (Sakhalin, Kamchatka, Magadan) because of the high prices of Sakhalin coal and oil, electric power in Magadan where gold mining is highly electrified, etc. Sakhalin's 'forestry and woodworking' also included paper and pulp, little developed elsewhere.

Much depends on the vagaries of national policy as to what funds and priorities are allocated to the S.F.E., as its history shows. Even in the main centres of the S.F.E., the Soviet power was only established in 1922, after nearly five years of bitter struggle; in outlying places, consolidation was even later. In the reconstruction period of the next few years the S.F.E. received little of the capital investment of the Soviet Union. In the First Five-Year Plan of 1928-32, however, when the

Table 3.13   Distribution of industry in the S.F.E. by Provinces
(per cent of total output, by value, 1964)

	S.F.E.	Khabar-ovsk	Mari-times	Amur	Sakh-alin	Kam-chatka	Maga-dan
All industries	100	29·2	30·2	9·1	16·4	7·6	7·5
Fishery	22·0	5·8	33·0	0·2	22·4	35·3	3·3
Other food	14·3	34·9	37·6	19·4	3·7	1·8	2·6
Forestry and wood	13·0	30·0	21·2	12·4	29·3	3·0	4·1
Machine building	20·0	50·0	29·0	6·3	4·9	3·6	6·3
Fuels	8·0	17·5	24·3	10·9	43·6	0·0	3·7
Building materials	5·8	28·7	32·7	6·2	19·2	6·6	6·6
Glass	0·2	7·2	8·0	50·2	–	–	34·6
Heavy metallurgy	0·8	100·0	–	–	–	–	–
Light metallurgy	6·5	38·7	30·4	8·5	12·3	2·5	7·6
Others	8·9	13·9	22·9	12·0	13·5	2·3	35·4

industrialisation drive began, its 'tempo' in the S.F.E. was double that of the country as a whole; the Region received 4·84 per cent of the national investment of capital. In the Second Five-Year Plan (1933-7) its share was raised to 5·8 per cent. In the first three and a half years of the Third Plan – interrupted by the war in 1941 – the figure rose again to 7·5 per cent. During the war the eastward emphasis broadly continued, in this respect. The S.F.E. suffered, of course, no direct war damage. In the reconstruction period after the war it was allocated only 0·76 per cent of the national capital investment. In 1959-63 its share was 4·3 per cent of the national total for the State and co-operative sectors. In the mid-1950s to mid-1960s the pace of industrial development in the S.F.E. slowed, becoming less than the national average; from 1962, however, a new upturn began, apparently gathering pace in the later 1960s. The projected capital investment in the S.F.E. for 1971-80 is 4 billion roubles.

One aspect is the structure of the work force. 26 per cent of the employees are in transport, distribution, catering, etc.; cf. 18 per cent on the average for the whole R.S.F.S.R. The transport ratio is the highest of any part of the U.S.S.R. In industry and building the ratios are also high, but a large proportion are on repair and maintenance work, and it is chiefly a question of a great mass of small, unspecialised workshops of a general-purpose nature. The predominance of male labour is especially marked. In the R.S.F.S.R. as a whole, in the mid-1960s, women were about 50 per cent of the work force, in Amuria 35 per cent, Khabarovsk 40 per cent, in the Maritimes 38 per cent. In various administrative districts the proportion of women in industry ranges between 29 and 34 per cent, in the construction industry between 22 and 29 per cent; these are low figures by Soviet standards. The light industries in which women should work are largely lacking. On the U.S.S.R. average in 1960, for example, about two pairs of footwear were produced per person in the whole population per year, but in the S.F.E. one pair in two years; on the U.S.S.R. average, some 30 metres of cotton cloth per person per year, in the S.F.E. 1·6 metres. There is great eagerness to use the women in industrial production, but great difficulty in providing the domestic and communal facilities which would make this possible.

The lack of skilled personnel is acute. In 1963 there were more than 87,000 'specialists' with higher training, including 34,000 engineers, 4000 agronomists, 11,000 medical workers, 30,000 teachers. 'Middle-grade specialists' numbered 161,000, half of them technicians. The educational facilities in the Region are considerable, but the shortage of cadres is persistent.

Erroneous planning or badly phased implementation gives recurrent trouble. For example, the construction plan for Luchegorsk coal-mining and power centre had been fulfilled 82 per cent during the first eight months of 1968, but the industrial part of the plan only 59·8 per cent. Then there is the extreme localisation, coupled with a general lack of functional specialisation.[5]

Metallurgy and machine-building are increasingly concentrated in the southern Provinces: 78 per cent of the relevant output in 1958, 88 per cent in 1964, almost entirely in the cities of Khabarovsk, Komsomolsk, Birobidzhan, Vladivostok, Ussurisk, Nakhodka, Blagoveshchensk and Svobodny. But this localisation still does not express the concentration of output. There were in the mid-1960s nearly 1500 factories and workshops classed as 'metals and machine-building', but of these only about forty were large, which, mostly in Khabarovsk Province, accounted for about 90 per cent of the output. Some of these larger units had certainly grown out of small plants of earlier days; it is hoped to continue that kind of growth with rationalisation. But the specialisation was still weak in the later 1960s, with few complete assembly units, most of the plants producing a miscellaneous range of parts or items. For example, the Svobodny car-parts works produced tractor-trailers, crankpresses, automotive cranes, forgings, stampings, castings, as well as car-parts; thereafter this plant was to specialise on cranes. The Dal'diesel in Khabarovsk (formerly Dal'sel'khozmash, i.e. Far East Agricultural Machinery) was still producing agricultural equipment, instruments, forgings, stampings, etc., besides diesel engines; henceforward it was to concentrate on certain types of diesels.

In the sphere of agricultural machinery, some specialised types are of particular importance for marshy, frozen and other soils; for these a rationalisation and concentration drive is being mounted. Also for the production of fishing gear (including tinplate for canning), all of which is produced on a small batch basis in scattered places, usually as the part-time work of shipyards and other units. The Belogorsk machine works and the Svobodny car-parts works make forge-presses, but send them mainly westward out of the Region. The Region manufactured in 1965 not more than 60 per cent of its own requirements of mining gear of all kinds. Equipment for roads, ports and wharves is produced only to a small extent in the Region.

It was only in the later 1960s that many plants were pressed to separate various functions (such as castings, electrodes, instruments, pitprops) into separate workshops. About twenty enterprises depend entirely on the foundry and castings items or components made at Amurstal'; this plant furnished in the mid-1960s some 20,000 tons a year of such materials, the Central Heating Equipment Plant in the same city furnished another 10,000, and the rest mustered between a few hundred and 5000 tons each. In 1967 the only outstandingly specialised plant was an instrument factory in Vladivostok. Any new plants that are built must be more expertly specialised while the functions of the older ones are being rationalised.

The machine output is still associated with the needs, primarily of shipping, secondly of other transport, although electrical and prime-mover equipment, lathes, agricultural machinery and mining equipment – in that order – have developed considerably. The first priority seems, however, to be the modernisation of the existing plants, followed closely by linking them up more effectively; the erection of many new plants is to follow only later. The shipbuilding industry of the S.F.E. is small; vessels must continue to come largely from European Russia's yards. Much of the output at all levels is shipped away to other Regions unprocessed or semi-finished, for further treatment in distant places. The power used per worker is low, despite a remarkably high degree of mechanisation – enforced by the lack of manpower – in some key places and activities.

On the consumer-goods side, the situation is more sheerly negative and dismal. The position of light industry (other than such curiosities as the production of musical instruments) is illustrated by Table 3.14.

Table 3.14   Light industry in the S.F.E.

	1952	1961	1963	Per capita, 1963 Far East	R.S.F.S.R.
Cotton cloth ('000 metres)	2,498	7,499	9,200	2·0	45·2
Knitted underwear ('000 pieces)	149	1,108	1,222	0·3	2·0
Knitted outerwear ('000 pieces)	170	334	387	0·08	0·6
Leather footwear ('000 pairs)	644	1,024	1,073	0·2	2·1

In the mid-1960s less than 10 per cent of the footwear requirements of the Region were produced within its boundaries. 200,000 pairs of felt boots (*valenki*) were made in a year in factories in Khabarovsk and Birobidzhan, but even for these material was imported. Other leather goods (including whale and reindeer skin articles) are to be found locally. About half the hides and pigskins produced in the Region are sent to European Russia, whence leather products are imported in return. There were a score of clothing factories; some thirty other industrial enterprises made clothing as a sideline. A clothing factory was opened in Komsomolsk in the early 1960s with 3000 workers, which was then the largest. The output of clothing was valued in 1963 at 40 million roubles, 67 per cent of it from the Khabarovsk and Maritime Provinces, which Provinces were still 25-30 per cent dependent on imports of clothing from outside the Region; Sakhalin and Kamchatka had to import over 30 per cent of their clothing needs from outside the Region.

Despite the growth in food industries after the war, most food products have to be imported from other Regions. The Region's main lines are flour milling, bakeries, meat, dairies, etc. Sausage-making and vegetable-canning are not satisfactorily developed. Local grain used to supply the local flour mills, but now as much as 60 per cent of their grist is imported; some 17 per cent of the flour consumption (by volume) and 50 per cent of the groats were imported at least until the mid-1960s, whereafter there was some increase in local capacity, but still far from enough, although at that time major centres claimed the following output of flour (tons per annum): three mills in Khabarovsk (200,000), Blagoveshchensk (160,000), Komsomolsk (80,000), Nikolayevsk on the Amur (40,000) and there were ten others. Sakhalin has only one mill, in Yuzhno-Sakhalinsk; Kamchatka and Magadan relied entirely on imports. The bakery industry is new and modern, as is the meat industry. The Zeya–Bureya plain provides about half the butter production. There are some twenty distilleries and thirty breweries, mineral-water plants, etc.; the alcoholic beverages are of indifferent quality, but the spa waters are good.

The sugar industry is a striking new development, but the production is well below the Region's needs. The growing of beet sugar has been extended, especially in the Maritimes, but much of the refining and milling is of sugar brought all the way from Cuba. A large soya-bean processing plant, working almost entirely for export to the rest of the U.S.S.R., was built in the Ussuri area before the war, another was set up in Khabarovsk and the old plant in Blagoveshchensk was refitted. The total capacity of these plants was, around 1965, 355,000 tons of finished soya preparations a year, but they were unable to keep working to that capacity. Until 1961 they were using beans imported from China, but then the import ceased and production was considerably reduced. Some soap is produced (46,000 tons from the Ussurisk Combine in 1964). Chemicals and pharmaceuticals hardly figure among the industrial activities. The quite good printing and publishing activities should be mentioned.

All the figures relating to the industrial scales have to be heavily discounted, for the large proportion represents mere repair and maintenance, rather than net output. The climatic and outpost conditions necessitate devoting a continuous and large amount of the scarce labour to preventing or repairing damage; the great distances delay the procurement of replacements, which are often unobtainable anyway, so there is endless patching of the existing plant and constant improvisation to keep it working. Even the major industries consist largely of repair services, and are insufficient even for that purpose. The ship-repair industry of the S.F.E. is comparatively large in total size, but small in scale for the most part and dispersed. It served not quite one-half of the repair needs of the Region in the mid-1960s. Non-marine repair facilities appeared somewhat more adequate, but did not cover the current requirements of the Region. A considerable proportion of the repair work was sent far outside the Region to be done, and the rate of writing-off damage or wear was necessarily high.

A large part of the metalworking and machine-making industry of the Region, similarly, represents repair work. The proportion was 29 per cent of the workers employed in the metal and machine fields, made up of 19 per cent on ship repairs and 10 per cent on other repairs. The proportion is high anywhere east of the Urals (Eastern Siberia recorded 25 per cent at the above date), much higher than in European Russia (5·6 per cent of the work force in the sector). More locally, this percentage varies extremely with the degree of industrialisation; only 10 per cent of the workers in metals and machine-building are on repairs in Khabarovsk Province, but 54 per cent in the Maritimes, 50 per cent in the Amur, while Sakhalin, Kamchatka and Magadan record even more than 90 per cent of their small work force in this category on repairs, so that the basic original production of the outlying Provinces in industry is almost nil, and that of the central ones much more modest than the numbers of workers and factories would suggest.

AGRICULTURE

The S.F.E.'s agricultural development is extremely weak. Its State and Collective farms cultivate only about 3 per cent of their extensive lands. Agriculture occupies about 15 per cent of the work force. Consumption of agricultural products greatly exceeds production. The Region had in 1966 self-sufficiency ratios of 90 per cent for potatoes, 40-50 per cent for grain, 32 per cent for meat, 30 per cent for milk, 19 per cent for eggs. In 1962, over 1·2 million tons of breadstuffs, mainly wheat

Map 3   Agricultural zones

and flour, were brought in from other Regions: about a half (675,000 tons) from Eastern Siberia, a third (460,000) from Western Siberia, plus 40,000 from the Ural and 45,000 from the Volga, even some from other parts of European Russia. In 1962 there were also imports of 40,000 tons of potatoes (from Siberia, the Ural, the Volga and the Central Black Earth Zone), 120,000 tons of meat and lard (from Siberia, the Ural, Kazakhstan, the Volga, the Black Earth area and the Ukraine) and 145,000 tons of sugar (from the Black Earth country, the Ukraine and the Volga). The only special crop of the S.F.E. was the soya bean, of which in contrast it provided 90 per cent of the Soviet Union's output, though it was a main contributor also of farmed furs, reindeer and honey.

The conditions are naturally varied, from the Arctic tundra to the southerly corner of Vladivostok, but only the long strip of the Trans-Siberian railway is agriculturally significant. Within this are two large granary areas, the area between the Zeya and Bureya rivers and the surroundings of Lake Khanka, then some mixed (predominantly market-gardening) zones around Vladivostok and Khabarovsk, also another general farming area in the Jewish Autonomous Area (Birobidzhan).

The whole area of the S.F.E. is 309 million hectares, of which about 160 million might be agriculturally useful. Of all this, if the extensive herding of reindeer is excluded, only some 7 million hectares is in agricultural use by State and Collective farms, of which 2·4 million under the plough, 1·1 million under fodder, 800,000 hectares in pastoral use. This relates to the collectivised sector; another 1·4 million ha under hay and fodder and another 800,000 ha of grazing in the private, non-collectivised and co-operative sectors must be added. Yields are significantly higher in the non-State sector. It is only in the Amur and Maritime Provinces that any significant part of the cultivable area has been utilised – about 55 per cent and 40 per cent respectively; cf. Sakhalin 7 per cent, Khabarovsk Province little over 2 per cent, Kamchatka only 0·5 per cent.

The Zeya–Bureya and Khanka basins represent together about 9 million ha of total area (about three-fifths of this in the former, two-fifths in the latter), of which some 2·7 million ha or less than a third is agricultural (including 1·5 million ha of arable). In addition there is about 250,000 ha of ploughland on the middle Amur and Ussuri lowlands. Apart from these, all the rest of the huge Region has only about 1 million ha of agricultural area, or perhaps 20 per cent of the Region's total.

Most of this remaining 20 per cent is on the upper Amur, the middle Zeya and some of the Ussuri tributaries. This relates to arable, but the fodder cropping and the grazing are similarly localised. Of the total of $2\frac{1}{2}$ million ha under hay or fodder, no less than 2·2 is in the southern part of the Region; of the 1·6 million ha of pasture, 1·4 is in the south. The Zeya–Bureya and Khanka areas specialise in grain and have relatively little land in other uses; they have between them some 600,000 ha under fodder crops or hay and 400,000 of pasturage, i.e. about one-ninth of their total crop area. In contrast, the middle Amur and Ussuri have 540,000 ha for fodder and 350,000 for pasture. On the upper Amur the land catering for cattle greatly exceeds the crop area, at 500,000 ha; similarly Kamchatka and Sakhalin have 600,000 ha in those categories, the whole northern mainland above Komsomolsk has nearly 600,000 ha under fodder and 450,000 of pasture.

The reindeer pastures amount to over 100 million ha. (Chukotia 48 million, the Koryak District north of Kamchatka 29, Magadan 20, Kamchatka 4) but much of this appears overgrazed. The reindeer herds were increasing in the early 1960s and the slight tundra growth was exhausted in places; longer-distance droving was planned, with the extension of winter outstations, etc., which would increase the food supply for the reindeer about 50 per cent.

The fodder crops are, however, broadly of very poor quality, owing especially to the marshy conditions in the south and in all the lowlands. On the Amur the yield of hay is 700-800 kg per hectare, in the Maritimes it rises to 1000, but generally the quality is poor and variable, so that grassy fodder from meadows does not satisfy more than 30 per cent of local needs and it is urgent to develop silage. Nor is the pasturage in much better case. In the south and in other lowlands, it too is subject to waterlogging and is covered with *maquis*. Not more than 1 million ha, of the total of 1·7 million of pastureland, can be utilised even in a good year.

At the beginning of the 1960s it was calculated that the practicable extensions to the agricultural area totalled over 2·2

million ha, nearly all (2·1 million) ploughland, the rest including 8000 ha of market-gardening, 100,000 of meadows and
pastures; i.e. some 30 per cent addition to the present utilised
area. This would be achieved by using 407,900 ha of fallow,
1·1 million of upland and marshy hay- and pasture-land,
200,000 of forest-clearing, 300,000 of bush-clearing and 200,000
of draining marshes. But all such improvements would be
enormously expensive and technically very difficult – prohibi-
tively so, for the foreseeable future. Some major works in the
Amur and Ussuri areas will be less uneconomic, but the most
vital needs are in the foodless outposts, where the costs rise
astronomically with the distances.

In 1960 the Amur Province had just two-thirds of the
ploughed area of the S.F.E. (with 1·5 million ha); this represented a 50 per cent increase over 1953. In the Maritimes 48
per cent of the agriculturally used area was ploughed. In
Khabarovsk Province the proportion was only 2 per cent, in
Sakhalin 7 per cent, in Kamchatka 6 per cent, in Magadan
0·2 per cent.

Before the war, cereals occupied 70 per cent of the sown area
– wheat alone over 50 per cent. Industrial ('technical') crops
represented 13 per cent, potatoes and vegetables the same percentage, fodder crops 4 per cent. During the war the rule was
the barest local self-sufficiency. By the mid-1960s more than
three-quarters of the sown area of the S.F.E. was in the
Bureya–Zeya and Khanka areas, which provided 80-90 per cent
of the grains and industrial crops; 64 per cent of these two
districts' sown areas was under spring wheat, followed by oats
17 per cent, barley 12 per cent, buckwheat 5 per cent, maize
(15,500 ha). Rice (found in the Khanka basin only) represented 3800 ha, millet (in the Zeya–Bureya) 5000. Soya was
practically the only 'industrial' crop in the Zeya–Bureya, where
it extended over 700,000 ha, but the Khanka had, besides
80,000 ha of soya, 7600 of sugar-beet. Between them the two
areas had 45,000 ha under potatoes and 15,000 under vegetables, i.e. 33 per cent and 4 per cent respectively of the S.F.E.'s.
totals. Their fodder area was 150,000 ha, 40 per cent of the
S.F.E.'s, of which 56,000 under annual grasses.

The vicinities of the major cities naturally return less under
cereals (33,000 ha altogether) and cash-crops (mainly soya,

Map 4   Sown area

90,000), having instead potatoes (55,000), vegetables (18,000)
and fodders (67,000). In all the northlands there are hardly any
vegetables (4400 ha), some 31,000 under potatoes, of cereals
hardly 1000.

Before the Revolution the Zeya–Bureya produced cereals and
other things on a pattern not differing from that of Western
Russia, while the Khanka followed the 'Korean' pattern (it had
a large Korean population, deported to Central Asian Russia
in 1945) featuring labour-intensive 'garden' cultivation with
vegetables, rice and millets. Soviet policy has aimed at mechan-

isation and at diversifying crops in all areas. In the last few years, ambitious schemes to extend the cultivation of rice, on the Amur and Ussuri as well as in the Khanka basin, have been launched; particulars will be given below, but the basic pattern should first be further considered.

Light snow cover with low temperatures characterises the southern S.F.E., permitting only spring sowings; spring wheat is the main item. Winter wheat was attempted in the Khanka area, never reaching more than 200,000 ha in extent; these efforts ceased in 1953. But spring wheat was constantly extended, representing in the mid-1960s about half a million hectares in Amur Province and 112,000 in the Maritimes. Oats, barley, buckwheat and millet followed, in that order; but rice, though it occupied only some 5000 ha or 5 per cent of the area under rice in the U.S.S.R., was already important. The 1966 calculations were that the possible area for rice was some 180,000 ha, of which 80,000 under rotation with other crops. The rice areas were then the Khanka plain and the Daubikhe and Ulakhe river valleys; besides additions there, rice was to be extended in Amur Province.

The area under soya was 840,000 ha in 1965, over 75 per cent in Amur Province, another 20 per cent in the Maritimes; the odd 40,000 ha was in southern Khabarovsk, where especially it was to be extended. Sugar-beet occupied only 7600 ha. Owing to the moisture, its sugar content is 17 per cent lower than the average in European Russia. Proposed expansion would concentrate rather on this plant's value as fodder. Regional self-sufficiency is not envisaged, the local plants depending greatly on the import of materials, which has helped Cuba but does not gratify local developers. Other crops are sunflowers, flax and perilla (for its oil, used in paints, cattle cake, printing ink and as a fertiliser); given the shortage of labour, these could be further developed only by mechanisation of harvesting or collection and better transport.

The area under potatoes (128,000 ha) and vegetables (35,000) totals 7 per cent of the sown area, not much less than the all-Russian average. Nearly a half of each is, however, in the Maritimes, a quarter in the Khabarovsk and Amur Provinces. In Sakhalin and Kamchatka, heavily dependent on imports (though local growing increased in the early 1960s), the vegetables area was about one-fifth of the potato area, whereas in the Maritimes and Amuria it was one-third.

Fodder crops at 376,000 ha represented in 1966 some 16 per cent of the sown area, half of this under annual grasses of low yield. Long-term plans were to develop greatly root crops, soya and beet residues, etc., to triple the area under fodder crops and raise its share of the sown area to one-third of the whole, mainly in Amuria and the Maritimes.

Yields are extremely poor – and irregular. Cereals yield some 800 kg/ha, spring wheat only 750, soya mostly 600-700. The yield of sugar beet is half what it is in the Ukraine, at 1200 kg/ha in the best years. The same applies to all other crops. All the devices of seed selection, soil improvement, drainage, etc., plus abundant fertiliser, would be required to alter this situation. Mostly phosphates are required; nitrogens and potash are ineffective without a phosphate base. Slag is very good, but not available. The requirements on the mechanical side are correspondingly formidable – a vast need for mechanisation in view of labour shortage, but requiring special machinery, notably caterpillar-track vehicles for the marshlands. More cheerful are the gardens, orchards and vineyards: in the Maritimes these total 9000 ha, in Khabarovsk 2500, Amuria 1400, Sakhalin 700 and even in Kamchatka 100. Wild or cultivated berries form a useful addition to the diet.

Animal husbandry is important. Planning has proceeded on the basis of increasing first the output of less transportable items (fresh meat, milk, eggs, etc.) for more local use, in the long run developing large-scale dairying and livestock exports to other Regions (Table 3.15).

Table 3.15   Livestock in the S.F.E.
(1963 – '000 head)

	Total	Zeya–Bureya and Khanka	Near the main cities	North and North-East
Cattle	921	500	300	100
(of which, cows)	(405)	(200)	(140)	(70)
Pigs	797	400	300	100
Sheep	240	200	40	–
Goats	31	12	19	–

The Okhotsk coast counted 45,000 reindeer, north Sakhalin

14,000, Kamchatka 171,000, northern Amuria 13,000, but Magadan 632,000. The total (some 900,000) represents 40 per cent of the U.S.S.R.'s reindeer.

At the beginning of the 1960s the cattle density, at 17 per 100 ha of agricultural area, was up to the R.S.F.S.R. average, but varied locally: 43 in Sakhalin, 23 in Khabarovosk and the Maritimes, 13 in Amuria, about 1 in Kamchatka, 4 in Magadan (which counted only 12,000 head altogether). The productivity was low: 2000 kg of milk per cow per year (the figures are usually given in this form), or some 16 tons per 100 ha. The yield in Sakhalin was higher, though dairying is on a small scale there. Meat and lard output was 2·1 tons deadweight per 100 ha of agricultural area on the S.F.E. average – which was a little above the R.S.F.S.R. norm, but well below the level in European Russia. Cows are predominantly 'Simmenthal' breeds; the 'humped' and 'shorthorn' kinds should be developed, to get more meat. 60 per cent of the meat output was pork at the end of the 1950s, apparently reduced to 50 per cent a few years later. The pigs are mostly large whites; Siberian and other varieties should be increasingly introduced to raise production. The pig densities are similar to the cattle densities noted above. The output of pig meat is about 1·5 tons per 100 ha of agricultural area, increasing lately to give some degree of Regional self-sufficiency.

The Zeya–Bureya and Khanka areas' sheep populations are about equal. The wool output is only about 8 kg per 100 ha of agricultural area (or 2 kg per sheep). This industry can hardly be extended, in view especially of the lack of dry pasture.

The poultry industry is fairly well developed. 47,000 eggs were produced, around 1963, per 100 ha of area under cereals – much above the national average. Geese and ducks are rapidly increasing in number. There is much bee-keeping, a good yield of honey.

Fur-bearing animals have long been hunted and trapped, in many places to near-extinction; therefore there is now a very large development of fur-farming. Few mink were produced in 1930, but by 1968 national output was 743,800 pelts, of which 634,700 in the R.S.F.S.R. In 1965-7 the Maritime Province earned a revenue from mink of 5·3 million roubles. In 1958 this Province delivered to the State 22,000 skins; in the subsequent ten years, 837,000. In 1968 half a million skins went to the auctions. The 1970 plan was fulfilled ahead of time; by 1976 it is hoped to raise the output by another 125,000. This relates almost entirely to farmed mink. The Kedrovski Farm is specially reputed. It uses 30,000 tons of *mintai* fish (unsuitable for human consumption) for feeding the mink on the farm. But three times as much is sent to other Regions, for this purpose; the State Fishing Trust makes a profit of 63 roubles per ton on exporting this fish-fodder westwards, though the business is handicapped by shortage of refrigerators.

Recurrent themes are the comparison between agriculture and industry, the low yield in agriculture and its low technical level. The shortage of manpower affects farming hardly less than industry, the rural population being small and scattered. The density of population on the Khanka plain is about 8 per square kilometre, on the Zeya–Bureya plain about 7. The Ussuri valley registers 4·5, a little further east in the southern Maritimes the figure falls to 2·6, not far outside Khabarovsk city it falls to 1. Industrial production in the S.F.E. has grown, from insignificant beginnings, as much as seventyfold since 1913; agriculture hardly threefold. The farming population has been dwindling; in 1956 it was 1·4 million or a third of the whole, in 1963 it was 1·2 million or 27 per cent. This proportion is much below the national average (which is above 50 per cent); only in the Amur Province is the agrarian population as high as 40 per cent of the total. High percentages in the outlying areas are of course not indicative; the huge Koryak National District in North Kamchatka registers over 70 per cent as 'agricultural', but the total population is about 35,000 and it lives by reindeer keeping, fishing and hunting.

Agriculture is much less specialised than industry; the only 'specialistic' rural products are soya beans and furs, apart from some pharmaceutical and gastronomical specialities for Oriental markets, mentioned below. The markets for the agricultural staples are too distant; western Russia can obtain these much nearer at hand. Technical progress (refrigeration and canning) has countered this difficulty in respect of fish; 95 per cent of the S.F.E.'s catch, which represents 30-34 per cent of the U.S.S.R.'s total, is exported, mainly to other parts of the Soviet Union, some to foreign countries. No such stimulus has been enjoyed by agriculture; no great rationalisation, improvements in production or distribution have occurred, no new products been added.

Agriculture accounts for only about 15 per cent of the Regional gross product. In the Amur Province, exceptionally, 40 per cent of local national income is from agriculture. The total scale of S.F.E. agriculture is considerable. In the mid-1960s the sown area was 2,384,000 ha, there were 921,000 head of cattle, 797,000 pigs. The whole agricultural production, except for soya beans, was used within the Region itself, being far less than the Region's own needs, and large imports have to be made. In cereals for human consumption the Region was about 70 per cent self-sufficient (as a whole – with tremendous distribution difficulties even within the Region itself), in animal feedstuffs only about 50 per cent. Some 'basic' self-sufficiency in potatoes was achieved (with, throughout, a very uneven distribution in different parts of the Region), in vegetables 55 per cent, in meat products only 33 per cent (supplemented, of course, by local game), in milk products only 30 per cent; in fruit and many other things there are severe deficiencies. The only areas with agricultural surpluses are the Khanka and Zeya–Bureya plains. In recent years, Western Siberia (and to some extent Central Asia, though Khrushchev's great hopes there were disappointed) began to deliver cheaper grain and the S.F.E. hoped to place more emphasis on dairying and meat production. Most recently, there has been some stress on the extensive production of rice. Most crops are not remunerative, the growers having no large local markets. The State gives better prices for soya beans and other 'technical' crops, but the production of these fluctuates. In 1960 the newspaper *Rural Life* stressed the great future of soya, which represented 31 per cent of total Kolkhoz income in the Amur Province in 1959. At the end of the Seven-Year Plan the area under soya in the S.F.E. was to reach 1·1 million ha, or 40 per cent of the sown area. The yield was low, 700-900 kg ha, which could be raised to 1400. Yet, even at the lower figure, the return from this crop was two or three times the return from cereals, with less exhaustion of the soil.

By the mid-1960s firm intentions were expressed for a 'massive' extension of agriculture in the S.F.E. The 'battlefield' was to be especially the marshlands. Early in 1967 the projected land reclamation was given as 1,216,000 ha, on which it was planned to settle many immigrants and establish 75 State Farms. Prompt results were claimed to have followed. From drained land, 1600 to 1800 kg of wheat per hectare and 1000-1200 of rice were obtained in 1969, it was asserted.[6] The Priamuria ('Amur-side') Kolkhoz had drained 10,500 ha, but much more experience was required The Amur Virgin Soil Project was organised in 1966. Some modern machinery was applied – under difficult conditions. The capacity of the dredge-scoops used there in 1968 was 0·15 cubic metre for first- and second-category soils, with temperatures down to −30°C. Soon the usual problems ensued of shortages and latefalls in planning. The Amur and Belogorsk (*tselinostroi*) Projects required in that year 35,000 cu. m of ferro-concrete, but Amur's Project-building industry could provide only 22,000; the rest could not be found. A large cement plant is planned at Vozzhayenka, but this work too was late.[7]

In the last few years the S.F.E. has thus been the scene of a massive 'drive' for increased agricultural production. Like Krushchev's famous 'Virgin Lands' campaign in Central Asia in the earlier 1950s, it stresses the opening of new areas, especially for growing cereals (including rice). The same terms are used, e.g. the main State agency in charge is called Tselinostroi ('Virgin Soil Construction'), but the new campaign is on a less grandiose scale – and claims of course to be more sensibly organised. However, there is the same stream of complaints and indications of broad failure, as illustrated by the following. In mid-1970 a Moscow daily reported these findings of three of its correspondents sent to the S.F.E.

In Khabarovsk Province between 1966 and 1969 the annual output of grain increased 72 per cent, that of soya 70 per cent, potatoes 44 per cent, other vegetables 22 per cent. The ploughed area was increased by 22,000 ha, 'enabling the proper rotation of crops, which had in many areas previously been very unscientific'. 'But you can't get away from the facts; the State plans for reclaiming land and establishing Collective Farms in the S.F.E. are not being fulfilled. In the first four years of the Five-Year Plan (1965-9) we should have set up 30,800 powerpoints for irrigation systems, but the result was 9000. In

Khabarovsk Province the basis for bringing new land into cultivation during 1967-70 was about one-half fulfilled.'

It is the shortfall in vegetables that continues to affect the local people most immediately. In Khabarovsk a Hothouse Combine is being built, originally planned to cover 50,000 sq. m. 'With what impatience the citizens wait for this. They still wait – for the thirteenth year now.' Meanwhile the size has been reduced to '30,000 sq. m, promised in 1972. In this Provincial capital one can't get vegetables even in summer' and the hothouse project is still in the bricklaying stage. 'The fact is extraordinary, but the explanation we received was simply astonishing. One worker of the Provincial organisation said: "You see, the Hothouse Combine is considered as a village (local authority) project to raise vegetables. But village projects do not have weight. The subordinates pass the buck to each other, it is hard to determine where the guilt lies." '

The Khabarovsk Tselinostroi and the Birobidzhan Tselinostroi, which were created to reorganise the State and Collective farms, handle half the agricultural products, but they prefer to 'raise walls in the towns, rarely visiting the branches of the State farms or the brigades in the Collectives'. The State Farms failed, prior to 1963, to build up capital funds. Up to 1968 they set up only temporary animal-husbandry installations, now characterised 'in the main by decrepitude (*vyetkhosti*)'. The U.S.S.R. Ministry of Agricultural Construction must, however, share the blame.

The report proceeds to identify 'two main factors inescapable in the S.F.E.' One is the problem of cadres. The agricultural population, especially in the Maritimes and Khabarovsk Province is streaming to the towns. Which is 'legal, but unnatural'; for 'village house-building is progressing very badly and the organisation of labour in general is primitive, especially in animal husbandry'. So 'the villager seeks the best conditions for himself – and finds them in industrial enterprises'. Big 'rice-engineering' projects are in hand, but labour cannot be found to work on them. The other factor is the grossly inadequate 'style and methods' of the authorities in charge. The 'long-suffering' Khabarovsk Hothouse Project 'will be remembered significantly' (*nesprosta*, meaning 'invidiously'; the context also suggesting 'there's more in this than meets the eye').

Examples are given. In Khabarovsk Province, Glavdal'stroi (the Construction Organisation for the S.F.E.) is setting up the new El'ban and Voznessenovski State Farms (south of Amursk on the Komsomolsk railway) costing respectively 20 and 12 million roubles; contracts are proceeding only at the rate of between 300,000–600,000 roubles a year. Glavdal'stroi was established as a special Regional section of the Ministry of Land Improvement and Water Economy, but it has no building industry to give it an infrastructure. In Ussurisk 'the material and technical supply-base shows only middling growth. The planned [expenditure] was 670,000 roubles, the realised 441,000. The Chief Engineer of the Trust said "It's awful to think, this bunch are going to build an automated machine-shop. How many years will that take!" . . . "We are a burden on the Trust. . . ." Official documents of the Maritime, Khabarovsk and Amur Provinces are full of such statements as "plan unfulfilled".' At Blagoveshchensk, the 'industrial unification project' is described as 'frozen up', and the construction of a trade school with 600 pupils, planned for 1969, was not achieved.

The new Tselinny (Virgin Soils) Kolkhoz in the Arkhara district of Amur Province received its first allocation of land, but this was only 7500 ha instead of the 22,000 planned. This is also an example of the lack of infrastructural provisions; 'the conditions here are unsuitable for normal work. There are no animal-houses, storehouses, schools, hospitals; and you can't get housing.' It is revealed that the draft plan represented a total expenditure of 62 million roubles; the Improvement Ministry considered this too high and reduced the items quoted, rather than cut down the area to be cultivated. The Mil'gunovski Collective Farm in the Maritimes has begun to deliver rice to the State; in 1968 it yielded 2·6 tons of grain from 500 ha, but for various reasons it was less successful in 1969. The Director is quoted as giving the same reason, lack of ancillary facilities: 'We've already sown 1130 ha. Heading for a big harvest – but trouble with the grain. We have no drying plant, no storehouses, don't know when we'll get them. But the sown area is increasing.' Further, he required tractor and combine drivers and repairers, but had nowhere to lodge them. No livestock were included in the plan, it was entirely for rice; this, comments the newspaper, 'is specialisation taken *ad absurdum*'.

Central policy always presses for the combination of local activities into 'complexes'; the correspondents from Moscow asked the Director whether the local State Farms could not be thus integrated. He replied 'My power is small' and showed them a telegram just received from Moscow saying that special attention was to be devoted to irrigation – everything else would be charged against the future profits of the Sovkhozes.

The Party Secretary of the Maritime Province wrote in *Pravda* on 4 May 1970 as follows. Large areas in the Province are suitable for rice, providing the required 8000-10,000 cubic metres of water per hectare. The 1966 Plenum of the C.P.S.U. decided on a large programme of land reclamation and improvement, with emphasis on rice production. In 1965, 8200 ha were under rice, now 17,000. Glavdal'vodstroi (S.F.E. Water Administration) organised two Improvement Trusts and one General Construction Trust, many building units with a 'column' of lorries, and Soyuzdal'giproris (i.e. a Hydraulics and Rice enterprise). The techniques began to be specially studied in the Science Institute in Vladivostok, making check-maps of the flow of water on a wide front, for a first experiment in the complex automatic regulation of water-levels. The study of plant diseases was also important. New varieties of rice had been produced; the 'Far Eastern', 'Maritimes-10 and -11' and the 'Northern' yield 4500 to 5000 kg ha and it is hoped to extend rice-growing further north, into Khabarovsk and Amuria.

However 'our system is too complicated and time-taking: for instance, the "Far Eastern" took 27 per cent of the whole rice area in the Province'. Much of the present extension thus consists of experimental work which is still unproved, for 'unfortunately', the Party Secretary added, 'it [the new 'Far Eastern' variety] is not yet officially adopted'. He proceeded to mention the serious lack of fertilisers and herbicides – though good results were claimed. In 1968 the average yield of the Sovkhozes specialising in rice was more than 3000 kg ha and they sold altogether 26,000 tons to the State – 2·6 times as much as in 1965. 1969 was, however, a bad year, unusually cold; the yield was only 2340 kg ha, nevertheless the State plan was fulfilled and all the State Rice Farms are paying concerns (*rentabl'nye*). He gave assurances that the Party's 'Agitprop' was constantly pressing the workers to do better.

The task for the next few years was to raise the yield to 3500-4000 kg ha and deliver more to the State. The Science Institute in Vladivostok, which has increased its project spending in three years from 600,000 to 1·9 million roubles, apparently cannot continue at that rate. It surveys all the rice areas, but has not been able to see to the provision of all the pumping stations and the farm buildings which were planned for populous farming areas; the provision of dwellings is especially vital, then the provision of dairies. The State was providing all the mechanical excavators required. Voluntary immigration must be fervently encouraged, in view of the shortage of workers; results are still disappointing.

A call went out in Georgia for 130 Young Communists; only thirty-two came forward, of whom only six finally reached the rice-farms of the S.F.E. In Vladimir Province the call went out for 150; seventy respondents were found, but they were all 'non-specialists' and had to be trained completely in the Far East. The Party Secretary considered that much more pressing efforts should be made – envisaging the voluntary emigration of whole families from Central Russia, rather than single youngsters.[8]

FORESTRY

Forests cover 117 million ha, 37 per cent of the area of the S.F.E. In 1958 the S.F.E. provided the rest of the Soviet Union with 713,000 metric tons of wood, in 1960 double that amount, besides some export to foreign countries. In 1963 the figure fell to less than 1 million and it was intended to keep it generally thus low, to cater for the Region's own internal needs, including the planned development of the paper and pulp industry. Much of the timber is, however, sent out – most uneconomically for transport over very long distances – unprocessed. The proportion was 60 per cent in the mid-1960s; great importance is attached to the development of local processing capacity of all kinds. Total stands in the S.F.E. are given as about 12 billion cubic metres, or 126 million per hectare (20 per cent above the average density in the U.S.S.R.), of which three-quarters is coniferous and the same proportion mature growth, though only about 10 per cent is of the top quality. The export (19 million cubic metres in 1963, an increase of only 12 per cent over 1940) represented only 18 per cent of the natural growth during the year. More selective felling became the rule during the 1960s, when over 70 per cent of the cutting was not for local use. In 1940, 70 per cent of the enterprises in the S.F.E. were cutting timber for their own direct use; by 1964 less than 20 per cent; i.e. over 80 per cent was being 'marketed', but this proportion could still be greatly raised. 40 per cent of the wood processing was, about 1965, in Khabarovsk, 21 per cent in the Maritimes, the Amur and Sakhalin had 16 per cent each, Kamchatka and the Kuriles 3 per cent each.

Though huge areas of timber remain untouched, the mature timber stocks are declining in the older centres of long exploitation. In 1959 in the Blagoveshchensk Forestry Collective the ratio of mature timber had fallen to 6 per cent of the whole, on the upper Daubikhe the cut was exceeding the growth.[9] These are extreme cases, though most of the more accessible areas are experiencing some exhaustion. Behind them, however, lie vast stores for the future.

FISHERIES

The fisheries may be considered in terms of the base areas where the catches are handled. In the mid-1960s, the structure of the fish-processing industry was broadly as follows. There were four main handling areas – the southern Maritimes, the Lower Amur, Sakhalin and Khamchatka – and one minor, Magadan. 40 per cent of the catch was merely salted, the rest frozen or canned (Table 3.16).

Table 3.16   Fisheries bases in the S.F.E.

	Share of total processing (%)	Proportion frozen or canned (%)
Maritime coast	60	63
Kamchatka	16	65
Amur river and mouth	9	66
Sakhalin	9	50
Magadan	6	50

The Maritime coast had three main processing centres and
one medium-sized one around Vladivostok and Nakhodka, one
medium-sized at Tetyukhe and a small one at the border of
Khabarovsk Province. Khabarovsk had three large centres at
Komsomolsk and Sovietskaya Gavan', smaller ones at Khabarovsk, Troitskoye, Bogorodskoye and four on the Amur estuary.
Sakhalin's centres are the large ones at Nevel'sk, Korsakov and
Dolinsk, medium-sized ones at Poronaisk, Aleksandrovsk and
Rybnovsk. In the Kuriles there is a large northern centre, a
medium-sized southern one. In Kamchatka, Petropavlovsk has
one large and one small centre, and other large ones are Ozer-

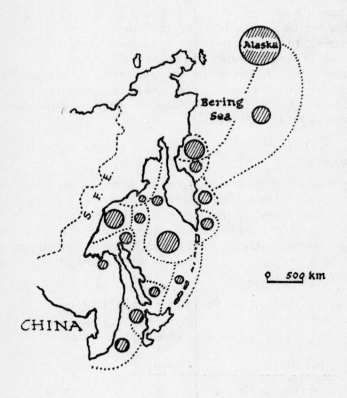

Map 5   Fisheries areas

noye, Ust'-Kamchatka and four on the north-east coast; on the
west coast there are four medium-sized ones, on the east coast
another at Uka. Magadan has one large and one medium
plant near its capital city, small ones at Yamsk, Nayakan,
Giziga.

The fishing grounds – apart from an increasing Soviet activity far into the Pacific and other oceans – are no less than
seventeen, each distinctly varied or specialised. Table 3.17
shows broadly the pattern in the mid-1960s, but this industry is
changing in every respect.

Table 3.17 Distribution of the total Soviet fisheries catch,
North Pacific
(in 1964, including marine products other than fish; approximate percentages)

Fishing grounds	Demarcation	% of total catch
1. Bering – Alaska	Karaginski Island – Bering Strait – Bristol Bay	12
2. Southern Okhotsk Sea	S.W. coast of Kamchatka	10
3. Aleutians	(Whaling and sealing only)	8
4. Olyutor Gulf, north	Karaginski Island – Olyutorski	8
5. Olyutor Gulf, south	Karaginski Island – Komandor Islands – Ust' Kamchatka	6
6. Petropavlovsk, north	Ust' Kamchatka – Petropavlovsk	6
7. Okhotsk	Off Okhotsk	6
8. S.E. Sakhalin	Dolinsk – Korsakov	5
9. Petropavlovsk, south	Petropavlovsk – N. Kuriles	4
10. N.E. Sakhalin		4
11. Amur river	Inland and mouth	4
12. S. Maritimes	Off Vladivostok	3
13. Central-eastern Sakhalin		3
14. Magadan	Magadan coast west of Kamchatka	2
15. Shelekhov Gulf		2
16. Kuriles		2
17. Tartar Gulf	West coast Sakhalin	1

Some 10 per cent is brought in from waters further south and
south-east.

Analysis by the types of fish is complicated. The Russian
names for local varieties do not readily fit English equivalents
(Table 3.18).

Table 3.18   Composition of the S.F.E. fisheries catch
(approximate percentages, by value, mid-1960's; for key to
fishing grounds, see Table 3.17 and Map 5)

Fishing grounds	Herring	Salmon	Flatfish	Other fish	Crabs	Whales, marine animals	Total
1.	10	–	60	30	–	–	100
2.	15	5	35	20	10	15	100
3.	–	–	–	–	–	100	100
4.	80	–	20	–	–	–	100
5.	–	95	–	–	5	–	100
6.	60	–	35	5	–	–	100
7.	100	–	–	–	–	–	100
8.	75	–	25	–	–	–	100
9.	20	80	–	–	–	–	100
10.	45	45	10	–	–	–	100
11.	–	50	–	50	–	–	100
12.	–	–	35	55	10	–	100
13.	40	60	–	–	–	–	100
14.	–	100	–	–	–	–	100
15.	–	100	–	–	–	–	100
16.	–	40	–	40	20	–	100
17.	–	100	–	–	–	–	100

The seasonality is still extreme. Winter catching has been
increased and fleets made more adaptable, especially the crab
boats, to switching types of fish by seasons; nevertheless about
three-quarters of the catching is in the second and third quarters
of the year. Some 86 per cent of the output was for human
consumption in the mid-1960s. The proportion frozen and
mildly salted was nearly 80 per cent at that time, but the low-
quality strongly salted fish still represented 15 per cent. Fish
meal is much needed for fertiliser and increasingly for feeding
animals on fur farms, for which the present processing output
is inadequate. Until the mid-1960s all the canning was *au
naturel*, thereafter just over one-third was done in oil, a quarter
in tomato. Catching is two-thirds by the State organisation,
one third by Collectives; the whole is controlled by the State
organisation Dal'ryba, concentrating on the southern Maritimes, where a good two-thirds of the repair and other services
are located.

A fundamental reconstruction of the fishing industry was

embarked on in the 1950s; the range was to be extended by modern mentods, the processing facilities modernised and rationalised. In the mid-1960s, though most of the fish was by then frozen or canned, a high proportion was still being merely salted (as much as 60 per cent in Sakhalin, 40 per cent in Kamchatka, 30 per cent in the Southern Maritimes).

In the recent history of the fisheries a striking feature is the (world-wide) decline of the salmon. In 1913 the total S.F.E. catch was 107,200 tons, of which nearly 90 per cent was salmon, about 6 per cent herring and about 5 per cent in the broad category called *chastik*, which in this Region is largely sea perch. In those days, there were no entries for whales, crabs, marine plants, etc. In 1940 the catch had nearly trebled (at 309,300 tons), salmon was (though nearly 20 per cent larger in quantity than in 1913) down as a percentage to 37 per cent, the quantity of herring was nearly nine times that of 1913 and its percentage up to 16 per cent; sardines (29 per cent), crab (14 per cent), whales (4 per cent), other marine products (very small), cod (4 per cent), plaice (1 per cent) and others were added to the list.

In 1955 the salmon catch reached a peak at 114,400 tons, but this was 27 per cent of a total catch which had doubled since 1940 (at 640,200 tons). Herring (21 per cent) and flatfish (19 per cent) had risen to a new prominence, cod to 7 per cent, whales (at nearly 80,000 tons) to 12 per cent, other sea animals and the 'other aquatic' (plants, etc.) to 1 per cent. In the following two years the total catch increased by some 30 per cent, to 815,600 tons, but salmon declined by some 13 per cent in actual quantity compared to 1955 and to only 19 per cent of the total; herring rose to six times the 1940 figure and to 36 per cent of the total catch; the rest remained at about the same percentages as in 1955, except that crab declined from over 37,000 tons or 6 per cent in 1955 to less than 30,000 or 4 per cent in 1957 (43 per cent of the Soviet Union's total catch of crabs).

There were subsequently changes in the statistical system; the subject is intricate. The fluctuations are very marked. The decline of salmon has continued sharply. The herring catch declined about 10 per cent in 1961 compared to 1957, but rose again by about 20 per cent in 1961. The catch of cod roughly tripled between 1957 and 1961, flatfish almost doubled, and 1962 showed about the same levels for both of these. The total catch rose to 1·7 million tons (about double 1957) in 1964.

The fisheries industry is one of the S.F.E.'s leading assets, but is affected by many variables which make its planning particularly difficult. In 1962 the State Fishing Fleet, accounting for about 85 per cent of the catch, totalled nearly 600,000 tons, of which over one-third consisted of medium-sized trawlers without refrigeration, some 20 per cent of similar ships with refrigerated holds, about 18 per cent of seiners, only about 7 per cent being large refrigerated trawlers and some 18 per cent being a mixed category of 'others'. In 1955 there were some six hundred small fisheries centres scattered all round the southern half of the Region, each producing on the average only just over 1000 tons of processed fish, though a few big centres were at the level of 25,000 tons. The total number of centres had been nearly halved by the mid-1960s and a large part of the output concentrated in modernised plants with an annual capacity of 20,000-30,000 tons. The ultimate aim is to reduce the processing centres to only fifteen – five in Kamchatka (where Ust' Kamchatka and Oktyabrski are especially large), four in Sakhalin (where Nevel'sk has been specially notable), and three each in the Maritimes and Kuriles, each to be very large and up to date. In the mid-1960s the catch exceeded the processing capacity by no less than 60 per cent.

A 'Round Table' discussion on the recent progress of the fishing industry, held in Vladivostok, was reported in the Press late in 1969. The total fisheries production of the S.F.E. was over 2 million tons; by the end of the Five-Year Plan (1970) it should reach 2·4 million, at some later date 3·1 million. There was, however, much criticism. The gap between the productivity of the fishing fleets and the inadequate refrigeration facilities remained serious. Repairs – and work ashore generally – were slow. Longer periods are spent at sea, provision for the 'cultural needs' of the fishermen is more difficult. The shortage of cadres is acute; the Head of the Far East Refrigerator-Fleet reported as follows: 'This fleet has a hundred modern vessels – but less than 4000 people to man them. We have to send ships to sea with crews five or six, or even ten short. Today we have not a single skipper, not a single mechanic, in reserve. There ought to be forty-two First-Class Diesel Mechanics – we have twelve. If a specialist is ill, we take one from a ship under repair, or recall comrades from leave . . . but still cannot get full complements.'

This situation applies over the whole field – the timber fleet, the Kamchatka cabotage, the Sovietskaya Gavan' fishing, the whalers, the repairers. In the factories the shift or replacement ratio is extremely low. 'The nose has become smaller than the forehead' (i.e. 'too much top-hamper'). Expansion outstrips labour capacity; in Nakhodka a new hull-shop was established, which is still short of 800 workers. (It is hard enough to recruit eight workers, even unskilled ones, in the S.F.E., let alone eight hundred.)

In 1959 there were 112,000 workers in the S.F.E. fisheries, now there are 182,000, but this is still insufficient. Specialists must be sought long ahead; 'they cannot be trained in a month'. 'Where are they to be found?' (The question remained un-answered at the Round Table.) Two-thirds of the present workers (who include, in Soviet fisheries, a high proportion of females) are young, 'attracted to shore occupations, fishing holds them only for their younger years', from romantic appeal. That appeal was not sufficiently publicised in fiction, the cinema, etc. Dockers are not to be had, though the work is mechanised and they are paid 'up to' 250 roubles a month. The average wage on large refrigerator ships is 327, on seiners 328 – more in a good season – and the food is good, including vege-tables and meat all the year round. 'We need new people as [urgently as] we need air.' The motor fishing vessel *Leninski Luch* operated in 1970 as far away as Africa; a sister ship had been built, but the plan had called for four in this class.[10]

However, earlier in 1969 the official organ gave the number of employees in the S.F.E. fisheries as 160,000 – of whom more than 60,000 were at sea. Output had tripled in the last ten years. In 1968 the S.F.E. marketed 300,000 tons of fish pro-ducts, including 310 million cans. 212 new vessels had been put into service during the Five-Year Plan (ending 1970), but the annual shortage of refrigerator-ship space still ran at 130,000 tons. 1969 was to have seen considerable 'regeneration' of the Vladivostok fishing fleet; but, whereas the first stage of this was projected to cost 49·7 million roubles, only 11·3 were allocated

SFE D

and only 9·8 actually used in the first three years. The 1968 plan had therefore not been fulfilled, and progress continues to be very slow.[11]

This concludes the preliminary general description of the Region as a whole. The following chapters describe, in more local focus, the life and problems of each of the Provinces.

CHAPTER 4

Trans-Baikal:
The Mongolian Threshold

The Soviet Union enters the Far East at Lake Baikal. That inland sea is surrounded on its eastern, northern and southern sides by the territory of the Mongolians within the Soviet Union – the Buryat Autonomous Soviet Socialist Republic. Beyond this to the south and east lie the frontiers with China, but with the interposition of the People's Republic of Mongolia, which is not a part of the Soviet Union but well connected with it. The penumbra of Mongolian presence and influence extends far to the eastward into Khalka, the northerly hump of Manchuria outlined by the curve of the Argun' and Upper Amur rivers, politically part of China.

The Soviet Union is in a position of strength and security in this area. After the mid-1930s the Mongolian People's Republic developed strongly on Soviet lines and under Soviet influence. It gave substantial help to the Soviet Union during the war with Germany and against Japan. Practical and cultural affinities deepened; even the Mongol language is now written in a form of the Russian Cyrillic script. In 1940 the railway was completed all the way from Ulan Ude in the U.S.S.R. to Ulan Bator, the capital of the Mongolian Republic. The two countries are closely linked.[1] In 1939 Mongolian and Soviet troops repulsed the Japanese Army on the Khalka river at the eastern end of the Mongolian Republic; in 1945 they joined in the swift move across Manchuria. They are confident that they could deal similarly with the Chinese if the occasion arose, particularly given the present technical superiority of the Russians.

Meanwhile the Buryat A.S.S.R. is more specifically integrated with the Soviet Union, as one of its constituent republics. It was established under Moscow auspices in 1923 as the Buryat

Mongolian A.S.S.R. In 1958 the word Mongolian was officially dropped from its title – a step which bluntly expresses its full integration with the U.S.S.R. Only 20 per cent of its population are now Buryats, i.e. Soviet citizens of Mongolian descent; almost all the rest are European Russians. Its area is over 350,000 sq. km. The population has shown a rapid growth – 673,000 in 1959, 789,000 in 1968 – especially the urban population, which was about 40 per cent in 1959 and is now about 50 per cent; the capital city of Ulan Ude (called until 1935 Verkhneudinsk) alone had 175,000 people in 1959, 235,000 ten years later. The central portion of the Buryat A.S.S.R. centring on Ulan Ude is considerably developed agriculturally, pastorally and in forestry; mining areas are further west (around Zakamensk) and far to the north-east (between Yeleninski and Tsipikan).

PACIFIC WATERSHED

Detailed consideration of the S.F.E. should, however, begin with the Province of Chita. This Province lies beyond the Yablonovy range of mountains, which may be said to form a watershed both literally and metaphorically. The waters do run from the Yablonovy crest towards the Pacific on the one side and inland on the other. Metaphorically also this is a watershed marking the beginning of the Far East; the ambience and the psychology change in that sense, even the ethnography, as Mongolian and Asian faces become more numerous among the people.

Chita Province was bitterly involved in the Civil War and the Allied Intervention (1919-20); the graves of Partisans and others are there in great numbers to attest it. This historical memory has never faded in Chita, and the present situation evokes fears that events could again take a similar turn. The south-east of Chita Province is face-to-face with the Maoist People's Republic of China, in easy sight across the river, where bellicose and vituperative noises sound in places within earshot or gunshot, or literally a stone's throw. Chita Province is still in Eastern Siberia according to the official demarcation of Major Economic Planning Regions in the U.S.S.R., which has the

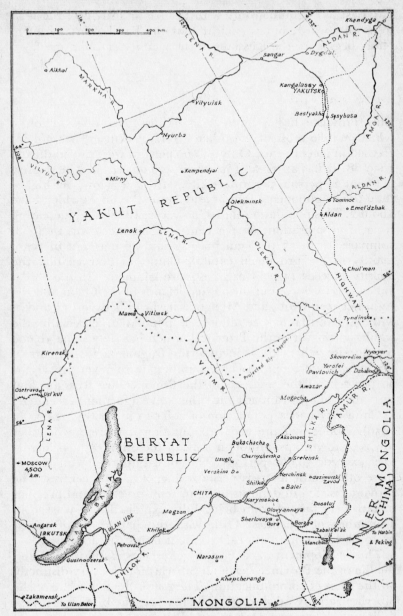

Map 6   Trans-Baikal and South Yakutia

Far East as beginning only with the Amur Province, the next to the eastward; but it is clear that the Far Eastern problem really begins for the Russians in the vicinity of Chita itself.

CHITA PROVINCE

This Province has a population of just over one million – which, unlike most of the other S.F.E. Provinces, has not increased in recent years. Only 40,000 persons were added during 1959-68. It has an area of just over 430,000 sq. k. The density of about $2\frac{1}{2}$ persons per square kilometre is very low, but higher than the neighbouring Buryat and Amur Provinces which have about 2. This population shows, however, a high and increasing ratio of urbanisation; 63 per cent were in the towns in 1968, compared with 57 per cent in 1952 and 46 per cent in 1939, mainly in the provincial capital, Chita; in that vicinity the density exceeds 15 persons per square kilometre. In the Shilka valley it is over 10, but in the steppelands of the Onon and the Agin between Chita and Mongolia it varies between $1\frac{1}{2}$ and 3, while the outlands are almost unpopulated, especially the whole north-east of the Province, which has only some 10,000 people altogether; these include the fragmentary survivors of the indigenous peoples (whose numbers were never great), for 90 per cent of the residents of the Province are Russians and Buryats, while Ukrainians and others take a further percentage.

Chita city had a population of 208,000 in 1968 (172,000 in 1959). About half the urban population is therefore in other towns or townships, although none of the other eight principal ones exceeds 50,000 persons. The most important category of these other settlements is perhaps that of mining centres. The Province is rich in deposits of light, semi-precious and precious metals, very far yet from being fully exploited, but worked in a number of localities. Otherwise the pattern is of mixed pastoral, forest, agricultural and light industrial activities.

The development in each of these respects is still modest and the life of the Province (as of all Siberia) focuses very distinctly on the lines of communication. These are, the main line of the Siberian railway all through the Province, the branch railways to Borzya, Kharanor, Dosatui and Priargun'sk in the south-east (connecting further to Choibalsan in Mongolia) and branch lines also in the central eastern part of the Province to Sretensk and Bukachacha; also the few roads (a motor road connects Chita southwards with Khapcheranga and westwards with Irkutsk), and finally the Argun' river, which forms the frontier with China, and some other rivers, which are, however, sinuous and not easy of navigation.

Until recently, the distance from any major industrial centre compelled concentration on transportable products and local finishing processes. The Province is all upland (700 to 3000 m) in parallel ranges. The climate is extremely continental and severe – hotter in summer than the Ukraine, colder in winter than Novaya Zemlya (– 25 to – 33°C) but always dry and sunny, apart from summer monsoon periods in which over half the rainfall (210-400 mm in various areas) is concentrated. All the northern slopes are much colder than the southward-facing ones. In the south especially, the rivers may have ten or fifteen times the head of water in the brief wet season (July-August) as in the driest periods; there are serious floods in September.

In winter all the smaller rivers freeze solid to their beds. The north of the Province stands on permafrost tens of metres deep, in the centre the frozen ground is limited to patches mainly in the forest, in the south to still smaller patches. Since at the other extreme the Borzya and other rivers in the south dry out completely in some warm seasons, their navigation season is only from three to five months in the year. Only the Shilka and Sretensk rivers, plus the small stretch of the Amur which comes within Chita Province, are usable by river boats of any considerable draught. The Argun', the frontier river, is uncertain and variable in all these respects.

Forests cover half the Province; 74 per cent of the area larch, 10 per cent pine, the rest birch, cedar etc., totalling 2 billion cubic metres of timber. However, most of this is remote from the settled areas, being in the northern and eastern uplands; the south is steppeland, the Mongolian steppe. These grasslands serve chiefly for pasturage (90 per cent of the grazing area of the Province) but also for arable (60 per cent of the planted area of the Province). The wild life is varied in all parts, including a considerable yield of furs in the north.

To all these difficulties of underpopulation, remoteness, geo-

graphical inconvenience (there is indeed one more not mentioned above – the Province is liable to earthquakes) must be
added two others. One is shortage of fuel. The Province contains a great deal of coal (7 billion tons, 4 of which in the
Kharanor area) but mined as yet to any notable extent only
around Chernovo near Chita and Bukachacha 200 km to the
north-east. There are hopes that at some future time there may
be hydroelectric stations at the confluence of the Amazar with
the Amur, on the Vitim and elsewhere.

Coal is dear; the Province's output ($3\frac{1}{2}$ million tons a year
in the early 1960s) is insufficient for its own needs (in 1962, 1·8
million tons were brought in from Cheremkhovo beyond Irkutsk and 0·3 million from Raichikhinsk equally far away to
the east). A thermal power station of 300,000 kW in Chita and
another of between 600,000 and 1·5 million in the Kharanor
coalfield should now be in operation.

The other problem is the cutting off of trade with China.
During the honeymoon of collaboration with the newly established Communist state in China and the high tide of Russian
supplies to it in the earlier 1950s, the route through Chita must
have been very active and prosperous, though neither Government has published specific details. By the end of the decade,
however, the partners had quarrelled bitterly, trade and aid
dwindled to a sorry trickle and remain so today. Not that this
is a new situation for the Chitans; this route has been hampered
and disputatious for forty or fifty years, the collaboration with
Communist China appearing as only a short interlude in a long
history of confusion, obstruction or blockade.

This area emerged fully from the Civil War only in about
1923. In the next ten years the situation in China was rather
chaotic; then the Japanese seized Manchuria under the puppet
Empire Manchukuo, renewing strife and chicanery, permitting
at best limited or sporadic communications on this frontier.
One graphic ultimate result may be cited: the well-known tea
factory in Chita formerly obtained its tea from China, but now
fetches it from the distant south-west of the Soviet Union.

Historically this sector has been the most stressful part of the
whole frontier, and Chita Province the hardest hit, economically and practically, by bad foreign relations. The people of
Trans-Baikalia have particularly strong revolutionary and

guerrilla traditions: this was the place of exile of the Decembrist rebels of 1825, a left-wing strongpoint in 1905 and 1918-23. All these factors are strongly felt today.

THE INDUSTRIES OF CHITA

A few kilometres west of the city of Chita is the lignite coalfield of Chernovo, the beginning of an area of light industrial development which extends into and around the city itself, but chiefly on its western side. The coal of Chernovo (1·7 million tons in 1965) sustains an electric power station on Lake Kenon. The industrial district contains clothing and worsted mills (12 million metres of cloth in the early 1960s) and a car-assembly plant. The western outskirts of the city contain the large and important railways workshops, a major centre of main-line maintenance since the 1930s. The two main railway stations (passenger and freight) are – unusually for Siberia – near the centre of the town.

Across the bridge over the Chita river lies the main factory quarter with food, woodworking and other light industries. The city is, however, mainly an administrative nucleus. It is also a main resort centre for all Eastern Siberia, being surrounded by pleasant hills with sanatoria, orchards and the like. The local apples are especially reputed. Typical of Siberian cities are the broad streets and large squares, planted with trees, the large administrative and 'cultural' buildings with their somewhat (to Western eyes) Edwardian architecture and Victorian internal décor.

Chita is still largely a railway town, serving especially the main-line Trans-Siberian traffic; at the beginning of the 1960s the Chita, Kadala and Chernovo stations handled well over thirty times as much outgoing freight as the Karymskoe station, which is the junction for the line to Borzya, and nearly five times as much incoming freight. There are also motor roads southwards to Darasun, Khapcheranga and Ulety, northwestwards to Romanovka.

EASTWARD DEVELOPMENT

About 25 km south-east of Chita, around Atamanovka, titanium

SFE D 2

and iron ores have recently been energetically prospected. Darasun (population 9000), further south-east along the Ingoda river, has mining and railway machinery factories and is the point where the road goes southward to Aginsk and Khapcheranga and the railway south-eastwards to Borzya, Kharanor and China, with the important narrow-gauge branch line to Dosatui (a grain and cattle area) and Priargun'sk on the frontier further east.

The next area of eastward-thrusting development is along the Shilka river from Darasun. The town of Shilka (population 17,000) 45 km west of Nerchinsk has railway shops and lies in a belt of livestock and cereal farming, with some mining developments, extending about 150 km to the north-east and about 250 to the westward. The same general description applies to the whole of the east of the Province, though between Nerchinsk, Sretensk, Balei and Bukachacha in the middle of this area there is more market and dairy farming. These towns are not very important in themselves. Coking coal is mined near Bukachacha (over 100 km north of Nerchinsk on a branch railway from Chernyshevsk) – one million tons in 1965 – but the deposit is small.

Nerchinsk (14,000 population), historic in Russian relations with China, is still a garrison town with some silver and lead mines, still worked by the convicts in the local jail. Beyond it on a branch line lie Sretensk and the nearby Kokui, which have a population of 15,000 between them, engaged in boatbuilding (including metal barges) and meat- and milk-processing factories. Further east there is less industrial development, though long-term plans envisage the development of metal industries using ores from the Argun' area and coking coal from Yakutia. Near Mogocha on the main railway (population 15,000) about 225 km north-east of Sretensk, gold and molybdenum are mined with good modern machinery and facilities. More promising, with a motor-road connection from Mogocha, are the copper deposits at Udokan. In the hilly country (running up to 1000 m) through which the main line continues to the eastern border of the Province, there is little activity.

To the north and north-west of Mogocha and Bukachacha lies the vast but very thinly populated north of the Province, where nothing happens except hunting, fur trapping and the breeding of reindeer, though a road reaches out into it from Mogocha. Of more interest are the lands to the south and south-east of Mogocha, Sretensk and Balei which compose the Priargun' sub-region, on the Argun' river which forms the first sector of China's north-eastern frontiers considered below.

UNDERPOPULATION AND UNDERDEVELOPMENT

Soviet writers refer to this Province, even more than others in Siberia, as underpopulated. In fact it has (with one million people) some 20 per cent more than either of its neighbours, the Buryat Republic and Amur Province, though distinctly less than the others next to the west and east. The Soviet criterion is undoubtedly in relation to the potentials of the Province, the lack of actual industrialisation, particularly main centres or bases of heavier industries and electric power, also the scatteredness of the population and activities.

The patches of development along the main Siberian line have already been noted. In the northern part of the western extremity of the Province is Petrovsk (population 30,000). It had an old ironworks (late eighteenth-century) drawing on local deposits, which fell into decline when the Siberian railway came, when it could not compete with the Ural products, but was renovated in the Soviet period with open-hearth furnaces and rolling mills. It has produced steel since 1940. There is a little coal near by at Tarbagatai–Novopavlovka, which produced 200,000 tons in 1965. Petrovsk depends, however, on pig-iron from the Kuzbas (or from China when available) and sends much of its finished product far to the west and east. It also has a pharmaceutical glass factory and meat-processing and prefabricated-housing plants. It must be considered, however, to be in the economic orbit of Ulan Ude (only about 75 km away) and is almost as near to Irkutsk as to Chita. To its eastward is a forestry area.

The southern part of this western end of the Province, all round the Chikoi river and beyond the Ingoda river, has only scattered agricultural development in the valleys, totalling 7 per cent of the area. The soil and the climate are unfavourable.

The main activity is pastoral – sheep and a few camels –
though there is some gold on the Chikoi and this was the first
area in which molybdenum was produced in Russia (in 1915).
The population is tiny. Khilok is a railway town with a population of 16,000, Yamarovka a spa.

The main – and increasing – concentration of manpower is
in the Chita sub-region. The next most important conglomera-
tion is the Shilka sub-region along the railway. Two-thirds of
the Shilka sub-region's population is classified as urban, but is
in small settlements. The largest is Balei (population 29,000), a
goldfield centre lying 56 km south of the main line (Priiskovaya
station) to which it is joined by a motor road. Balei is a pretty
town. There are some sizeable goldmines, but the operation is
mainly by electric dredges in the Unda valley. At Vershino–
Shakhtaminski (founded 1948, population 5000) molybdenum
mining has been developed; it is about 100 km south-east of
Balei, less than half-way to Priargun'sk on the frontier.

On the other side of the Trans-Siberian, 80 km north of the
Shilka station, is Vershino–Darasunski (population 12,000)
where there are rich underground workings of gold, containing
other metals. 60 km further north are the large Usugli fluorite
deposits, which are worked. Still further north is Bukachacha
(population 13,000) on the branch line from Chernyshevsk.
Arbagar (population 4000) is only 9 km from the main line,
25 km west of Nerchinsk; it has a light railway link with the
electric plant at Kholbon (population 5000) which supplies
Balei, Vershino–Darasunski and other localities. Bukachacha
and Arbagar are coal-mining areas; the former produced 1
million tons in 1965, the latter 200,000.

Eastwards from Sretensk, 120 km down the Shilka, is Ust'
Karsk (population 4000), a minor centre of the gold industry,
operating with small dredges. In the Shilka sub-region generally, agriculture and herding are fairly equally developed, in
specially favourable valley or steppe areas. The whole area
north of this, beyond the Yablonovy range, is virtually unpopulated.

Turning to the central south of the Province, there are the
railway and trading towns of Borzya (population 24,000) and
Olov'yannaya (14,000); the latter, as its name indicates, was
formerly a tin producer. About 70 km north-west of Borzya is

the actual tin-mining area of Sherlovaya Gora (population 13,000) which produces also precious stones (its name means, in the local language, black tourmaline) and other metals. A refinery was planned here for the late 1960s, after the opening of a new lode in 1967. In the east of this sub-region, or already in the Argun' sub-region, is the fluorspar mining area of Abagaitui near the frontier and Kalangui (population nearly 6000).

At the other, south-western, end of this sub-region is the newly developed wolfram mining area of Angatui up the Onon river about half-way between Aksha and Khapcheranga, which latter is another tin centre with a population of 7000. The coal area at Kharanor is about 55 km north of the station of that name. Good minor roads link Sherlovaya Gora, Kolangui, Abagaitui and some other places in this vicinity, west of which there is a transport gap until Khapcheranga, which is on a good road to Chita.

The whole Argun' (Chinese frontier) area of the Province contains about 500 inhabited places, none of them of any significant size; nearly all are mining settlements. The total population of this sub-region is just over 100,000. Klicha, about 100 km east of Borzya, has a population of 7000. Kadaya, another 100 km north-east near the frontier, has 3000, nearby Gorny Zerentui another 3000; both places were founded in 1958. A little further north, still near the frontier river, are the Gazimurski and Nerchinski Zavod old mining settlements (population 4000), now not prosperous; they have some solid buildings recalling their earlier days.

Further south is Priargun'sk – on the Argun' river, as its name now proclaims, though it was formerly called Novo–Tsurukhaitui – on the narrow-gauge branch railway to Kharanor, with a population of about 5000. These townships thus form another strategic nucleus from the manpower and supplies points of view: numerically not very imposing, but the miners and ranchers of this area are reputed by tough people, who certainly showed revolutionary and guerrilla capacities in earlier times. The whole of southern Chita is now the U.S.S.R.'s main source of lithium.

In short, this is a thinly manned frontier Province of somewhat patchwork development, without a heavier-industry base of its own, but producing rare metals which are now of vital

importance to the Soviet Union. Its people are reckoned to be
high-spirited pioneers, and the destiny of the area hinges
strongly on the alliance with Mongolia. This is one of the main
bastions of the Soviet frontier.

AGRICULTURE AND TRANSPORT

Apart from mining and light urban industries, agriculture is the
basis of the life of the Province; but all these depend on transport. Rural settlement until the Revolution was largely a
monopoly of the Cossacks, who moved in among the Mongol
nomads: peasants from Russia represented only about 1 per
cent of the immigration into the Chita Province up to 1917. In
the Soviet period the emphasis was largely on the growth of
mining and the towns. Nevertheless the agriculture is notable,
especially for its large scale. This is partly because of the extent
of cattle and sheep farming, but tillage is also extensive. However, the Province is very mountainous and poorly watered:
thus only about 17 per cent of the total area (7·5 million ha) is
in agricultural use. Some 30 per cent of this is ploughed, 20 per
cent is for hay, 50 per cent pasture.

Livestock is the remunerative part; over three-quarters of the
agricultural income of the Province is from livestock, nearly a
half from sheep. There are three million sheep in the Province,
found especially in the south-east where the terrain is an outpost
of the Mongolian steppe. Their quality is not, however, high;
the average weight per sheep in the early 1960s was about
40 kg, the wool-clip only 2-3 kg.

Cattle numbered 570,000 head in 1965 and appear the better
investment; they increased in numbers by 12 per cent in 1961-5,
and also improved in quality. The live weight per cow averaged
only 280 kg in the early 1960s and the annual milk yield less
than 500 kg (the Russians report milk output by weight), but
the milk yield at least has been raised, to a claimed 1500 kg
recently. The Plan target for the 1960s for the whole Province
was 330,000 tons of milk, 140,000 of meat.

The production of wheat is notable; this crop occupies some
400,000 hectares, 40 per cent of which is in the south-east and
Shilka areas. Thus the frontier area of the Province is also of

importance as a centre of meat and cereal production. Besides wheat, oats must be mentioned as the second most important cereal. Animal feeding stuffs are a major concern; root crops are much propagated and do well.

However, a difficult transport situation affects the distribution of all products. The difficulties of the severe climate, the inadequacy of the rivers and the general relative shortage of labour-power are common to the whole of Siberia and the Far East, but the main additional feature of Chita is its topography – mountains in close parallel ranges.

THE CENTRAL SUB-REGION

The city of Chita, with its adjoining coalfield and industrial zones, is thus clearly the foremost sub-region. Chita is an administrative centre, transport node and railway base. Its Chernovo lignite, over half the coal output of the Province, coming from both shafts and open cuts, serves mainly local needs. The industries of Chita have been primarily the processing of rural products: meat from near Chita itself and partly from Mongolia, the making of sheepskin clothing, furs, wool, leather (using hides from the meat-plant and from Mongolia) and a shoe factory. Chita flour mills supply the Province and neighbouring parts of Baikalia and the Far East. Later the railway workshops, substantial enough to handle locomotive and all other repairs and refits, were joined by further metal-working plants. The machine factory makes mobile compressors and refrigerators, the lathe factory specialises in screw-cutting machinery.

This sub-region has, however, as much as 11 per cent of the Province's cultivated area. It produces 20 per cent of the Province's potatoes, one-third of the vegetables, its famous apples yield as much as 30-50 kg per tree; it also produces fodder crops and has many dairies, claiming a milk yield much higher (at 1750 kg per cow per year) than the rest of the Province.

THE CENTRAL SOUTH

This sub-region includes the Aginsk Buryat National Area

(capital Aginsk, population 6000), a very dry zone, with only one reliable river, the Onon. About one-third of its area is forested, the rest upland steppe good for pasturage. 90 per cent of the agricultural income is from livestock. There are herds of horses as well as sheep and cattle; the Mongols eat horseflesh and drink fermented mares' milk (*kumis*). This area has a quarter of the Province's sheep, one-sixth of its cattle and horses. Agriculture is chiefly represented by fodder crops (some 12 per cent of the Province's total); though 20 per cent of the sown acreage in this area is under wheat, 70 per cent is for fodder. A little gold and wolfram are mined, limestone and marble quarried. There is a gravel road from Aginsk to the railway at Mogoitui.

The rest of the sub-region consists of the Onon and Borzya river basins. Despite the sunny climate (growing season 136 days a year), the extreme dryness and extreme temperatures inhibit agriculture; in winter there are only a few centimetres of snow, temperatures go below – 50°C, in summer not more than 250 mm of rainfall, temperatures up to 40°C. The concentration is on livestock and meat, the sown area (270,000 ha, about 8 per cent of the Province's total) is largely devoted to fodder crops. However, another 1½ million ha is pasturage and on this the number of sheep is about double the number of cattle.

The mining developments in the sub-region in two areas – in the east Sherlovaya Gora and Kolangui and in the centre Angatui – already mentioned, depend on the Kharanor lignite. This coal, discovered in 1885 is in seams near the surface. 60 per cent of the deposits could be mined by open-cut methods. The output is about 3 million tons a year, which could be raised to 10. This coal is very cheap at the pit-head (less than one rouble a ton) but difficult and expensive to move very far. The whole area depends for power on the Kharanor electric plant.

The area of Khapcheranga depends rather on tin (which is there mined underground) and some other metals, locally refined. These are to some extent yielding diminishing returns, the metal-content of the tin ores is poor and the future depends on opening up new deposits – of which there are many in the area. The Mordskaya electric plant 25 km west of Khapcheranga uses local coal. There are two handicaps of which it is hard to judge the exact effects; one is the obsoleteness or exhaustion of older installations, the other the shortage of water. In the Angatui fields there are a number of old pits now used only as reservoirs for holding water. Per contra, there are such important developments as the mining and processing of tantalum at Orlovsk, begun in 1965.

THE ARGUN' DISTRICT, FACING CHINA

This area, between the Argun' and Gazimur rivers, is especially an area of scattered 'polymetallic' mining, in small and dispersed settlements. Many of them date back to the eighteenth century, e.g. the *zavody* (factories, originally in the old sense of trading posts) of Nerchinsk and Gazimur. Also some places in the south, e.g. Borzya, once Borzinski Zavod. This is therefore an area of distinct and long-standing Russification.

Some of the older sites are derelict, but there are various new developments. Near the ore-enriching plant of Klichka, which draws its material by a narrow-gauge railway from the mines 5 km away, new workers' quarters of two-storey flats are to be seen. At Kadaya there is also a concentration-plant, drawing on the Mikhailov mine 25 km away; though some of the old workings and smelters in this vicinity figure mainly as large accumulations of old slag, up-to-date plant has been introduced and the slag is being reworked for lead, zinc and some more precious metals.

Similar regenerations are planned or under way in the other so-called polymetallic centres, such as Gorny Zerentui with its nearby Blagodatski mines (distinguished architecturally by its old stone-built jail) and Akatui (also a former prison town, but similarly developing both mining and ore-enrichment plant, drawing on some of the richest ores in the region). Intended developments at Novo-Shirokinsk north-east of Gazimurski Zavod seem to be still in the projected stage, but at Solnechnoe north of Nerchinski Zavod a new fluorite mine was recently opened. The first stage of a new electric power station was completed at Priargun'sk in the early 1960s with 24,000 kW capacity, joined to Dosatui by a narrow-gauge railway.

However, Argunia is also a notable agricultural zone; one-third of this sub-region's area is agriculturally utilised. Plough-land totals 340,000 ha, but fodder and pasturage represent a million hectares. Sheep predominate; the sub-region has 20 per cent of the Province's count of sheep, though their yield of wool is low. Cereals represent 70 per cent of the sub-region's sown area of 244,000 ha, half of which is under wheat, most of the rest under oats.

Really there are two agricultural zones. In the south are broad pastures where 70 per cent of the grazing animals are sheep, 30 per cent cattle. In the upland north-east these proportions are reversed, and market gardening is developed to serve the mining settlements.

SHILKA: MINES AND CEREALS

The adjoining Shilka sub-region is similar, but has much better transport links; it straddles the Siberian main line, also has a minor outlet in navigation below Sretensk to the Amur. Balei with its goldfields is served by an adjacent farming area. Considerable underground and surface workings, with refinery capacity, have been added in this long-worked area. Vershino–Shakhtaminski, in a more cramped situation in steep forested hills, uses the Bugdainsk molybdenum deposits, easily worked on open casts. The gold workings at Vershino–Darasunski are underground, producing other precious elements also, now extracted by improved refinery equipment.

This region has something of the aura and prosperity of gold. In the early 1930s local people still carried little pouches of gold and the ambience had in general some 'Klondike atmosphere', which it has perhaps not altogether lost today, though everything is now much more under modernised State control.

There is also hard coal of fair boiler quality, though somewhat outlying, at Bukachcha and Arbagar. Nerchinsk and other areas were also long famous for silver, but recently no particulars have been published. Soviet planning envisages a greater future ultimately, if and when this area can be linked with the coking coal and other reserves of Yakutia far to the north, providing perhaps at last 'a complex upper-storey metallurgical and heavy-industry base' in this Province. Such dreams have been fulfilled before in the Soviet Union, though the local difficulties are great.

Other focuses already mentioned above are Kokui's river-boat building yards and the Ust' Karsk shallow-dredge gold-field. There is also, however, a notable agrarian activity in this mixed forest-steppe region, which has more moisture than other areas. The 'Nerchinsk ploughland' was already distinc-tive in the seventeenth century; so there is some longstanding agrarian, as well as mining and garrison, Russification of the area. At present the emphasis is rather on stock raising, never-theless the arable quality is relatively high; wages of the diggers of fields, as well as those of the diggers of gold, are higher in this sub-region than those of herdsmen and shepherds.

The steppelands are widely utilised (1·2 million ha), pro-portionately less for pasture than in the south but more for planting. The sub-region furnishes a quarter of the Province's output of cereals, one-third of the wheat (by value). The wheat is mainly in the centre of the sub-region, where it forms 40 per cent of the harvest. The sub-region produces also 40 per cent of the Province's buckwheat. It has one-fifth of the province's cattle population, one-third of the pigs.

THE NORTH AND THE EAST: THE OUTLANDS AND THE FULL FRONTIER

The remaining sub-region is the remote north called the Vitim–Olyokma–Amur sub-region, by the names of its three great rivers. The Amur is in this Province only for its first 80 km, but that is an important headwater position. This sub-region forms no less than 40 per cent of the Province's area. Two-thirds of it is forest (taiga). It is very cold and mountainous. Of the rivers, only the Shilka and the Amur are significantly navigable, transport links are slender. The population is very small (50,000) and concentrated in the south-east. In the north dwell some Evenki, living largely on their 10,000 reindeer (50 per cent of their income) and hunting (15 per cent). In the south are Russians, only slightly more numerous but better off; their kolkhozes depend up to 70 per cent on wheat, but the amount involved is small, in this chilly air and soil.

Kliuchevsk (population 4000) has gold dredges working on the Mogocha and other rivers, Ksen'yevka (7000) works its gold by hydraulic processes. Davenda (5000) produces molybdenum. Mogocha (population 15,000) is the railway centre. Its electricity plant depends on coal brought from a distance.

On the northern rivers, gold mining may be extended in future. A hydroelectric power station (Mokskaya) may ultimately be established on the middle Vitim with 1·8 million kW capacity. The Udokan copper and other deposits may also become increasingly important. Transport development is the key; the main northern traffic is at present by road from Chita to Romanovka, thence by small boats down the Vitim (sometimes unfrozen for as little as one month in the year) to Nelyata in the far north of the Province. The great dream of the whole Region is that a second Trans-Siberian railway might be constructed, taking a large sweep north of Lake Baikal, thence probably along the Upper Vitim and Kalar rivers; which might bring it through the Udokan area and permit the development of a large industrial base there. Some work is proceeding on this tremendous project, but its progress is one of the deepest and most guarded secrets of the Soviet Union.

Meanwhile the southern half of Chita Province is – from the Westerner's point of view, approaching as this book does out of Europe – the first apex of the Russo-Chinese front, which broadens out from here to the Pacific.[2]

CHAPTER 5

Amuria: First Face to China

IN the Amur Province the eastward traveller finds himself more fully in a Far Eastern setting; not merely formally, because the Soviet Far Eastern Region is entered (from the westward) there, but in many practical and psychological senses. As, moving eastward, the Mongolian heartland is left further behind and the Chinese presence becomes stronger and more immediate, the confrontation of the two countries and races is more directly felt. All along the Amur through Blagoveshchensk, Khabarovsk and the Ussuri to Vladivostok, Peking, Maoism, the hundreds of millions of Chinese, are no longer abstractions but matters of close and urgent concern.

The Amur Province has an area of 364,000 sq. km, 12 per cent of the S.F.E. and about 15 per cent less than the area of Chita Province, Its population is just over 750,000, i.e. 16 per cent of the S.F.E. and only three-quarters of the population of Chita Province. The interior of Amur Province has not been fully prospected and is almost entirely lacking in transport facilities, but the south is known to be rich in resources and is significantly developed.

RICH LANDS ON CHINA'S BORDER

The wealth, actual and potential, is especially in minerals – even if these are somewhat over-emphasised in Soviet discussions, which always focus keenly on the possibilities of industrialisation. Prominent is the lignite coal at Raichikhinsk about 150 km south-east of Blagoveshchensk, the total reserves of which are reckoned at 500 million tons. This is in the comparatively well-populated south-eastern part of the Province. The coal is near the surface, easily worked by open cuts. The area is well served by railway. The Raichikhinsk coal – 12 million tons in 1965, representing some 40 per cent of the Region's output – is to some extent exported to the Khabarovsk, Maritime and Chita Provinces, as well as supplying the basic fuel for Amuria itself.

Extensive workable iron deposits (totalling over 200 million tons) exist at Garinsk 150 km north-west of Svobodny; these could also be worked by open-cast methods and are of good quality (50 per cent iron content) but there is no railway nearer than the main line at Svobodny, which in turn is about 180 km from the coal at Raichkhinsk. Gold has long been worked on the upper Zeya and its tributaries the Urkan and Selemdzha. Limestone, clays and sands are almost everywhere in the Province and are utilised in the south for building purposes. There is a considerable potential in bauxite, but an aluminium industry is only a hypothetical prospect pending development of electric power. There was a prospecting boom in the Amur Province in the 1960s, disclosing distinct potentials in light metals, lead, silver and mercury, yet undeveloped.

Amuria is also a vast timber-land. Forests cover two-thirds of its area (24 million ha), representing a total stock of two billion cubic metres of lumber. Three-quarters of this is larch or birch, some is pine and fir. Much of this reserve is not of high quality and it is readily exploitable chiefly in the south, near the railway – the areas south of the railway also send it along the Amur river.

The development of electric power is a great question. Sino-Soviet co-operation is not now in prospect. The Amur and the Zeya, especially, could be utilised for large hydroelectric projects. Altogether the Province has a practicable ultimate capacity of 6 or 7 million kW. The Zeya station is expected to begin working in 1975, at 1·75 million kW. Hydroelectric projects would also be multi-purpose: they would help to eliminate a chronic problem which seriously vitiates the economic life and the safety of the population in many southern parts of the Province, namely the disastrous summer floods and the general marshiness.

At the same time the south of the Province is a considerable agricultural area, one of the largest food bases on the long frontier. 2·3 million ha are farmed, 1·5 million sown. Agriculture in this Province has recently pressed ahead. The above

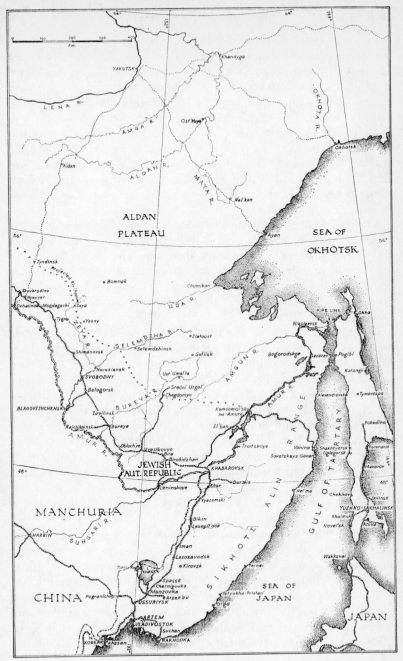

Map 7   Amuria, Khabarovsk, the Maritimes and Sakhalin

figures are double those of 1953, and represent a larger agricultural area than is found in the Khabarovsk and Maritimes
Provinces put together. This crop-base of the Amur Province
is, however, concentrated in one part especially: the rich, quite
long-settled black earth country of the plain of the Zeya and
Bureya rivers. Two-thirds of the cultivated area of Amur Province is found within that plain, and 80 per cent of the cultivated land in that Zeya–Bureya plain is under the plough,
making it a granary area of great importance to the Soviet Far
East. The other cultivated areas are scattered – along the line
of the Siberian railway only, the hinterland areas having very
little agricultural activity.

The arable area could be extended in future by some 300,000-
400,000 ha, but only by long and costly improvement work,
not yet in prospect. Even after drainage and other improvements, the marshy humus, podzol and clay lands of the south
respond only to prolonged cultivation. The Zeya–Bureya lands
are largely deforested, with only copses of birch and oak remaining on the plains.

Especially because of the flood danger, villages in the south
in the Amur valley are characteristically on high ground or
ridges (relki). In the southern Zeya–Bureya area there are older
Cossack settlements (such as Poyarkovo and Konstantinovka)
and the villages are larger, with around 1000 people. Places on
the rivers are better organised from the Soviet point of view,
with Collectives and State Farms, many of them thriving on the
river traffic or the railways. Konstantinovka affords a typical
example of the river villages. It is built on two ridges or 'dunes',
because of the annual flooding. Yet, though flooding is such a
consideration throughout the south of this Province, in some
years the monsoon can be very perverse and there may be
serious summer droughts.

On the ridge at Konstantinovka nearer to the river the work
depending on water transport goes on: a small fish plant, an
oil depot, a warehouse for vegetables, a silo and a mill. Here
many river channels run down to the main stream, which have
to be dyked, but the dykes are often overflowed in the flood
season. The population then retires to the higher of the two
ridges, which is never inundated even in the worst floods. It
holds the administrative offices and activities such as the dairy

and the brickworks, which do not depend so directly on the river transport.

On the plains there are only agricultural settlements, but they approach in many places the densities found in European Russia; from the nineteenth century, peasants were settled in scattered 'hut' (*khutor*) villages of about 300 persons each.

The villages on the plain have rather a steppeland character: extended hamlets on broad roads, originally the 'tracts' so characteristic of Siberian communications. Their main business is the processing of agricultural commodities. A typical example of a small town there is Tambovka, a crossroads site with broad leafy streets on a rectangular pattern. It is still a market centre, though others have arisen in the area (such as Ivanovka and Voskresenovka). It has a population of 5000, only half of whom are collective farmers, other activities being repair shops for agricultural machinery and the nearby Agricultural Experiment Station serving the whole Region. A large incubator installation was set up in the early 1960s.

The population of the Amur Province is predominantly Russian and Ukrainian. 63 per cent of the people live in towns, especially in the south-east (Blagoveshchensk, Belogorsk, Raichikhinsk, Svobodny) which has a total of a quarter of a million persons, the only other main centre being Skovorodino far to the west.

In contrast to the large hydroelectric potential, the present electricity supply appears particularly small. There are only two major stations at present, which are thermal plants; the large one (capacity unknown) is located at Progress (Raichikhinsk), the other is a small one (12,000 kW) at Ogodzha far to the east. There are in addition hundreds of small local plants, operating expensively on imported oil.

Industrial development is strongly concentrated, like the agriculture, in the south-east of the Province, north of Blagoveshchensk and eastward along the railway. The large towns or townships are all in that part – a salient of modernisation facing the northward movement of progress in Chinese Manchuria, based on Tsitsihar and Harbin about 600 and 700 km south of Blagoveshchensk. The only exception to this concentration in the south-east of the Amur Province is Skovorodino, some 400 km to the north-west, the transport node for the

mining area to its northward, with goldfields and lumber industries. Most of the other settlements in Amur Province are gold-
mining centres, scattered in the north.

Table 5.1   Industry in Amur Province
(in 1962)

	Percentage of	
	Industrial output (value)	Industrial work force (numbers)
Food industries	38	14
Machinery and metal	21	25
Forestry	12	18
Wood and paper	5	6
Coal	9	5
Light industry	5	7
Building materials	4	7
Glass and ceramics	1	2
Others	5	15
	100	100

The Trans-Siberian railway is still the lifeline of this Province,
even more than of other Provinces. It parallels the Amur river
at 40-130 km distance and puts out vital spurs to it at Skovorodino to Dzhalinda in the west, Belogorsk to Blagoveshchensk
and Zavitinsk to Poyarkovo in the south-east. The few roads
are feeders to the railway. Most notably, from Nyevyer starts
northward the vital motor road running to Aldan and eventually right up to Yakutsk, and on to Magadan some 3000 Km
away. Another goes from Tygda to Zolotaya Gora (Gold
Mountain) about 150 km north, others from Belogorsk to
Blagoveshchensk and Svobodny to Ekimchan in the north-east
of the Province.

Water transport is a useful supplement on the Amur, Zeya,
Selemdzha and Bureya rivers. The Amur can be navigated by
small boats for the whole of its length, but larger vessels and
the main traffic are restricted to the stretches below Blagoveshchensk and even there they are blocked by ice in winter.
Air traffic, almost entirely for passengers, is considerably developed and increasing year by year. Blagoveshchensk has
regular air services to Moscow and to the principal Far Eastern

and Siberian cities, besides some local lines within the Province. However, the Province remains largely a transit area. The main stream of through traffic is along the great Siberian railway, supplemented by the Amur river traffic. The Amur Province has also a considerable and growing transit trade, both ways, with the vast hinterland of Yakutia to the north, of which it is the main outlet, as there are no major connections between Yakutia and either Eastern Siberia or the other Provinces of the Chinese frontier, the only other land connections of Yakutia being with Magadan Province far to the north-east.

The Amur Province is divided into three sub-regions, very different in their basic conditions and their levels of development, as summarised in Table 5.2.

Table 5.2   Sub-regions of Amur Province
(percentages, 1962)

	Sub-regions		
	Upper Amur	*Zeya–Bureya*	*Northern interior*
Population	34	56	10
Area	16	16	68
Industrial production	33	56	11
Number of workers	23	73	4
Agricultural production	17	69	14
Arable area	8	86	6
Wheat production	8	88	4
Soya bean production	5	92	3
Cattle	16	74	10
Forests	18	8	74

These figures clearly show the concentration of both agricultural and industrial wealth in the lowlands of the Zeya and Bureya rivers, to which the other sub-regions are mere outliers, though broadly rich in minerals and forest resources. The following account proceeds as before from west to east.

THE UPPER AMUR

The administrative districts of Svobodny, Tygda, Shimanovsk and Skovorodino form the Province's western frontier area, over 500 km long from south-east to north-west and from 60 to

140 km in northward breadth from the frontier river, straddling
the main railway line. Transport is comparatively well developed in this sub-region; besides the main railway and the main
river there is the branch track from Skovorodino to Dzhalinda
(Reinovo station) on the river, motor roads from Dzhalinda
northwards to Nyevyer near Skovorodino and all the way on
to Yakutsk far to the north, also from Tygda to Zeya and Zolotaya Gora in the middle part of the sub-region.

The wealth of this sub-region is forestry. The growth thickens
from east to west. Around Svobodny in the east are deep valleys
wooded with oak and birch, with pine and larch only on the
upper slopes, interspersed with arable areas; in the west the
timber is better and more plentiful, yet the actual development
is less. The sub-region has more than 3 million ha of forest area
altogether; more than half of this consists of the *taiga* kinds of
larch, pine is the second most common genus. The main lumbering base is the network of tributaries of the Amur and the
Zeya, on which more than half the primary output is rafted. At
Svobodny most of what comes down the Zeya is put on the
railway. What comes down the Amur is largely unloaded and
processed at Blagoveshchensk, to go on mainly in the form of
building materials by rail rather than on the river, both eastward and westward.

Nevertheless this sub-region does not have a dominant position even in timber. Khabarovsk and the Maritimes are large
producers, better provided with transport links within their
own borders; while Siberia, Kazakhstan and Russia further
west can much more conveniently and economically draw on
central Siberia. Paper and cellulose industries have not yet
developed in Amuria, there is only sawing and the making of
pitprops. a little furniture making, matches in Blagoveshchensk,
house-timber at Shimanovsk. Moreover, the quality is not high
and is deteriorating. The best trees have been heavily selected
already in the busy areas, leaving the inferior timber – and even
some 'clutter' (*zakhlamlenie*) of old roots, twigs or debris. The
growth being, however, far greater than the cutting, the forests
in the less intensively worked areas are old, overgrown and
'stale'.

Agriculture is only important in the Svobodny area, which
is really part of the 'granary' of the Zeya river lands, though it

has more woodland interspersed with patches of cultivation. These woodlands cannot, however, be much further cut without increasing erosion, which is already acute; thus the food-supply area cannot be extended much to the west, where the forest grows progressively denser. The climate is continentally extreme throughout the Province, with a short growing season. At its latitude (54°N, i.e. the latitude of northern England and of Labrador) this is the coldest part of the world, but decidedly like the latter, not the former, and even colder. Agricultural man-power is very short; here and in the Zeya–Bureya basins, farm work has been mechanised much more than elsewhere.

The main centre of this sub-region is evidently Svobodny, which is almost an extension of the adjacent Zeya–Bureya sub-region, adding in effect to the preponderance of that sub-region. Svobodny (population 60,000) is a main transport and distribution centre, having also metal industries. It is on the right bank of the Zeya, which, with its confluent the Selemdzha, links the railway with the goldfields in the remote interior. Timber comes down these rivers and the Amur in large rafts. Svobodny also has a car-parts plant and an iron foundry, besides working up the agricultural products of the neighbouring area.

The other towns – Shimanovsk, Sivaki, Tygda, Nyevyer and Skovorodino – are mainly railway places, with some food industries which deal especially with soya beans, apart from meat-packing and milling. They are mostly small, scattered and old-fashioned. The same applies to the electric-power plants, which run at high cost in this area. Other industries are few; gold mining in the north is obviously important, though its output and conditions are kept secret.

The profile of the Upper Amur country is clearly defined by following, as before, the main railway artery from west to east. The Province is entered about 7000 km east of Moscow. The first settlement is called Yerofei Pavlovich, the Christian names of Khabarov, the great explorer who arrived here in 1649. Urusha is only a railway point. At Takhtamygda, 150 km from Yerofei Pavlovich, there is an iron forge providing building materials. Even this remote locality provides a graphic illustration of the long-distance working of the contemporary Soviet economy; its ironworks produced construction materials for the

Aswan dam in Egypt (for which machine and instrument works still further away in Khabarovsk Province furnished more significant deliveries). The Seven-Year Plan provided for the development of new lumber industries in this area.

Skovorodino, formerly called Rukhlovo, began its modern existence in 1909. This place exemplifies the unpropitious climate of the Region. In the first winter after the new town was built in 1909, much of it collapsed; it stood on permafrost, which alternately chilled and flooded the interiors of the buildings and twisted the foundations. Since the 1930s a Permafrost Research Station has been working at Skovorodino, which has done much to advance 'the conquest of frost'. Otherwise Skovorodino (population 13,000) is an administrative centre and an important railway point, including the branch line running south to join the river at Dzhalinda.

The next town, Nyevyer, 16 km east of Skovorodino on the railway, lies on the Greater Nyevyer river which runs into the Amur. Nyevyer – to give it this spelling, in order to avoid the discouraging sound in English of the transliteration 'Never' for this quite active locality – is also dubbed Yakutski, being the terminus of the good motor road to the Aldan goldfields northwards. This road crosses the Stanovoy range and the Chul'man deposits of coking coal, also some iron deposits, on its long way to Yakutsk in the far north, and beyond.

The railway line swings south-east after this, into mighty coniferous and birch forests with trees up to 35 metres in height. Taldan is a forestry centre, Gonzha a good mineral-water spring with a sanatorium. Magdagachi about 180 km east of Nyevyer is an important air base, the white buildings of which are clearly seen from the railway. Tygda 108 km further along the line is a district centre and is engaged in the building industry. To the north-east of Tygda is the site of the first hydroelectric project in the S.F.E., on the Zeya river at the town of the same name about 90 km north of Tygda, where a dam a hundred metres high with thirty-metre sluices is under construction.

At Ashumun the permafrost zone ends, the forest changes to oak and pine. At this place (where the railway is nearest to the frontier in this Province) sleepers are hardened and other timbers are processed. A step further into the Pacific Basin and its monsoon climate brings the railway to Shimanovka (population

15,000) where the rain is heavy in summer and the winters are long, cold, dry and sunny; floods are serious in summer and the land south of Sivaki is generally marshy (so is the Chinese territory on the other side of the river).

The sub-region ends with Svobodny, a much busier locality (population 62,000) near fields of brown coal, iron and gold, a centre of river navigation, with machine and metal industries. The Zeya river is 1200 km long, with a huge catchment area; it floods badly in summer and autumn, rising as much as ten metres, sometimes in huge 'walls' of water which cause great damage and disruption. At Svobodny (meaning 'free', referring to the history of non-convict settlers there) the railway enters one of the most favoured and fertile areas of colonisation in the S.F.E. – the plain of the lower Zeya and Bureya rivers.

FOOD AND MINERALS

The Zeya–Bureya area is by far the most important of the Province's three economic sub-regions. It comprises many administrative districts, being strongly developed in various parts: Seryshevo, Belogorsk, Ivanovka, Tambovka, Mikhailov (Poyarkovo), Bureya, Octyabr' (Yekaterinoslavka), Arkhara, Zavitinsk, Romny (Pozdeyevka) and Mazanovski (Novokievski Uval). These areas have only one-sixth of the territory of the Province, but over half the population, two-thirds of the agricultural output, three-quarters of the livestock, 80 per cent of the sown area and considerable metal and food-processing industries.

This sub-region may be divided into the plain and the uplands. The plain (rising to 190 metres) is 20-80 km wide on the left banks of the Amur and the Zeya, mounting to the Amur plateau in the west and on the other sides to the Bureya, Turan and Dzhagda ranges. It has many small rivers; in the summer rains (July and August) many of its lowlands are flooded. Its eastern part, the Arkhara lowland, is permanently marshy. The meadowlands produce fodder (800-1000 kg/ha, the grass growing two metres high); the crop season is 157-164 days a year, with 630-420 mm rainfall. There is a large output of soya beans.

One-third of the sown area is generally under wheat. Other cereals are oats and barley, mostly in the north. The importance of the soya bean is hard to estimate in the conditions of the present stage of development. This useful plant ripens in September or early October in dry sunny weather, resisting the autumn night frosts, after cereal harvesting is over. It is highly nutritious for cattle as well as for men, so is used for fodder locally; the local processing facilities are surprisingly inadequate and a high proportion of the export is in unprocessed form.

The Zeya–Bureya sub-region has three quarters of the cattle of the whole Province. They pasture on river-islands and in fields, also on the soya stubble, but lucerne and timothy are widely grown and are now claimed to be the main fodder in many districts; perforce, perhaps, where the wetness is so bad that the cattle have to be kept largely in stockades or stalls. Another instance of the mastery of waterlogged conditions has been the recent extensive development of duck farming.

The nearer uplands run to almost 200 metres, the outer ones to 700. They have a drier climate with a shorter growing season. They are much less developed – with one big exception, the great lignite area of Raichikhinsk where seams are near the surface and almost horizontal, one to six metres thick and easily worked on open cuts. The output is transported both by the Amur and the railway. Another coalfield area which is reputedly still larger, at Erkovets in the north-east, awaits development.

The Siberian railway enters this sub-region from the west through the black-soil area centring on Seryshevo, an intensive agricultural zone; it boasts crops of 2500 kg of wheat or 50,000 kg of tomatoes per hectare in the warm wet summers – but endures a fall of temperature of no less than 85°C by mid-winter, when the ground may be frozen three metres deep. One crop predominates in the warm season, showing dark green in the springtime. This is the soya bean, prominent all the way from this locality to the Pacific. It occupied 573,000 ha in the Amur Province alone in 1966. Cattle are quite numerous, increasing year by year. In summer the meadows are resplendent with flowers, in damper places the grass grows taller than a man. The area, resembling the Ukraine and the Kuban in western Russia, was famous centuries ago under the name of Dauria (from the indigenous tribe); voluntary Russian settlers came there long ago, as well as Cossacks and deportees.

The eighteen-metre-high silo of a flour mill surmounted by a television mast is the contemporary landmark of Belogorsk (population 50,000). It has also meat-packing and macaroni factories and a score of other minor plants; but more important is its Amur Agricultural Machinery Plant 'Amursel'mash', which specialises in modern equipment for mechanised dairies and ranches. A vegetable cannery, capacity 25 million tins a year, was added in the 1960s. Belogorsk is the junction for the Provincial capital Blagoveshchensk. It is perhaps curious that this name has been retained, with its religious suggestion ('the Annunciation'), but it may be simply construed as 'good news' (though, according to local folklore, the original 'good tidings' received here was a report to the garrison commander that a number of people had been duly massacred according to his orders).

Blagoveshchensk was established in 1856. It is a pretty town located where the Zeya joins the Amur, with white houses and good tree-lined streets, a local metropolis (population 125,000). There are eighteen technical schools and four technical high schools, an opera house, a theatre, cinemas, a museum housing a rich collection of Siberiana, large old-established flour mills. The industries include also a match factory with the well-known brand name 'Iskra' ('The Spark' – which can be taken irreverently, though it is the name of an historic Bolshevik publication) and a distillery (which in times past did much business across the frontier into China) but also, higher up the scale of industrial importance in Soviet eyes, the Amur Metallist Works specialising in gold-mining equipment, an electrical equipment works, knitwear, the prefabrication of buildings and the main river-shipping facilities.

The river Amur at Blagoveschensk is frozen for about five months of the year, but busy with traffic when it is open. It is about a kilometre wide at this point. Opposite is the Chinese town of Heiho (also known in Russian as Sakhalyan) and further east another Chinese town, Aigun. There is a well-known acoustic effect at Blagoveshchensk: sounds, whether of the thoughts and songs of Mao or of other activities, carry clearly across the water in the one direction, the more technologically sophisticated noises of the U.S.S.R. in the other. Blagoveshchensk, though founded in 1856, was reached by the railway only in 1913. The flood danger was in evidence from the beginning; the first street (Ridge Street, the Relochnaya) was on the long rise in the ground above the Amur. It now spreads on both the rivers, the factories mainly on the Zeya, but extending always to the north and north-westward where the ground is higher and unflooded. The old town on the central southern frontage (Lenin Street and the quayside), the ship-repair facilities and storage are menaced by floods every year; the existing embankment has continually to be raised.

The next point on the main line east of Belogorsk is Zavitinsk, a town of 19,000 people situated in a region of virgin soil which is another potential granary area. In this area flooding and chronic dampness present particular technical problems. Ordinary combines and harvesters bog down in the summer and autumn rainy seasons. The factory at Birobidzhan further east in the Jewish Autonomous Area of Khabarovsk Province produces special machines in this category with outsize caterpillar-tracks designed for these localities. An 89-km branch line from Zavitinsk serves Poyarkovo on the Amur. For obvious military reasons the riverine areas are not on any tourist itinerary and few details are available about them.

Just over 8000 km after it left Moscow the railway comes to Bureya, which is important not only as a repair centre serving the railway and the mining operations but as a gateway for the supply of coal. 40 per cent of the coal output of the Far East passes through Bureya, coming from the Raichikhinsk fields, 32 km away on a branch line. Mining began in 1932 when it was all by hand; but now the workings are entirely mechanised, from the cutting at the coal-face to the loading on the railway. This is perhaps the cheapest coal in the Soviet Union, costing one and a half roubles a ton at the pithead. Scores of trainloads of Raichikhinsk coal come every day to Bureya, for forwarding both eastwards and westwards. Only 20 per cent is for local consumption; some minor proportion is shipped by river from Poyarkovo, most by rail from Bureya. It is loose stuff; planned improvements include processing more of it into briquettes.

Raichikhinsk itself had 27,000 inhabitants in 1966 and there are many linked settlements in the vicinity. The electric power station, located in the township named Progress half-way to Bureya, also serves Blagoveschchensk. A new glass factory was built at Progress in the 1960s. From Bureya, besides the Raichikhinsk branch line, there is another to Kivda (14 km), as well as a roadway westward to Blagoveshchensk and eastward into Khabarovsk Province.

The railway then crosses the Bureya river, which is 700 km long, torrential in its upper reaches, with a catchment area offering possible sites for three or four hydroelectric stations of 1·5 million kW capacity. Beyond the river the famous Siberian cedar trees and the Amurian liana are especially in evidence in the countryside. Arkhara is a lumber town at the foot of the Little Khingan mountains on the Arkhara river, beyond which lies the border of Khabarovsk Province.

Clearly the whole south-east of Amur Province constitutes a strong part of the middle of Manchuria's northern frontier. On the Soviet side it is a base for the supply of food, fuel and materials, as well as offering a relative concentration of manpower, especially skilled manpower. As a source of timber, the area has limitations which have already been indicated. As a source of food and agricultural materials, its further development depends on considerable additional work and investment, primarily and physically in land reclamation, drainage and the clearing of bushes and deep grass.

The activities on the Raichikhinsk coalfield have grown increasingly 'complex' or integrated, now showing an extensive minor conurbation, recently greatly modernised with two- and three-storey housing and other buildings and amenities. Metallurgical processing possibilities might enhance the local industrial prospects; rapid progress continues. The future depends, however, on bringing to this area other mineral ores and materials, in relation to which it is necessary to consider the remaining economic sub-region of the Province, the long deep belt of mountainous *taiga* which runs all along the north of the riverside areas.

THE NORTHERN INTERIOR

Two-thirds of the whole area of the Province thus remain to be described; but its tally of economic and other developments is quite scanty. The northern interior forest-upland (1500 metres) includes the administrative districts of Dzheltulatsk (Tyndinsk, north of Nyevyer), Zeya and Selemdzha (Ekimchan–Ogodzha, far to the north-east). This is a zone of permafrost, with a growing season little over one hundred days, bearing only small crops – rye, potatoes and some vegetables – in the river valleys. Three-quarters of it is forested; timber reserves total two billion cubic metres, but they are of poor quality. Gold is worked, in undisclosed quantities and ways. Iron is found at Garinsk no more than 150 km from Svobodny, but these and other items (mainly light metals) still await development.

The whole area in the triangle formed by the Stanovoy range north of the upper Zeya and a line drawn on the map from Maiski right down to Bureya, with its third side the Turan range on the eastern border of the Province, is widely marshy. The Zeya hydroelectric plant may have complex drainage effects but will provide much electricity. In the north-eastern limb of the Province, the Ogodzha thermal plant using local coal has a capacity of only 12,000 kW.

The entire interior region broadly lacks not merely transport, but people; it has perhaps 100,000 inhabitants, or one per 3 sq. km, evenly scattered, occupied in gold mining and hunting. A few stretches of motor road are open throughout the year, but the main one which runs through marshy tracts from Svobodny to the Selemdzha goldfields works only in winter. In summer boats are used along the Selemdzha river, though road transport resumes at Norsk. The patches of habitation and development are: Solov'yov in the Dzheltulatsk (Tyndinsk) area, Dambuka and Zeya, Maiski in Mazanov district and Tokursk far up the Selemdzha near Ekimchan.

In sum, the outer reaches of Amur Province form a largely empty hinterland to the richer and more activated lands along the great river.[1] Still further to the north, but with some vigorous connections to the Amur, spreads the vast cold land-locked expanse of Yakutia, which must be considered later.

CHAPTER 6

Khabarovsk: The Meeting of the Waters

THE vast Province of Khabarovsk is separated from the Sea of Japan to the south-eastward by the Soviet Maritime Province which centres on Vladivostok. To the eastward it has its own shoreline, on the Gulf of Tartary which separates the island Province of Sakhalin from the mainland; and to the north-eastwards a very long coast of its own, all the way to a point due north of Japan and Sakhalin on the Sea of Okhotsk. To the south-west the frontier is also drawn in water. The Amur river continues to form the northern frontier of China with Russia until it is joined near the city of Khabarovsk by the Ussuri, which, coming from the southward, forms for a long way the other, eastern, frontier of China's Manchuria.

The territory of Khabarovsk extends southward up the Ussuri (which river originates at a point almost as far south as Vladivostok, but flows northward away from that port) as far as Bikin about 200 km south of Khabarovsk. The Amur itself turns north-eastward near Khabarovsk, to flow eventually into the Okhotsk Sea.

All these confluences suggest the image used in the title of this chapter. There is one specific local manifestation which is worth mentioning particularly; it seems to embody most vividly the appropriateness of the metaphor. The Amur, after reaching its southernmost point at Amurzet in the Jewish Autonomous Area of the U.S.S.R.'s Khabarovsk Province, is joined near Leninskoe by the river Sungari, flowing out of China and causing, in the unfrozen seasons, a symbolic phenomenon. The waters of the Sungari are generally a deep yellow, those of the Amur a Siberian grey-blue; their meeting and mixing are sudden, the stream beyond is strong and turgid. The present

writer's Japanese *haiku* of many years ago on this, freely trans-
lated, runs:

> The southern stream, a wooden hue;
> The northern waters, steely blue.
> A muddy mix – I feel
> The south lacks trees,
> The north is short of steel.

Khabarovsk is a vast Province (825,000 sq. km, or 27 per
cent of the S.F.E.). It is the hinge of the frontier with China,
on which hangs the Maritime Province centred on Vladivostok,
Russia's only unfrozen door to the Pacific. It is a vital part of
the Soviet structure, and would be particularly exposed to
Chinese attack in the event of war. On the west, Khabarovsk
Province adjoins the Amur Province. It begins with the very
interesting, materially and strategically significant Jewish Autonomous Area. This area is strikingly developed agriculturally
and industrially; it is another granary and focus of development, like the south-eastern part of Amuria, virtually a continuation of that key zone of local Soviet strength.

The western border with the Amur Province is all mountainous, right down to the river Amur where the Little Khingan
range puts out a spur from China into the Jewish Area. Thereafter the Amur frontier passes through lowlands to the great
city of Khabarovsk, where it turns the corner of the 'horn' of
Manchuria at its north-eastern tip. The frontier then becomes
the Ussuri river. It continues through lowland at first to
Vyazemsk, then a short further upland area leads to the southern border of Khabarovsk Province, which is at Lesopil'noe
('the Sawmills') on the Bikin river, one-third of the way from
Khabarovsk to Vladivostok. But the Province extends the best
part of 2000 km to the northward of Khabarovsk, beyond
Okhotsk, and is about 700 km wide from the west to the east,
where it comes to the Pacific coast on the Gulf of Tartary. The
whole coastline of the Province is about 2500 km; nevertheless
maritime activities are not correspondingly developed. The
coast has many bays, but few of them furnish good harbours or
inland connections, the only exception being Sovietskaya Gavan'
('Soviet Haven') and its nearby Vanino, fine ports linked by
rail with Komsomolsk on the upper Amur.

Lowlands cover the eastern half of the Jewish Area, the large plain of the Amur below Khabarovsk to Komsomolsk (220 km wide in the south, 100 in the north), the rest of the narrower Amur valley down to Nikolaevsk and another valley-line north from Komsomolsk to the Okhotsk Sea; also low-lying is the Ussuri area immediately south of Khabarovsk to Khor. All these are marshy, with waterlogging and flood conditions similar to those in southern Amur Province. The swampiness extends far into China on the other side, over most of the north-eastern horn of Manchuria as far as Chiamussu.

The whole development of Khabarovsk Province is, however, very strikingly concentrated; primarily in its southern part (still along the Trans-Siberian and the river) in Khabarovsk itself and the Jewish Area, secondly in Komsomolsk (with moderate extension to Nikolaevsk on the Amur estuary), thirdly in the Vanino area. A branch railway connects Khabarovsk with Komsomolsk (300 km north), with a continuation to Sovietskaya Gavan' (about the same distance further east). The population is to a striking degree urban, to a proportion, mounting swiftly over the past decade, of nearly 80 per cent. The total population of the Province was 1,245,000 in 1956, 1,336,000 in 1968; but no less than one-third is in the capital city of Khabarovsk, much of the rest in the other main towns. The overall density of population is 1·5 persons per square kilometre. The neighbouring Maritime Province has nearly ten times that average density; the Amur Province not more than one and a half times.

However, this quotient is obviously due to the huge area of virtually unpopulated northlands included in Khabarovsk Province; the south around the Amur 'corner' has no less than 90 per cent of the Province's population, the density in some places there reaching 30 to 35 per square kilometre, the level of many areas in European Russia. These features reflect the considerable industrial development and immigration centred very largely on Khabarovsk, secondly on Komsomolsk. For the same basic reasons the average age is low and the proportion of females high. The density for all the rest of the Province is extremely low – 0·4 persons per square kilometre. The villages generally contain from one hundred to a few hundred people, occasionally 1000; some fishing collectives on the lower Amur are larger, running to 1500-2000. Russians greatly predominate, together with considerable numbers of Ukrainians and others from the western U.S.S.R. who are well integrated in the Province; the aboriginal peoples are of many groups (Nanaitzy, Ul'chi, Nivkhi, Udegeitsy, Orochi) but few in numbers and generally declining.

The huge northlands are so desolate and unpopulated, lacking all modern transport except air and coastal shipping connections (though there is also inland navigation on part of one river, the Maya), that their development is at present insignificant. Only the southern half of the Province has been at all fully surveyed or prospected; the north is not only vast, it is also complex in its geology. This huge territory must contain enormous mineral resources, virtually inaccessible as yet, especially in coal, iron, tin and building materials.

There is, however, one other major area of interior development, linking with the south-eastern part of the Amur Province rather than with Khabarovsk; namely the vast deposit of good coal (two billion tons) about 350 km north-west of Khabarovsk around Sredni Urgal', hardly tapped as yet. It is separated from the Provincial capital by two difficult mountain ranges (up to 2600 metres) but is joined by a railway to the Trans-Siberian at Izvestkovaya in the west of the Jewish Autonomous Area. There is one large mine at Sredni Urgal', which produced 1·2 million tons in 1965.

The position of the east coast area is even less defined. The Sikhote Alin' range which runs parallel to the whole coast through both the Maritime and Khabarovsk Provinces is also rich in minerals, timber and quarried materials. There is the railway from Sovietskaya Gavan' to Komsomolsk, but sea traffic is primarily drawn towards Vladivostok (and to some degree Sakhalin). Overland transport direct to Vladivostok a thousand kilometres through the massif is out of the question, even the much shorter distances to the Komsomolsk–Vanino railway present grave difficulties; only the river Khor and its tributaries give some access for this interior to the main line and the Ussuri.

Thus coal mining is so far being developed significantly only in the Urgal' area and beginning in the lignite deposits near Bikin 150 km south of Khabarovsk on the railway and in the adjacent parts of the Maritime Province, totalling nearly three billion tons of reserves. At Nadarovka 40 km south of Bikin, a large open-cut mine was being developed in 1969, a new town called Luchegorsk was established in 1966 and a large electric station (Primorsk) is being completed, with a capacity of 1·2 million kW. Iron has been located in no less than ten places in the Jewish Autonomous Area, but detailed surveys have been completed only in the Kimkan area of Obluch'e district and in the South Khingan spur in the Oktyabr'ski (Amurzet) district. The Kimkan deposit is reckoned at 190 million tons of ore, of 36 per cent iron content. There are smaller iron deposits far to the north at Nikolaevsk near the Amur mouth.

Tin is widespread in the Province but worked as yet mainly on the Myaochan range near Komsomolsk, in the Amurzet district of the Jewish Area and in the east-coast Sikhote Alin' range. Building materials are also widespread and are won in the more inhabited areas near the railways, but there is special dependence on cement and limestone from the Jewish Area (Teploye Ozero and Londoko, where there is dolomite). Clay is taken for brick-making in many places; Khabarovsk naturally draws on deposits nearby to the southward, two kilometres west of the railway at Korfovski station.

Evidently transport is the most crucial problem. The rivers play some part, but the railways are most vital; primarily the great Trans-Siberian, with its spurs to the Amur wharfages, the branch line from Izvestkovy ('the lime quarry') in the Jewish area to Chegdomyn (Sredni Urgal') and from Birobidzhan to Leninskoe. Next, the great line to Komosomolsk; as an example of matters being more complicated than the simple map, this line does not set out from Khabarovsk itself but from Volochaevka a little to its westward (the Amur valley being very watery). At Komsomolsk the river has to be crossed by ferry in summer, though lines are laid on the frozen river in winter, before the traffic can proceed from Pivan' on the other side to Vanino.

Roads are comparatively few and poor. One accompanies the whole Trans-Siberian railway line and there are good local connections over such comparatively short distances as Birobidzhan to Novy, Birobidzhan to Birafeld in the Jewish Area and Khabarovsk to Sarapul'sk (75 km north-west).

Table 6.1 Location of activities, Khabarovsk Province
(1961, percentages)

Sub-regions	Area	Population	Workers	Industrial output	Agricultural output	Sown area	Cattle	Forest area
(a) The south:								
1. Khabarovsk	4	32	25	34	8	15	13	6
2. Jewish Area	4	15	11	10	43	56	36	4
3. Ussuri	5	11	11	7	10	22	21	9
Total, the south	13	58	47	51	61	93	70	19
(b) 4. Komsomolsk	11	22	36	37	11	5	16	20
(c) 5. Central coast	17	15	11	8	20	2	11	25
(d) 6. Urgal	8	2	2	0	3	1	2	13
(e) 7. The far north	51	3	4	4	4	0	2	23
Grand total	100	100	100	100	100	100	100	100

Thus there are seven economic sub-regions to be considered in Khabarovsk Province; but the whole development is concentrated primarily in the frontier areas in the south and to a lesser degree in Komsomolsk and on the central coast, while the wide north remains comparatively blank. Table 6.1 relates to several years ago; the shares of the southern areas have since increased.

Table 6.2   Types of industrial activity in Khabarovsk Province (1962, percentages)

	Output (value)	Number of workers
Machine building	30·6	33·1
Other metal processing	6·2	9·2
Total, metalwork	36·8	42·3
Fish processing	5·4	4·4
Bakeries	5·0	2·5
Other food industries	12·0	3·9
Total, food	22·4	10·8
Lumbering	6·1	10·2
Woodworking	7·2	10·0
Paper, pulp	0·1	0·1
Total, forest products	13·4	20·3
Iron and steel	2·6	2·4
Coal	0·6	0·9
Oil	3·5	0·7
Other fuel	0·1	0·1
Total, fuel	4·2	1·7
Light industries	9·4	9·3
Building Materials	5·8	6·2
Others	4·4	7·0
Grand total	100·0	100·0

Within its industrial sector concentrated in Khabarovsk, Komsomolsk and the Jewish Area, the Province has a surprisingly high proportion of the more sophisticated products. Machine and metal industries of modern kinds are well established in the major cities. Food industries take the second place, forestry the third; light industries are very limited. A Soviet study – again, relating to several years ago but showing proportions that are even more applicable today – gives particulars (Table 6.2).

JEWISH AUTONOMOUS AREA: FAR FROM ZION

The 'Hebrew Autonomous Province of the Khabarovsk Country' (*Yevreiskaya Avtonomnaya Oblast'*, *Khabarovski Krai*) is unique. It was created by Stalin's decree as an alternative or counter to the actual or potential influence of Zionism. This area was to provide a Socialist homeland for the Jews within the U.S.S.R. and to attract like-minded Jews from other parts of the world into the Soviet fold. Though the name is retained and Yiddish still the official language, there is now nothing specially Jewish about this sub-province. Everybody speaks and uses Russian; it is unknown exactly how many of the population (of 174,000 in 1967) are now of Jewish extraction, but the census of 1959 had less than 9 per cent. The rest are Russians, Ukrainians, etc.

One of the milder manias of Joseph Stalin in the 1930s was the establishment of autonomous homelands within the Soviet Union for special ethnic groups. In anger, he would later 'liquidate' some of these as sweepingly as he had established them. Members of several groups in western and southern European Russia, suspected of collaboration with the German invaders, disappeared at the end of the war, many being deported to Siberia. The Jews did not come into that category, being the chief objects of Nazi genocide; and the other National Areas in the S.F.E., those of the Koryaks in the north of Kamchatka, the Chukchi at the farthest eastern extremity opposite Alaska, the Yakuts and the Buryats were quite out of the reach of German political warfare.

The Khabarovsk Jewish Area was founded in 1934 as an Autonomous *Oblast'*. It existed quietly under pioneering conditions, until recently; in the last few years it has shown dynamism, its rich resources are beginning to be significantly tapped, and in face of the new confrontation with China it has become an area of major military importance, not generally on tourist itineraries even for Russians, a zone of special secrecy.

The area is also referred to as Birobidzhan; from the names of two small rivers, the Bira and the Bidzhan, the capital city of the Area is called Birobidzhan. Its total extent is 36,000 sq. km. The average density of population is thus about three times that of Khabarovsk Province as a whole. The urban proportion is slightly less – 71 per cent. Two-thirds of the population is along the Siberian railway which traverses the northern part of the Area, about a quarter in the settlements along the Amur in the south, leaving only about 10 per cent in the small and scattered settlements in the upland western and marshy eastern parts.

The capital Birobidzhan (established in 1928 at the former insignificant railway halt of Tikhon'kaya) has 47,000 people – 24 per cent of the whole population. In 1959 Birobidzhan had 41,000, the whole Area 163,000. Birobidzhan certainly stands in the middle and is the communications link. The west of the Area is rich in tin, materials for cement, and forests (cedar, larch, pine and fir). The foothills and river valleys have more valuable timber such as the Mongolian oak and the Amurian lime tree. The basins of the Urmi and Kur rivers, north of the Area itself, are also drawn on for processing timber. There are several centres for this in the Area, but the major woodworking focus is at Nikolaevka where the Area reaches the city of Khabarovsk and the main branch railway to Komsomolsk; the installations there were to be greatly refurbished by 1970.

The rest of the Area is a major agricultural zone. Its agricultural output is greatly extensible. The whole eastern half contains much unused land. Also, however, much formerly used land that has long lain fallow; for previous efforts at agricultural extension have not always been successful, even though the Area provides such a great part of Khabarovsk Province's rural output. Further progress would require much work and outlay in drainage, clearing undergrowth and levelling the ground. The plain abounds with low smooth rises, of fertile turf and podzols but covered with broadleaved woods or *maquis*.

The middle of this area, about one-quarter of the whole, is the least swampy and holds the best expectations of extending cultivation. Heavy caterpillar-treads have to be fitted to the agricultural machines in many localities.

The sown area was actually doubled, for the little 'Jewish' state as a whole, in the period from the mid-1950s to mid-1960s; but the increase was largely for fodder crops. The acreage under fodder or pasture exceeds that under all other crops. In the marshy areas this is of course extremely marked; in the Smidovich district in the middle of the plain, for instance, the proportion is actually 90 per cent, only 10 per cent being under non-fodder crops, in Birobidzhan district it is over 80 per cent, in the Leninskoe and Oktyabr'ski (Amurzet) districts it is around 70 per cent. Such high proportions of fodder might suggest a flourishing livestock industry; yet the quality of cattle raising is rather low. The best farms have a population of eleven or twelve cows per hundred hectares, producing annually two and a half to three tons of meat and a little over two tons of milk; but the poorer farms return only two or three cows per hundred hectares, yielding between 0·8 and 1·1 tons of meat and 1·8 to 2 tons of milk.

Yet Soviet accounts stress the value of this Area as a 'food base' comparable to the Bureya–Zeya sub-region of Amur Province. Certainly the intensity and efficiency of cultivation on the relatively limited sown area are fairly high, even very high by Siberian standards. A significant proportion of this is under wheat; another large proportion is under soya beans. It is hard to judge the actual contribution of this Area in agricultural supplies; though some percentage figures are given, overall yields and quantities are not divulged.

The stress in the early 1960s was distinctly on the future potentials of the Area, rather than its actual achievements. Such potentials were avowedly contingent on a great deal of reclamation and improvement work. Much work of that kind, accompanied by the organisation of agricultural undertakings into larger and better equipped units, has been proceeding in the last decade, so that the Area is now making a rising agricultural contribution; but reclamation and improvement in any case take time to result in increased output. Confirmatory statistics are not offered. It is clear that, in the early to middle 1960s at any rate, the *total* food resources of Khabarovsk Province – even if the Jewish Area was a substantial contributor – were relatively poor. The perspective given was that the maximum extensions in the Area would suffice eventually to make the Province as a whole self-sufficient agriculturally.

Meanwhile the Jewish Area contains interesting industrial and mineral activities. These are concentrated along the railway line, which enters the Jewish Area at Obluch'e, a railway town of about 15,000 people with streets and high blocks of flats on a steep hillside. It is connected by road with Khingansk a few kilometres away, where tin ore is mined. All this is near the frontier and still nearer to the southward there are the Sutar river gold-workings. About 40 km further east at Kimkan there is a large deposit of iron ore right along the railway, awaiting development; meanwhile Kimkan is a sawmill centre.

The next station Izvestkovy is (as its name indicates) actively concerned in limestone-quarrying, but is also the junction for the 356-km branch line northwards to Chegdomyn and the Sredni Urgal' coal basin. For the next hundred kilometres eastward the railway passes along the valley of the Bira, which is amply lined with grey-green limestone – enough to give material, it is said, for cementing over the whole of Siberia. This is worked especially at Teplo-ozersk ('warm lake'), the main cement works along the Amur.

The area is well forested; its lumber goes mainly west to Kimkan and east to Bira for processing. Its rivers are very rich in fish (incidentally, again a 'meeting of the waters', this being the first fishing area in which eastern, Pacific or Chinese, varieties mingle with the western ones). A 'Fish Factory Combine' was established here in the early 1930s, the hatcheries of which have since put hundreds of millions of young salmon and other fry into the Amur.

The railway enters the plain just before the city of Birobidzhan. The main agricultural development lies to the southward, on the important 122-km branch line to Leninskoe on the Amur. Old wooden houses near the station remain to show the character of the one-time village, beyond them are good modern streets – lined largely with monotonous prefabricated buildings. Building prefabrication is one of the main activities of Birobidzhan. Others are food processing (which is the oldest established), knitwear, calico cloth (this town has the only spinning and weaving factory in the whole S.F.E.), clothing, shoes and confectionery.

Machine industries have recently been inaugurated in Birobidzhan. Under the Seven-Year Plan Birobidzhan's old truck and tractor repair plant was converted into the new 'Dal'sel'khozmash', i.e. Far Eastern Agricultural Machinery Works, which produces caterpillar-tracked machinery for cultivating rice and other cereals and for other operations in swampy terrain, as well as the ordinary run of implements and parts. The town has accordingly technical schools and civic facilities of all kinds; and market gardening flourishes in the suburbs. Owing to the situation right on the river, however, the flood danger is vividly present; embankments and channels are common features of a landscape reminiscent of Holland.

This palustrine setting continues generally for the next 70 km eastward along the railway, after which the station of In, serving the settlement of Smidovich, presents the traveller with a most striking monument to war and foreign invasion. Between In and Volochaevka there was a famous victory of the Red Army and guerrillas, early in 1922 in three days of fighting in 45° of February frost. On top of the Yun' Koran' peak rising steeply from the plain to the north there is a silvery statue of a Red Army Liberator facing the east, towering over a barbed-wire entanglement.

Between Volochaevka and Dezhnevka stations, the 350-km branch line takes off for Komsomolsk on the lower Amur. From this point, the environs of the great city begin. The Jewish Autonomous Province extends here at its eastern extremity right up to the Amur, just at its northward turn, within a few kilometres of Khabarovsk, the largest city in the Soviet Far East.

KHABAROVSK: THE CENTRAL CITY

Khabarovsk (after the explorer) and Nakhodka (the new port near Vladivostok) are now the only places in the Soviet East open to foreign visitors. The factory and military areas of Khabarovsk are out of sight of the imposing centre of the city. The huge squares and broad straight tree-lined streets, so characteristic of Siberian cities, are here laid out in even more gigantic proportions.

The train from the west climbs a high man-made embankment out of the plain, over-watered by the confluences of the Amur, Ussuri and Tunguska rivers, to reach the bridge across the Amur into Khabarovsk. Crossing the enormous river, it plunges through a tunnel suddenly into the town. Khabarovsk is splendidly situated on several hills. The urban district extends over some 40 km; centring on the great Station Square, this really constitutes a sub-region in itself. A great part of the economic and social activities of the Province are carried on within the city. In this section of this chapter, however, the whole adjacent sub-region is considered, which is of the same size as the Jewish Area.

Apart from the main squares and boulevards, the sports stadium (25,000 seats) which is another matter of local pride, the excellent museums and libraries (the Provincial Library has one and a half million books), the Polytechnic with 12,000 students, the airport which is the hub of all the Region's air traffic, indeed all the city amenities, this capital of a Province one and a half times the size of France is the central industrial base of the S.F.E. Vladivostok, the other great industrial base, is situated far out at the end of the Trans-Siberian limb. Khabarovsk contains, especially, the main factories making machinery: Energomash (Electric Power Machinery), Dal'-dizel' (Far East Diesel Works, once the Tsarist arsenal), Amurkabel' (the Amur Cable Works), the oil refinery and others represent a remarkable – even precocious – industrial and technical development. For they draw their materials from very distant sources and send their final products also largely far away to distant corners of the country. The heavy industry, even the medium industry, of Khabarovsk have greatly outstripped the local absorbtive capacity.

Light industry consists of food-processing activities, tailoring and shoe factories. The need has recently been felt to increase the electric power supply, which depended a few years ago on one large and a few small stations. A more inevitable dependence is on the railway, which handles no less than 90 per cent of all Khabarovsk's freight: mainly coal (largely from Raichikhinsk, as well as Urgal' and the nearer Bikin), oil, metals, building materials, foodstuffs and consumer goods. Timber is brought down the Ussuri and Tunguska rivers for processing.

Khabarovsk's population is growing very rapidly; it increased by 10 per cent between 1965 and 1968 alone, to 435,000 in the City administrative area, which totals 130 sq. km, extending 35 km along the right bank of the Amur with a width of up to 5 km in the central part and up to 2 km in the north and south. Urbanisation is extending mainly in the south, the industrial belts are in the south and north. Around them, agricultural activities have developed to feed the city; no less than one-seventh of the whole agricultural output of the entire Province, one-fifth of the vegetables, a quarter of the milk and meat, emanate from this metropolitan sub-region.

Since Khabarovsk contains one-third of the whole population of the Province, these high proportions still do not represent local abundance; further food supplies are drawn chiefly from the Jewish Area, even from Amuria. Much of the local land is used for fodder crops, but the output is low in this category and the official aim is to replace this with arable; but the same difficulty arises as in the areas further west along the Amur, for no less than one-third of the land in this sub-region is marshy, the work of improvement would be long and costly. The industrial output of Khabarovsk is certainly large and important; and is growing. It was to increase by no less than 74 per cent during the Seven-Year Plan. Many new factory constructions are visible on the outskirts.

CHINA'S EASTERNMOST FRONTIER: THE LOWER USSURI

After Khabarovsk, the frontier with China turns south; the territory of Khabarovsk continues to a point south of Bikin. In this stretch, near Khor, is the furthest-east point of China's territory – some 1000 km further east than Shanghai, almost on the longitude of Kobe in Japan. This part of Khabarovsk Province, comprising the administrative districts of Vyazemsk, Lazo and Bikin, is the next sub-region to be considered. The Ussuri plain, broad in the north, is narrowed in by uplands south of Vyazemsk. The soil of the plain is poor and denuded, two-thirds of its surface marshy. The growing season is 140 to

150 days; there is some patchy agriculture, so in this area also the aim is to reclaim and improve, the target being an additional 200,000 ha of cultivated area. The turf soil continues into the uplands further south, but this higher ground actually has a longer growing season and less damaging frosts than the lowlands, because it has more forest cover. It also has patches of cultivation, either ploughlands or pasture and hay fields; but these could not be extended without some heavy clearing of the forests, moreover the terrain is broken and there is not the necessary population.

The sub-region extends, however, far back into the mountains to the east; all this, particularly the large basin of the Khor river, is primarily a timber-producing area. Forests cover 80 per cent of the surface of the whole sub-region: 2·7 million ha in the Khor basin alone. More than half is spruce, estimated to represent total reserves of 250 million cubic metres, nearly all ripe for cutting. Wood is floated down various rivers, there are a few roads; and some local railway facility in the Obor area.

Most of the townships are therefore sawmill centres. Nevertheless, the contribution of agriculture is relatively important; this sub-region furnishes no less than 20 per cent of the agricultural output of the Province, though it has only 5 per cent of the area. It must be noted that the total output of food in the Province, which is undisclosed, must be low. The proportion for this sub-region, the Khabarovsk Ussuri, is augmented by the production, in its southernmost part, of rice, which occupies some 200 ha in this sub-region and yields two and a half to three metric tons per hectare. Nearer to Khabarovsk, the crops are potatoes, vegetables and soya beans; otherwise there is some grain and livestock. The best fodder yields are no more than 1·2 to 1·5 metric tons per hectare, many areas yield far less and the pressure is to get these ploughed.

Last but not least, there are the important lignite deposits in the south of this sub-region, beyond Bikin, which remain still untapped. The whole population of the sub-region is only 120,000, giving a density of 3·3 per square kilometre overall, but two-thirds live along the Trans-Siberian railway and the road beside it. Almost the only industries are woodworking and transport services. The former employs more than half the workers of Bikin (population 19,000) and a larger proportion of those of Vyazemsk (18,000). A score of much smaller settlements exist even more exclusively for the timber trade, with no processing facilities, sending out lumber mostly in the round.

Pursuing the journey along the Trans-Siberian railway, the following features are of interest. Near Korfovski station, clay is taken for making bricks. In the Khekhtsirski mountains in this area is a large Nature Reserve (46,000 ha) with wild boar, reindeer, bears and other wild life. The area also shows the variety of forest resources other than the spruce which is the main cut at present. The famous red-bark cedar lives for six hundred years and grows to a height of 42 metres. The 'velvet tree' has a soft bark which is a substitute for cork. The river willows reputedly grow to a girth of 'three embraces' (*tri obkhvata*) – i.e. it takes three men with outstretched arms to encircle them. The more common varieties of vegetation are represented in a vast range.

Verino station (68 km from Khabarovsk) and Pereyaslavka village are the centre of the Lazo district (named after a Civil War hero) which contains good timber. Khor is the location of a Lumber Combine with a hydrolysis plant. In the vicinity there live – or lived till recently – a few survivors (1400 persons altogether in 1968) of the indigenous Udegeitsy. These forest people were great watermen, but their dug-out canoes have now been replaced by motor boats. The motor road to Vladivostok beside the railway presented great difficulties of construction in this riverine area: this part of it was only completed in 1935.

Vyazemsk and Bikin are modest places, with low buildings, railway towns with lumber yards; though Bikin brings the first sign of the more southerly type of agriculture, with its small but efficient cultivation of rice. 14 km beyond Bikin is the last station in Khabarovsk Province, Zvenievoi – for the village of Lesopil'noe ('the Sawmill').

CITY OF THE YOUNG PIONEERS

Descending, now, the Amur northward from the capital city, we come in 320 km to Komsomolsk na Amure, the second centre of the Province, with nearly half the population of the city of Khabarovsk. It is also a considerable industrial base. The name means city of the Komsomol, i.e. the Communist League of Youth. This city was created, in a typical adventure of the Stalin era, out of nothing and far from anywhere, as a 'shock-brigade' assignment. In its establishment and all through its subsequent remarkable progress, younger people and youthful enthusiasm have indeed played a great part. In the early 1930s a call was issued for young volunteers from all over the Soviet Union, to which thousands responded. Their new city, in a pleasant but cold and remote location formerly the hamlet of Permskoe, grew rapidly; in 1939 it had a population of over 70,000, in 1967, 209,000. The railway joining it to Khabarovsk was completed in 1940, the continuation to Sovietskaya Gavan' in 1945. Communications with Sakhalin and Kamchatka were thereby shortened by a thousand kilometres.

In the 1930s, according to the publicity, enthusiasm of a similar sort quickened construction in the town of Amursk about 30 km to the south, where a large sulphite pulp cellulose and cardboard plant began production in 1967. A nitrogen fertiliser plant is projected at Amursk for the 1970s, when natural gas (for hydrogen for ammonia synthesis) is to be brought by pipeline from Sakhalin. The northern half of the middle Amur plain, comprising the Komsomolsk, Amursk and Nanaisk (Troitskoe) administrative districts, is considered as the Komsomolsk sub-region, together with the adjoining uplands.

Moreover the construction of another railway to join Komsomolsk with the Urgal' coalfield some 300 km to the west has begun. A section (Komsomolsk–Khurmuli–Evoron–Duki, still within the Komsomolsk administrative district) was completed by 1966. It is presumably the eastern end of the proposed new Trans-Siberian line north of the present one, the planned route of which is secret but is believed to pass through Chekunda on the Bureya a little south of Chegdomyn. Nearly three-quarters of the sub-region is *taiga* forest (totalling seven million hectares). On the left bank of the Amur to the Bureya range is predominantly larch, on the right bank to the Sikhote Alin' mainly fir. The new line would tap enormous resources of timber.

The town of Komsomolsk extends for 20 km along the left bank of the Amur, on both sides of a small tributary, the

Silinka. On the other side of the Amur is Pivan'. Trains are carried across by rail-ferries in summer, but in winter the river is firmly frozen and tracks are laid over the ice. Recently the construction of a bridge was begun. Komsomolsk's industrial development boasts especially the construction of the first heavy metallurgical plant in the Soviet Far East, namely Amurstal', the Amur Steel Works, which supplies principally the needs of ship-repairing and the fishing industry. Its sheet-steel and tin-plate are sent to all the main towns of the S.F.E., but are insufficient for that Region's needs. Originally, it was planned as a full iron and steel complex, but it evolved as a steelworks only. The other principal factory installations are the Amur-litmash (Foundry and Machinery plant) making hoists and transport equipment and the Metallist Works furnishing all kinds of machinery; like the leading Khabarovsk factories, both these last deliver their products not only to the S.F.E. but to distant places. Their production capacity is in excess of current effective demand within their own Region. The other 'giant' industrial feature of Komsomolsk is its oil refinery, on which transport and agriculture in the S.F.E. greatly depend.

The lumber industry is naturally active; two large Combines cover all aspects from the making of railway sleepers (for which Komsomolsk is the Region's greatest centre) to the making of furniture. There are cement, ferro-concrete and brickworks, gravel quarries. In the 1960s several new industrial and resi-dential suburbs were developing, a new river-steamer port was projected, so the local demand for building materials was still rising. In the past decade a garment factory was established, the Amurlitmash Machinery Plant was reconstructed and began a new phase of expansion. River traffic increased, especially with the areas in the lower reaches near the estuary, where there was some economic progress. The meat plants and dairies also under-went improvements.

A major recent development is the increase in activity in the upland Myaochan area, where there are useful deposits of tin and other light metals, centring on the settlement of Gorny ('Mountainous'), established in 1958, now a neat place with regular three-storey houses, mines and an ore-enrichment plant. A concentrating plant began working at Gorny in 1963. An-other mining town was established, at Solnechny (Molodezhny mine) nearby, in 1966, where another concentrator went into operation in 1969.

New developments of such kinds are much emphasised in the Soviet Union, but the older basic activity of fisheries still continues to be very important. There are a number of fishermen's settlements all along the Amur, which mostly work nearly all the year round. The total catch in this sub-region is 5000-6000 tons, an important but dwindling part being autumn salmon; carp varieties, sheat fish and pike make up the rest. This supplies mainly Komsomolsk and Khabarovsk, though some is sent to more distant places. The fish stocks are somewhat depleted; lumbering operations on the smaller tributaries of the Amur interfere with the spawning-grounds. Roads and light railways are almost entirely lacking; until or unless these can be provided fishing and forestry are alternative, not complementary, activities. The industrialisation of Khabarovsk and Komsomolsk have also gone far enough to raise the problem of water-pollution.

The population consists very largely of Russians, Ukrainians and other Soviet westerners though there are a few indigenous Nanaitsy well settled in this sub-region. 80 per cent of all the people are in the urban area of Komsomolsk; more in surrounding market-gardening areas, while the outlying parts of the sub-region are almost uninhabited, except for small forestry and fishing settlements and a few significant mining developments such as Gorny. The conditions of further progress are transport improvements – roads, new railways and the improvement of navigation on the Amur. The area for expansion here is mainly eastwards towards the Pacific coast.

MARITIME KHABAROVSK

The part of Khabarovsk Province which extends from the Amur and Amgun' rivers to the Pacific Ocean is called Maritime Khabarovsk (Khabarovskoe Primor'e) and includes the Ul'chski (Bogorodskoe), Nikolaevsk, Polina Osipenko and Sovietskaya Gavan' administrative districts. The long coast further north is separately considered, as Okhotia. Maritime Khabarovsk depends on three towns: Komsomolsk, Nikolaevsk and Soviet-skaya Gavan'. It has a total area of 160,000 sq. km, the coastline from the Golden Cape near Adimi in the south to Cape Alexander in the north being over 2000 km. Fully 90 per cent of this area is mountainous *taiga*. The Amur lowlands in the north are swampy.

The population is 180,000, or slightly over one per square kilometre, but nore than half of it is concentrated in the Soviet-skaya Gavan' and Nikolaevsk urban districts. The rest are scattered along the railway, on the Amur and along the coast; the ports of Vanino (Sovietskaya Gavan'), Nikolaevsk and Mago, also Lazarev at the nearest point to Sakhalin, have a considerable traffic with each other as well as outside the sub-region. The climate makes all work and movements seasonal. Even the sea is icy most of the year, even the railway connection is broken at Komsomolsk in early spring when the ice floes come down the river. For shipping in general the Amur is navigable only in summer.

There are a few gold-mining settlements up the Amur off the railway; forestry bases are everywhere. The agricultural centres are modest: Bogorodskoe, Takhta, Mariinskoe, all in less marshy riverside areas above Nikolaevsk, are mere villages of two or three thousand people. On the Amur and around Sovietskaya Gavan' there are small groups of indigenous people (Ul'chi, Nivkhi, Orochi) now conducting some agriculture besides their ancient occupations of fishing and hunting. Some of the coastal groups participate in modern fishing activities in the Okhotsk Sea and have fish-processing plants in their Collectives.

Fishing is the main industry of the sub-region. The lower Amur used to be a great area for salmon, especially the Siberian (*keta*) and humpbacked varieties, but, as elsewhere in the world, the salmon population has sadly decreased in recent years. The movement continues to be, in reduced numbers, in summer (from July) and autumn (from August) with the busiest season in early September. In winter fish are caught under the ice. The stocks are seriously depleted; the organisation of hatcheries and the extension of fishing out to sea are urgent tasks. Meanwhile the processing centres are too few and specialise too greatly on salmon: the two principal ones are near the Amur mouth. The main recent development is at Sovietskaya Gavan', where a substantial cannery handles other fish besides the formerly dominant salmon.

The second industry is forestry, the sub-region having ten million hectares of forests representing a billion cubic metres of timber, of which more than half is forseeably exploitable. Much of this is larch and fir, including much good material for paper and pulp. Such an industry would have to look to exports to foreign countries for its main markets.

Prospectors for minerals are active, but no major operations have yet resulted. New gold-workings were opened on the left bank of the lower Amur in the 1960s, but at the same time some of the older workings closed. A few continue to operate on the Amgun', where prospects appear brighter.

Nikolaevsk-on-the-Amur has not had a brilliant history. It was founded in 1850 as an advanced military post. It was the scene of a much-publicised massacre during the Civil War. It has not developed as a port, as its location would suggest it should. The adjacent waters are shallow, sand-barred and ice-bound far out from shore. Recently it has been notably modernised, with some good living quarters and new ship-repair facilities; the population is about 32,000. It occupies a narrow stretch of the left bank of the river, mostly devoted to the port activities which are its main – but not luxurious – livelihood. Mago 40 km upstream is a main timber wharf; in recent years it has developed some considerable export of lumber to Japan and other parts of Asia. On the opposite bank to Nikolaevsk is Konstantinovka, with repair and machine shops. Otherwise the locality has just a few fishing villages. A grandiose scheme for possible future implementation is the construction of a ship canal through some of the lakes in this area, shortening the distance to the sea and improving the throughway by coming out clear of the sandbars.

Sovietskaya Gavan' has recently developed much more substantially. It was given the status of a town only in 1941, since when its population has multiplied four times (absorbing also some adjacent villages) now reaching 52,000 (exclusive of nearby Vanino, which counts a further 12,000). The site is a large bay with numerous indentations, along which there is a considerable boat traffic. Sovietskaya Gavan' is on the south shore. It has good modern buildings. The main port activity shifted, however, to Vanino, on the middle part of the bay. Even after the completion of the railway (1945) ship repairs and lumber remain the principal occupations. Some gold has been found along the nearby coast.

THE NORTHERN WASTES

North of the Amur-Amgun' delta there is a vast and empty land. This is the Okhotsk sub-region – nearly half a million square kilometres of mountainous tundra. It is divided into three very large administrative districts: Chumikan, Ayan and Okhotsk. The total population is only 40,000, or less than one person on the average in more than a hundred square kilo-metres; in fact over 30,000 of these are in a few small settle-ments on the coast, the most important at the farthest end of the Province's coast around Okhotsk (namely the fishing villages of Ul'ya and Tsentral'ny, Urak, Novoe Ust'e, Okhotsk, Inya and Shilkan). The interior is practically uninhabited: 28 mil-lion ha of mountainous (500 to over 2000 metres) taiga, 16 million ha under forests, the rest tundra or sub-tundra, ex-tremely cold with a short and slight remission in summer, without any road or railway. Less than 1 per cent of the area is used in any way by man, and that mainly for the keeping of reindeer.

Geologically the area is unsurveyed, though hypothetically rich; lead and zinc deposits have recently been identified. Food, other than fish and a small part of the potatoes and vegetables, also other supplies – including even the vats for packing fish – have to be brought to this coast all the way by sea (except for an air service to Okhotsk). Fishing in the Okhotsk Sea is limited to the summer (young herring in May-June, older herring in July, salmon in August and September). There are some pro-cessing plants in the villages, which employ two-thirds of the local work force and send their products to all parts of the Soviet Union. Okhotsk has some ship-repair facilities.

The fishing industry is the only significant resource of this area, now and for a long time to come. The possible yield of the Okhotsk Sea for this sub-region is taken by Soviet planners to be some 80,000 tons of fish a year; the present production is not definitely known, but is some small fraction of that figure. Most of it is in the simplest form – salted herring and salmon. The salt has to be brought from a great distance. Though Nikolaevsk and Sovietskaya Gavan' are much nearer, both the slender exports of this sub-region (fish) and the relatively heavy imports (salt, other equipment and all sorts of articles of consumption) are routed mainly to and from Vladivostok, which is much the most powerful centre of development for the whole Pacific fringe of the Soviet Union. Northern Khabarovsk Province does not even have any land-surface communications with the great interior area of Yakutia, as do the neighbouring Provinces of Amuria and Magadan. There is, however, the important prospect of another link into Amuria, which has been briefly mentioned above but requires the following additional references.

A NEW DOOR TO THE WESTWARD

The remaining sub-region of Khabarovsk Province is the Urgal' mining area in the southern part of its western border, containing a rich coalfield around Chegdomyn, including coking coals, through which the new northern Trans-Siberian line may be laid. This would transform the economic and general pattern of Khabarovsk Province, especially its central and southern parts, though as yet the Urgal' delivers its coal and timber via the Jewish Area and Bureya. The Urgal' coal is good lumpy stuff.

This sub-region is mountainous, 90 per cent of its area is 1200-1500 metres above sea level. The rest is the plain of the Bureya basin. The output of coal is about one million tons a year – at that rate the known reserves would last a thousand years. Khabarovsk obtains some coal from the Urgal', but still draws much more on Raichikhinsk in Amuria. The railway from Izvestkovy to Chegdomyn and a road continuing northward to the Umal'tinski and Sofiisk gold workings are the main artery of transport, though many of the rivers are good for rafting timber. Chegunda is a centre for that activity, and at Sogda on the railway there are sawmills.

The whole population is only 25,000, of which all but 2000

are in the townships of Chegdomyn, Tyrma, Sredni Urgal',
Sogda and Sofiisk'. Clearly agricultural development is incon-
siderable; mining and forestry are the assets of this sub-region.
Apart from the coalfield, the mineral prospects are really
limited; most of the ores appear poor, they could be worked
only when enough electric power is provided. The forests,
covering two-thirds of the area (80 per cent larch, some fir) are
now being more considerably developed.

In sum, Khabarovsk is a most extensive and varied Province.
The huge northland is empty and has little cohesion with the
rest. The great city of Khabarovsk dominates, as one of the
major centres of the Trans-Siberian railway and the frontier.
The city's industries are rather remarkably developed. In some
technical respects they are (to quote a native saying) 'too big
for the local boots'. The Jewish Autonomous Area is another
busy centre, from the standpoints of food supply, complementary and general activities. Development also overflows from
Khabarovsk to some extent into the Ussuri area towards Vladivostok and more markedly into the area of Komsomolsk. From
the latter, by (to quote again a local comment) 'a knight's
move' around a corner, some developmental activity flows
across to the seaboard.

A much greater base of economic and other developments
exists in the next Province to the eastward – in Vladivostok and
the Maritime Province. The main strength of the S.F.E. lies so
greatly in its south-eastern end that Khabarovsk, considerable
as it is, perhaps figures principally at present as a gateway to
the richer terminal Province – the Maritime lands which are
the subject of the next chapter.[1]

CHAPTER 7

The Maritime Province: Pacific Seaboard

THE Maritime Province occupies a very important position on the Pacific. Development of all kinds in the rest of the Russian Pacific seaboard – Sakhalin, Kamchatka and Magadan – depends greatly on the fine port of Vladivostok. So may foreign trade, though latterly the neighbouring new port of Nakhodka has been the main route for this, Vladivostok being an area of secret naval operations. At the same time the Maritime Province, especially its south-western part, is well favoured by Nature with agricultural and mineral wealth, a comparatively mild climate and good conditions for transport. Consequently the south-west has advanced industrially. The rest of the Province is colder and much more inaccessible; it is mountainous, right down to the coast which (north of Nakhodka) offers at best only a very narrow strip for development, with few favourable locations. This key area is in an especially exposed position in the confrontation with China.

This Province comprises only 5·3 per cent of the whole territory of the S.F.E., but has one-third of its population. The numbers reached 1,669,000 in 1968, a density of just over 10 per square kilometre. It produces nearly a third of the gross national product of the S.F.E., far more than 45 per cent of the output of the fishing industry by value (with one-third of the fish catch in volume). It has 28 per cent of the sown area of the whole Region, 41 per cent of the cattle, 40 per cent of the pigs. It handles 80 per cent of the sea freight. On the same latitude as the northern Black Sea coast in European Russia, it is one of the Soviet Union's southerly parts.

The Sikhote Alin' massif occupies almost the whole Province, but the lowlands (the Suifun and Ussuri valleys and the plain around Lake Khanka) form a notable agricultural base, close to the railway, the ports of Vladivostok and Nakhodka and the mines. The climate is distinctly of the monsoon type, the summers being warm (though reaching 39°C at the warmest in August, the summer average is seven or eight degrees lower than in the same latitudes in European Russia) but rainy. Half the yearly precipitation occurs in July, August and September. Snow in winter is light, though the winds are cold and strong. The winter is of course fiercer in the upland interior, where there can be 40°C of frost, though 25 is more normal. The weather is, however, very variable. Even in the uplands there are about 130 frost-free days in the year, elsewhere 170 or 180. The autumn is beautiful; the winds are then stilled, the sun is bright. In the warm season the food markets are quite unlike those of Siberia, offering such local products as rice and maize, sugar beet, soya, even water melons and grapes.

The Vladivostok area has naturally the strong local colour of a seafaring and foreign trading community, to an extent certainly not felt in inland Siberia – and hardly anywhere else in the Soviet Union. The nearest Soviet parallel is Odessa (the name of which reminds of Ulysses, and its ambience is quite 'Mediterranean' – Leningrad is the only other large foreign trade port but Leningrad, though majestic, has more northern phlegm and more of the claustrophobia of central Russia). The Asian and sub-tropical influences in the Vladivostok area and the nearby borderlands of China and Korea are also evidenced in such curious local activities as the production and export of ginseng (a 'root of life' in Chinese and East Asian medicine), some special deer-horns (of supposedly aphrodisiac properties) and some sea-foods (which are especially appreciated by Oriental gourmets). Details on these and other items are given below.

More basic exports, mainly to the rest of the Soviet Union, are coal (the Province has thirty identified deposits totalling 3·7 billion tons, a few million tons are currently produced), other minerals such as tin, fluorite, cement materials, a range of light metals, fish and lumber. Of these, only timber is significantly exported to other countries. To sustain and expand these lines of production, considerable industrial activity has developed, but much more is needed. The present and future requirements are machinery for fisheries, food industries and mining, parts and equipment for ships and other means of transport.

Transport activities of necessity represent a large part of the Province's gross national product and number of enterprises, much more than in the rest of the S.F.E.; industry represents 85 per cent, against 15 per cent for agriculture. Fisheries represent 25 per cent of this Province's total output, against 22 per cent for the S.F.E. as a whole; other food industries 20 per cent, against 14 per cent for the Region as a whole.

Nevertheless the agriculture is very important. It includes a higher proportion of animal husbandry than other Provinces of the Region, including such activities as the breeding of fur-bearing animals and of deer as well as cattle and poultry. The Maritime Province has 3800 ha planted to fruit and berries (65 per cent of the total for the S.F.E.) 31,100 under maize (95 per cent) and 12,000 under sugar beet for both factory and fodder use (80 per cent). Its averages are higher in agriculture generally than those of the S.F.E. in general or particularly those of the other Province which is really in question in this connection, the Amur Province.

Table 7.1   Levels of agriculture in the S.F.E.
(1962)

	Amur Province	All Provinces of the Soviet Far East	Maritime Province
Numbers per ha of sown area of:			
Cattle	0·23	0·38	0·52
Pigs	0·18	0·33	0·46
Per cent of sown area devoted to:			
Cereals	46·6	42·6	41·7
Potatoes and vegetables	2·7	7·2	10·7
Fodder	12·6	16·2	19·7
Output of cereals (kg per hectare)	5·9	6·8	8·7

Only in the proportion of the area devoted to cereals is the Maritime Province below the average or below the Amur

Province; but it cultivates cereals much more intensively and productively.

It is convenient to begin with the area traversed by the railway. Along it lie three of the four significant sub-regions of the Province. First the Ussuri sub-region, including the whole basin of the river of that name with its confluents the Ulakhe and the Daubikhe in the south, the Iman and the Bikin in the north. This excludes the lowlands immediately around Lake Khanka (where the Chinese frontier turns westward across the northern end of the lake), which form a distinctive area, classified separately as the second sub-region of the Province. Thirdly there is the metropolitan area of Vladivostok itself. The fourth sub-region is the mountainous and coastal area north-east of Vladivostok and Nakhodka.

THE UPPER USSURI FORESTRY AREA

This comprises the following five administrative districts. Iman is an important town, with a surrounding district under the same name. Adjoining it to the east up the Iman river is the Red Army (Krasnoarmeiski) district, the capital of which is the village of Novopokrovka (the appellation Red Army does not signify that it is specially a garrison area). Then there are two administrative districts around the head of the branch line which goes east from Manzovka to Varfolomeyevka, namely the Chuguyevka and Yakovlevka districts. Finally there is the Anuchino district around Arsen'iev (Daubikhe).

The area thus defined includes 46 per cent of the whole area of the Province (78,000 sq. km) with 15 per cent of the population (230,000 persons). This population is mainly gathered in those towns along the railway where the tributary rivers come into the Ussuri on its right bank. The railway is the main livelihood, the rivers making supplementary contributions. The long plain of the Ussuri is from 30 or 40 to 150 km wide on the Soviet side, undulating gently at its edges to the uplands on the east, which rise to 1500-1700 metres. Where the Ussuri forms the frontier with China (i.e. below its confluence with the Sungacha – above that point the Sungacha becomes the frontier) the wider left-bank valley is Chinese territory.

The sub-region is slightly drier than the coastal belts in springtime but suffers downpours, therefore floods, in the summer. In its upland parts there are marked local differences of climate, hence of crops and conditions; there are sheltered pockets of agricultural development, while other places are too exposed. The southern slopes are generally more favourable than the northward-facing ones. The uplands are chiefly engaged in forestry, using the rivers (which range from only a few kilometres to 300 km in length) for the floating of timber towards the railway. This activity is, however, extremely seasonal; on the smallest rivers (torrential in the high mountains) good rafting conditions are found only on as few as three to ten days a year, on the larger rivers only fifteen to twenty days, even on the Ussuri only twenty-five to thirty days.

Nevertheless the output is large. $2\frac{3}{4}$ million cubic metres of timber were floated in this sub-region in 1963: the Ussuri took nearly a third (800,000), the Iman 600,000, the Ulakhe 550,000, the Vak 250,000, the Daubikhe 227,000, the Fudzin 190,000 and the Bikin 130,000. In most localities four-fifths of the area is forest; even in the river valleys where human settlement and exploitation are most marked, the proportion is around one-half. The sub-region has about 60 per cent of the forest area of the whole Province, and the types of timber are more diversified than anywhere else in the S.F.E., including many of the better-quality woods. Forestry operations through all stages from cutting to milling are specially developed in this sub-region, which accounts for three-quarters of all such work in the Province.

The Bikin area is the least worked; only about 14 per cent of its presently workable area is actually used, whereas on the Iman and the Vak the proportion is 30 or 40 per cent. The figure for the Ulakhe is similar, but on the Daubikhe it reached 65 per cent some years ago and may now have exceeded the economic limits, i.e. begun to cut into areas where the cost is really higher than the return, or beyond the requirements of conservation.

However, the cutting is generally very selective. Only soft-wood is taken, at the average of 60 cubic metres per hectare of worked area, out of a total availability per hectare of 216 cu. m in the domains under the Ulakhe State Forestry Enterprise and

121 in those of the Lower Daubikhe. Unselective felling is
carried on in not more than 20 per cent of the forest area,
almost entirely in the domains along the railway line, where on
the average 123 cubic metres are taken per hectare. Over 90 per
cent of the output is coniferous wood (cedar 51 per cent, fir 28
per cent, silver fir 13 per cent), the rest being ash, birch, elm
and maple.

The reserves are large and varied. In the north the trees are
mainly firs and deciduous in the upper reaches of the main
rivers more than 600 metres above sea level: fir, silver fir,
Daurian larch, some lime, maple, ash and birch. The quality
and the variety improve towards the south-west where there
are more broadleaved trees; there the dominant kinds are
Korean cedar below 600 metres elevation, mixed with ash, the
'velvet' tree (cork-oak), nut trees and elm. Practically all the
cedar of the Province is in this sub-region.

Two large sawmill centres thus dominate the industrial life
of this sub-region; namely Iman in the north serving the basin
of the river of the same name and the Vak, Lesozavodsk ('the
Forest Factory') in the south serving the basins of the Ulakhe
and Daubikhe. In these railway and river junction towns nearly
90 per cent of the labour force is in the woodhandling and
woodworking industry, which accounts for a similar proportion
(over 80 per cent) of the local gross product. Iman (population
28,000) is the larger of the two, having nearly double the output
(by value) of Lesozavodsk (population 35,000). Until recently
at least, Iman certainly had the more imposing installations: a
five-storey sawmill (the fifth storey added a few years ago)
handling 130,000 cubic metres a year, a building materials and
veneer combine, a bonding shop and a furniture factory. These
have not, however, been working at capacity; the scale of plant
has been somewhat larger than the local availability of materials
and of skilled workers or other complementary requirements.

Nevertheless Lesozavodsk has handled a much greater volume
of lumber – about 300,000 cubic metres of sawing material a
year. Though Iman registered a much greater *value* of production, chiefly because it had a higher proportion of more highly
finished materials, Lesozavodsk produces house-building timbers and veneers, wooden boxes, barrels and staves. It is also
the chief furnisher of skis to the S.F.E. The above particulars

relate to about 1966; major developments were then planned and may since have been started, especially in Lesozavodsk. Still in the planning stage for Lesozavodsk are pulping facilities (hydrolysis and 'vibrator' equipment plants), cement-fibre and wood-shaving processes.

More actual, to all appearance, are steps to improve access to and utilisation of both the large river basins, especially the southern one serving Lesozavodsk, which depends greatly on the branch railway to Varfolomeyevka, to which an extension has been in hand to Novo-Mikhailovka. This would tap new interior areas; meanwhile older ones (the domains of the Breyevski Forestry Enterprise in Chuguyevka district and the Fudzhino-Nottinsk Enterprise) are being improved. The middle Iman is being tackled first, the less-developed Bikin river area later. More intensive felling is spreading over wider areas. In its train, processing plants are to be extended: first cardboard factories (the first of these on the Province was planned in the 1960s at the Burlit station in the Bikin basin), later cellulose-paper mills. The improvement works have to include a great outlay of labour and materials on new railway construction, river improvement (to facilitate flotation and rafting), reconstruction of old timber yards and the provision of new ones. There is already a well-equipped modern yard at Lesozavodsk. Projected new yards are at Iman, Sysoyevka (for the Daubikhe basin), Burlit for the Bikin and Novo-Mikhailovka for the Ulakhe.

This builds up a picture of an enormous and rich forestry activity. For perspective it must be emphasised that this is very far from sufficient. The Maritime Province still has an annual deficit of one to one and a third million cubic metres of wood, imported from other Provinces. It is desired not only to make up that deficit and increase consumption within the Province but to generate a large surplus for export. There is strong pressure both to extend the area and intensity of exploitation and to rationalise the location of forestry activities (which are uneconomically scattered at present) into a few main centres, old, new, or yet to be established. Recently under construction, a complex at Novo-Mikhailovha in Chuguyevo district planned to produce annually 160,000 cubic metres of sawings, 52,000 of veneers, eight million of shavings, chips and small pieces, fibreboard, furniture, rosin and other items. Similar new enterprises may follow in the Iman and Bikin areas.

While forestry is thus the most obvious activity in this sub-region, its other rural pursuits are important. It is the Province's centre for hunting. The Alchansk State organisation for this has its central post at Burlit; the Central Iman organisation with a main post at Kartun in the Red Army district and another at Krasny Yar employs native Udegeitsy people and uses the Bikin basin. The fur trade is very predominantly in squirrel, representing over 95 per cent of the production of furskins in the Province. The Upper Ussuri contributes over 200,000 squirrel skins a year, 80 per cent of the production of these in the Province, also more than half of the Province's production of kolinsky mink.

The forest areas also produce berries, nuts and fruit. The annual output of 'Amurian' grapes is 2600 tons, of 'Chinese' citrus 1600, of bilberries 2000. Nearly all this is directly consumed by the people locally, a welcome variegation to their diet.

The sub-region is largely unprospected geologically, but the Sikhote Alin' massif is presumed to be rich in minerals, particularly in light-metal ores. Known deposits of tin began to be test-worked in the 1960s at the Dal'nii ('Distant') mine in Chuguyevo district, the Tayozhny ('Taiga') mine in the Iman basin and on dredgings on the Shetukhe river. Some small gold workings have operated on the middle Iman since 1929. A much larger perspective is the recent development of the Bikin brown coal deposit. The Nazarovka village area in the Iman district is the centre, but the coalfield extends into Khabarovsk Province. Total reserves are given as three billion tons, in seams $1\frac{1}{2}$ to 70 metres thick, accessible on the surface in many places. At least one major cut was started in the middle 1960s and the intention was to build at this location the largest electric power station in the Province.

Another significant centre of development is Arsen'iev further south, a growing town with about 40,000 inhabitants, relatively well served with transport. The northern parts of the sub-region have practically no roads or railways, other than the main rail and highway. In contrast Arsen'iev is on the Manzovka–Varfolomeyevka branch line, which has already been extended some distance with a view to taking it eventually all the way to

Tetyukhe on the coast. Moreover there are roads from Arsen'iev to Tetyukhe, Kavalerovo, Chuguyevka and Yakovlevka, all with bus services and lorry traffic.

Agriculture is however extremely weak in this sub-region. It is limited in area to the valleys of the Ussuri and its tributaries. The valleys are highly liable to flooding, while in the foothills man is still fighting the swampy forest, the *taiga* and its undergrowth. Many of the village areas in this sub-region grow only half of their food, some no more than a quarter; they rely greatly for the rest on hunting, fishing and side-occupations.

Fortunately the adjoining Khanka area is fertile. In the north there is some dairying and growing potatoes and vegetables, in the south more cattle and cereals. Wheat takes up 23 per cent of the sown area of this sub-region, soya 17 per cent, oats 14 per cent, potatoes and vegetables 13 per cent. Sugar beet is produced in the south. The ploughland is on the slopes or terraces. The lower land, liable to flooding, is mainly for pasture.

Most of the output is consumed very near where it is grown; only a little is picked up by the railway. The Ussuri area produces a quarter of the Province's rather inadequate crops of vegetables. Potatoes and vegetables are sent from the Ulakhe area to the mining zone of Tetyukhe and Kavalerovo in the north-east. Sugar beet and soya are processed at Ussuriisk in the south, there are also some vegetable canning and salting or pickling plants. The planners want to extend animal husbandry. Bee-keeping is quite a characteristic local activity on the Ussuri. Some collective apiaries have 14,000 swarms of bees, each yielding up to 190 kg of honey in a good year, forming a main source of income. There is a buzz in August when the lime is blossoming and in September in the late herbage.

Clearly the great axis of this sub-region is the main railway track. Only the Varfolomeyevka railhead area links with the north-eastern part of the Province. Burlit–Volochayevski station near the northern border is the centre for the prospective development of the paper industry, adjoining the Bikin coalfield. Near Lastochka is a well-known mineral spring the water of which is highly reputed – the S.F.E. equivalent of Borzhomi (the Perrier or Vichy of Western Russia).

An important recent development is the opening of tin and

tungsten mining of the Tatife river, far up the Iman in an area called Vostok; planned to be fully opened in 1971. Iman, besides having sawmills and woodworking industry, is also the upstream terminal of regular river-boat services to Khabarovsk. Lazo is named after a Civil War hero, a great leader of the Red Partisans (guerrilla forces) in this area. The other side captured him and executed him, according to the Soviet account, by throwing him into the fire-box of a locomotive. Such was the cruel and bitter record of the Civil War, the memory of which is still strong in this area. The memorial of Lazo is prominently visible from the train, on the east side of the track. Ruzhino is the name of the station at Lesozavodsk, the other main woodworking centre. The vicinity is subject to disastrous floods in summer. Shmakovka is the station for the well-known spa of that name, a full hour away by bus. The hills to the east are the beginning of the large natural basin which contains Lake Khanka; a little later, just about 9000 km after it left Moscow, the line passes out of the upper Ussuri sub-region into that of Lake Khanka.

THE FERTILE LAKELAND

South of its Ussuri sub-region, the Maritime Province bulges, above Vladivostok, about 150 km to the westward. This is still the frontier with China – almost all the way to the sea, only the last 50 km of the frontier being with North Korea. Within this westward bulge is the large (65 by 75 km) Lake Khanka. The Chinese frontier runs across this lake near its northern shore. The low-lying lands around the lake form a fertile and well-worked agricultural area, distinctive and important enough to be counted as a separate sub-region.

The Khanka sub-region comprises the seven administrative districts of Mikhailovka (in the south, just north of Ussurisk and 130 km north of Vladivostok), the Ussurisk district itself, Khankai (Kamen'-Rybolov), Spassk, Kirov (Shmakovka), Pogranichny ('Frontier', on the west) and Chernigovka (Muchnaya, south of Spassk). This takes in a little of the Ussuri valley in the north, in the west some of the foothills of the mountains of China's eastern Manchuria and, in the south, part of the valley of the Suifun river, which flows in from China and is separated from the lakeside lowlands to its northward by the Khorol'sk hills, which rise to about 200 metres. The area of this sub-region is 27,000 sq. km, 16 per cent of the Province.

Apart from these hilly areas, the rest is level lowland, especially in the central parts near the lake, with some slight flat-topped elevations. On the periphery there is a frequently changing landscape; there are still many flat lands, but more sudden rises. This is the best agricultural land in the whole of the S.F.E. – intensively settled and cultivated for more than a century, though the climate is not so favourable as the soil. The spring has periods of drought lasting ten days or two weeks. The winter snow cover is usually light (average about 27 cm) but in some years there is little or none and frost is severe. Hence there are practically no winter crops. In late summer and early autumn, just at the reaping and harvesting seasons, there is copious rain and extensive flooding of the farmlands. The lake then spreads far to its south and east; the rivers also overflow widely.

Long-range planners envisage elaborate hydraulic systems to regulate the main rivers, even to lower the level of the lake; also to cut a canal from the Suifun to the lake, for navigation as well as drainage, opening navigation from Vladivostok through to the Ussuri and enabling reclamation of many marshy areas for extensive growing of rice. These are not yet immediate priorities: the sub-region is comparatively well provided with transport, having more railway and road facilities than any other part of the S.F.E., so can still develop considerably on the basis of its existing transport network.

The soil is peaty, with thin top layers of humus (18-25 cm at best), rather heavy in composition. This, with the climatic conditions, causes the soil to dry out in spring and be over-moist in summer and autumn, shrinking, crusting and cracking when dry, swelling and becoming soggy after rain. The underlayers are thick and impervious. Skilful ploughing is necessary; and the use of plenty of chemical fertiliser could greatly improve productivity. Good deep-ploughing skill seems to be available locally; but chemical fertilisers are not available to the Khanka farmers to any great extent. Nor is animal manure; but the use of silage is much developed.

There is a good deal of woodland, largely underlaid with swampy ground; but in this area of comparatively old settlement it has been heavily cut. Though all parts of the sub-region still have 8 per cent of their area under trees and some as much as 20 per cent, felling is now prohibited altogether in some areas and restricted in the rest, for conservation.

Oats, barley and buckwheat have been cultivated in this area for several generations. Overall, the sub-region may now surpass Amuria as the main agricultural base of the S.F.E., though it still takes second place to the Zeya–Bureya area as a provider of grain in particular. It furnishes 50 per cent (by value) of the total output of crops in the Maritime Province, on 70 per cent of the sown area, 75 per cent of the cereal output of the Province, 80 per cent of the soya beans, 85 per cent of the sugar-beet, about 60 per cent of the potatoes and vegetables, about one-third of the meat and milk.

As the agriculture is diversified, the failure or shortfall of one crop is usually offset by better results in another, the collectives in this area have a steadier livelihood than others. 56 per cent of the arable land of the sub-region is ploughed, one-third of the arable land in the uplands, less than one-fifth in the southern lake-shore area. The rest is fairly equally divided between hay-making and pasturage. Although the production of cereals for the market is not the first priority in agricultural planning for this sub-region, as it is for the Province as a whole, about half the sown area in the Khanka sub-region is in fact devoted to grain: spring wheat 19 per cent, oats 17 per cent. Rice and buckwheat, though distinctly suitable to the area, each take less than 1 per cent of the sown acreage. The average yield of spring wheat is 1100 kg/ha, but the maxima for the best farms and the best years are 1800 to 2000. Oats have the best average yield, with 2200. Perennials do much more poorly. The comparatively low yield of wheat is ascribed partly to unbroken sowing over many years (wheat was the great staple of the settlers in the last century and is still 'habitual'), partly to insufficient manuring, partly to weather conditions (drought in the germinating period, dry winds later, flooding in harvest-time) and the incidence of fungoid affections of the grain.

Maize is also cultivated, with preference for the varieties ripening before the other main cereals, but these require much sunshine. The authorities press for the cultivation of the later-maturing varieties – yielding a larger mass of greenstuff as well as of cobs – with a view also to their use as silage, though from other points of view such varieties are less suitable for the local rural work-cycle.

Buckwheat has long been cultivated. Early in this century it took 17 per cent of this sub-region's sown area. In about 1910 the Maritime Province was producing up to 200,000 poods (3276 metric tons) of buckwheat groats in a good year. This is a 'beneficent' crop: it is harmful to pests which affects other crops and is melliferous, i.e. it produces much nectar or pollen. Yet the area in the Khanka country under buckwheat has greatly diminished since the Revolution, to little over 3000 ha – though it is still half the Province's total. The yield varies between 370 and 680 kg/ha. Recently there have been efforts to increase this crop in area and yield.

Most interesting is the cultivation of rice in this sub-region, organised in two State Farms. Rice has been cultivated in the Province, especially in this locality, since 1917. One is the Khanka, which has recently developed new ricefields near the lake, the other the Santakheza Sovkhoz. The rice area on the plain has recently been extended. In the Morozovsk and Platonovo-Aleksandrovsk hills in the Khanka district and those of Kharikovsk in the Frontier district old irrigation channels have been rebuilt and new ones made. The total area suitable for rice cultivation in this sub-region is 100,000 ha.

The sub-region produces 80 per cent of the Province's soya beans, all of which can be handled by the oil and fats plant in Ussurisk. This plant's requirements are not always met, because the crop varies from year to year with weather conditions and because the beans may be put to other uses on the farms. Industrial crops occupy some 20 per cent of the sub-region's sown area, if soya beans for oil and cattle-cake are included. Sugar-beet has been cultivated for factory processing since 1930, and is the most profitable crop, except vegetables. The sub-region produces over 50 per cent of the Province's output of vegetables and potatoes, taken together; these two crops occupy 9 per cent of its sown area. They are marketed in Ussurisk, Spassk and Vladivostok. They are much used in crop-rotation on the plain, where the yield would be high but for the constant danger of floods, which come just at the time of picking and lifting, make the work arduous and cause much spoilage. Most of the output is used immediately by the local growers; the larger settlements have canning, or at least bottling and processing facilities. Most of the rest goes to the Maritime Province's own towns but some is exported to Kamchatka and Magadan.

The ordinary types of farm machinery are hardly suitable for this marshy area; limited progress has been made in devising and applying special equipment, such as the caterpillar-treads produced in Birobidzhan. Even before such equipment is brought to bear extensively on the land, a great deal of clearing and preparatory work is necessary, especially eliminating the swamp grass and water-plants. For this the large-scale application of herbicides – even poison gases – is advocated. An equally vital aspect is soil improvement, simply by the provision of large amounts of various fertilisers. Neither the herbicides nor the fertilisers are yet available on any large scale; regarding the machinery, much experimentation has been carried out and some special equipment is working.

The Khanka sub-region has 60 per cent of the cattle in the Province, 57 per cent of the pigs. Meat and dairy production is the general emphasis, though some areas concentrate entirely on producing milk for supplying Ussurisk, Spassk and Vladivostok. The annual yield per cow varies between 2000 and 2500 litres, with a fat content of 3·8 per cent. Poultry and beekeeping are important. There are even some sheep. The activities are certainly variegated. Nevertheless, though this sub-region has 45 per cent of the hay-land and fodder output of the Province, it is short of animal feeding stuffs, since the total is not large. If the yield of soya and other beans, maize and silage increases, the local people wish and need to devote all this to animal feeding. Alternative possibilities, little exploited as yet, are wastes from the processing of fats and oilseeds at Ussurisk, the discards of the distilleries, or fish-meal.

53 per cent of the Khanka sub-region's inhabitants are in villages, against 29 per cent for the whole Province in the areas under Village Soviets – it was said above that 80 per cent of the Province's inhabitants are 'urban', but some 9 per cent are in villages close to towns, or mining villages, etc., administratively or practically townships. The Khanka sub-region con-

tains 47 per cent of the village population of the Province. The biggest agricultural settlements are Chernigovka (population 11,000) and Khorol' (7000). Some of the 'district' (*rayon*) capitals count up to 5000 inhabitants, the Village Soviet ones only one or two thousand. Most of the villages are on the road-ways (Vladivostok–Khabarovsk and Ussurisk–Khorol'-Turii Rog on the north-west corner of the lake), or the railways, in the river valleys and near the lake-shore. On the higher western side of the lake they are right on the shore, but in the lower-lying south and east the villages (Astrakhanka, Kamen' Rybolov, Platono-Aleksandrovka, Santakheza, Gaivoron) have to stand some kilometres back from the shoreline.

Two considerable towns have already been mentioned as important for their connections with this sub-region. In the north, on the mainline railway, is Spassk (or Spassk-Dal'nii – the station is called Yevgen'ievka) with 42,000 inhabitants. This was a great centre of the Red Partisans in the Civil War; the setting described in their stirring song 'In the valleys, on the hilltops', an old favourite in the Soviet Union. A cement factory was established there at the beginning of the century, now the basis of the activity which makes Spassk the largest supplier of building materials in the Maritime Province. It produces over a million tons a year of cement of all kinds, including recently a million metres of asbestos-cement piping and over 100 million roof-tiles, but the capacity is still expanding. This suffices to supply all the needs of the Province itself and to provide some exports to Sakhalin, Kamchatka and Magadan Provinces. There are also bricks and asbestos products, made from materials from nearby quarries.

Santakheza a few kilometres south of Spassk is the location of the large State Rice Farm and Experimental Station. Rice has been grown there for more than fifty years. This has been on an 'American' rather than a 'Chinese' basis, i.e. more extensive, more mechanised and less labour-intensive than the familiar and basic one further south in Asia. The individual rice-fields are not strikingly larger than those of south-central China (though larger than in the southernmost parts of China). Indeed they are hardly larger than those in Manchuria across the border. But on this spacious plain-land they are 'gridded' out in seemingly endless sequence as far, in places, as the eye can reach. This enables large-scale mechanised operations, so far as the first stage of rice-growing is concerned, the sowing. Sowing is done to some extent by aeroplane. Beyond this, it is not clear how far the Soviet Russians have been able to modernise and mechanise the production of rice; but they have certainly made special efforts.

The mechanisation of rice-growing has been much studied and experimented with in several parts of the world. The Soviet version is that it presented a very great challenge, which the U.S.S.R. has brilliantly overcome. There seemed to be insurmountable obstacles. To hold the water the fields cannot be too big and must be surrounded by low walls, preferably mudwalls which can immediately be opened or changed at any point. Walling, sowing, transplanting and gleaning all had, it seemed, necessarily to be done by hand. It is claimed that sowing by tractor is now the rule, bulldozers and graders are applied to set up and constantly maintain or adapt the irrigation network. On the same basis, anti-pest sprays are operated on a mass scale. Caterpillar-tracked combines do the harvesting. The Research Station has perfected early-ripening high-yield varieties of rice: reducing, in sum, the amount of man-days of labour required per hectare from 120-150 to only 9-12, and keeping all the workers dry and free from rheumatism. There is not enough detailed information to enable close scrutiny of the results. If the Soviet Rice Farms have received this special equipment, they have been luckier than the other farmers in this swampy plain. These State Farms have certainly done well. They are accounted to be 'millionaires'; this means, in Soviet parlance, they have an output in millions of units, or a revenue of a million roubles or more. The rice area has been considerably extended under the current Plan. The production of rice is considerable, but hardly plentiful.

Manzovka, 60 km south of Spassk by rail, has the distinction of being the only railway crossroads in the whole of the S.F.E., or even in the whole eastern half of Siberia. The line from Manzovka north-westwards to Novo-Kachalinski (Turii Rog, 127 km) was finished in 1941, opening up the best agricultural lands on the southern lakeside. The cross-line on the other side, eastwards to Varfolomeyevka (106 km), was laid by 1940; it traverses a forest area and comes out in the basin of the

Daubikhe. The Khanka area thus has as good a transport network as any other part of the S.F.E., except the more immediate vicinity of Vladivostok.

South of Manzovka is one of the largest State Farms of the Maritime Province, still named after the founder of the Chinese Republic, Sun Yat-sen; originally a soya-bean farm, it now produces also wheat, milk and meat. This is the last watershed on the Trans-Siberian journey; the small rivers here bring muddy rain water from the mountains to the eastward on the one hand into Lake Khanka, the Ussuri and the Amur to the northward, on the other hand to the Suifun and the Sea of Japan.

The other main town connected with the Khanka lands is Ussurisk (founded in 1866; previously called, in the days of the cult of personality, Voroshilov, in Tsarist days Nikol'sk Ussuriski). It has a population of 124,000. The branch line to the west (to Pogranichny-Grodekovo) is the Maritime Province end of the Chinese Eastern Railway, which used to be the 'great shortcut' across Manchuria between Vladivostok and Chita, but the Chinese no longer co-operate in through traffic. Meanwhile it serves the Khanka sub-region well. At Lipovtsy 50 km along this line there is a mining settlement with an annual output of about 700,000 tons of good slow-burning coal (20-30 per cent ash, calorific value about 5000) mostly from pits, though there are a few open workings; this goes to the power-stations in the south of the Province. To the north-east of Ussurisk there are two other coalfields, Rettikhovsk and Chikhezk, both providing brown coal (of a calorific value of about 3000) on open cuts with seams two to twenty metres thick.

Ussurisk is a considerable industrial town. Its foundation is in the food-processing industries, which still represent three-quarters of the local income. There is a fats and oils plant, a meat factory, sugar and mixed feeding-stuffs factories. The fats plant, dating back to 1927, is now the largest food-factory in the Province; it produces butter, margarine, meat and soya products. There is also some development of machine-making industry – recently reaching 10 per cent of the town's income – railway and automobile repair shops and woodworking industries. Ussurisk is quite a centre for the training of specialist workers. It has the Province's central agricultural research station and forestry station, a special school of agricultural mechanisation as well as a general agricultural school and various specialised middle schools. There is a theatre, cinemas, sports stadia and other 'cultural' facilities. Outside Ussurisk, moreover, there is the Far Eastern section of the Siberian Branch of the national Academy of Sciences. Fifty kilometres from Ussurisk, on the Suputinka river (which joins the Suifun and the Rakovka at Ussurisk) is the Suputinka Reservation of the Academy of Sciences, extending over 617,000 ha. It is mainly a forest area, with all the Far Eastern trees in their natural conditions, but also rich in animal life, including wild tigers and leopards. The Siberian tiger is still found in the Region generally, though much more rarely than in the past. One of the small halts on the railway is named Tigrovy, 'the tiger place', where many a fine animal has been bagged in days gone by. The Suputinka Reserve has also a special experimental plantation of ginseng, the 'magic' medicinal root which has such a legendary repute in Korea, China and other parts of the Far East. Ginseng is mainly grown a little further south and west in the Maritime Province. In the western frontier areas of the Province there is some production of another item in the same category of Oriental pharmaceuticals, a special kind of deer horn called *panti*. Further particulars of these will be given below.

Mining is developing in this area. At Rettikhovka, to the north-east along the railway, an open coalpit was cut in 1961 and reached an output of 1·2 million tons in 1965. Another pit, at Pavlovka–Novoshakhtinski some 50 km west of Ussurisk, was opened in 1967; its capacity is given as 1·2 million tons. At Voznesenska, 50 km north of Ussurisk, fluorspar has been produced since 1963. Tin, lead and zinc have been produced and concentrated nearby at Yaroslavski since 1958.

THE GOLDEN HORN

The next sub-region is that of the Provincial capital, Vladivostok, and its immediate environs. A main part of the beautiful harbour of Vladivostok is called the Golden Horn, reminding of the fact that Vladivostok was a substitute for Constantinople in the mind of the Tsar, who longed for an ice-free southern port. Balked of Constantinople, he turned after Russia's defeat in the Crimean War to the other end of his domains and secured Vladivostok. So runs a popular but not ill-founded simplification of history. The metaphor of a cornucopia is also useful as an allusion to the relative prosperity and comfort of Vladivostok.

This area is more formally called the southern coastal sub-region. It comprises the following administrative districts: Khasanski (on the Korean frontier to the south-west), Nadezhdinsk, Shkotovski (Petrova) and Partizanski (Yekaterinovka), also the City and Town Soviets of Vladivostok, Artem, Nakhodka and Suchan. The main foundations of this area are its two fine ports Vladivostok and Nakhodka. Vladivostok was secured by the Russians in 1860. Nakhodka is a very recent development; in response largely to its being a splendid natural harbour, but also apparently to some extent in the desire to segregate foreign traffic and foreign contacts to it, away from Vladivostok whose naval and other activities appear to be specially secret. The development of Nakhodka for foreign trade is, however, rational, as the facilities of Vladivostok are mainly crowded with fishing fleets, the shipping to Sakhalin, Kamchatka and the far north-east factories and other installations ashore; it is easier to expand operations in the large Nakhodka bay (formerly America Bay) 120 km by sea from Vladivostok.

The Trans-Siberian runs straight to Vladivostok, its terminal. There is a branch railway to the eastwards starting at Baranovski 90 km north of Vladivostok and running round the coast to Khasan and Korea. At the frontier 238 km away there is Kraskino, administrative centre of the Khasan district; nearby, at the Khasan Lake, the Soviet Army defeated an attack by Japanese troops who crossed the frontier in July–August 1938. In the other direction a branch line takes off from Nadezhdinskaya for Nakhodka; with southward spurs to the coast also from Nadezhdinskaya to Tavrichanka and from beyond Artem to Dunai. Peter the Great Bay is ringed by these two railway lines.

Vladivostok, 9320 km by the Trans-Siberian railway from Moscow, is a main city and industrial centre, an ice-free port (more exactly, there is ice in winter, but it is fairly easily kept open by ice-breakers). Obviously it is a main base for Soviet interest, of every kind, in the Pacific Ocean. The West naturally visualises this in terms of Soviet 'expansionism' – fleets and submarines, atomic tests, wide-ranging fisheries, whaling, trade or scientific ventures and the like, all over the world. Active as the Soviet Union is in such respects, Vladivostok and its vicinity are structurally important to the Soviet Union also from a more home-based or self-contained point of view. There is no other harbour, no significant industrial, mineral or food supply base, nowhere with the communications and organisational strength, on the whole Pacific coast of the U.S.S.R., comparable with Vladivostok and Nakhodka. Sakhalin, Kamchatka, Magadan, the whole S.F.E., depend vitally on this southernmost part of the Maritime Province.

Vladivostok's sea-cargo turnover is much smaller, however, than that of Russia's European ports (Leningrad, Odessa and Riga). No less than 50 per cent of Vladivostok's export tonnage is oil, the other items are coal, cereals and general cargoes of consumer-goods and supplies. Two-thirds of these exports go to Petropavlovsk in Kamchatka, Korsakov (South Sakhalin) and Nagaevo (the port for the town of Magadan). The imports are fish, oil (by coastal shipping) and a few mixed cargoes. Thus Vladivostok greatly serves the needs of the Okhotsk and Bering coasts; but its commerce with foreign countries has been small in Soviet times. It is a base for the fishing fleets and whalers (usually four whaling ships were based there in the early 1960s) and passenger connections to the North-East. The Vladivostok rail terminal in the middle of the port has a freight turnover of about five million tons a year, of which the greater part consists of arrivals, being largely supplies going on by sea to the North-East. Nakhodka was built when Vladivostok's facilities became overloaded after the last war; it has now a larger traffic than Vladivostok. 40 per cent of its cargo handlings are for foreign trade either way, it is the port for both freight and passenger traffic with Japan. Its main outward shipments are cement and other building-materials, coal and timber, the inward ones cereals, building materials and metals.

Port and railway work is the main livelihood. There are five or six fisheries bases dealing chiefly with catches brought in by the seiner fleet. 70 per cent of the catch is, however, from deep-sea fleets with ranges of thousands of kilometres, equipped and maintained in Vladivostok and Nakhodka and delivering their catches there. A large fish-processing plant has been built at Nakhodka, in addition to older ones at other coastal points. Near Vladivostok there is an agar-agar factory.

Vladivostok had 410,000 inhabitants in 1968 and was growing rapidly (367,000 in 1963, 265,000 in 1959). It is also a centre for education, having the Far Eastern section of the Siberian Branch of the Academy of Sciences, planning institutes, six other higher educational institutions, many special and middle schools, etc.

The city is at the end of a peninsula 30 km long with an average width of 12, with suburban development spreading all up it. About ten islands lie off the peninsula continuing its south-eastward direction; the nearest, Russian Island across the strait called the Oriental Bosphorus, is far the largest (about 15 km long from north-west to south-west by some 12 km broad, heavily indented). The whole area is hilly. The Golden Horn is an inlet at the base of the peninsula and the main town stands on this, in a narrow belt of coast only a kilometre wide all along the Golden Horn and round the corner into Amur Bay on the west (into the head of which the Suifun river flows). The main station and port are in this belt, in the city-centre. The topography explains the curious description of Vladivostok by the modern poet Tvardovski:

> Fires. Hooters.
> In a belt into the hillside.
> A railway station
> Cut like a fortress.

The railway and the port are towards the west, in the area called Cape Egershel'd. Across the Golden Horn, on Cape Churkin, is the fishing port with its cold-storage facilities. The shoreline east of the railway terminal has the ship-repair yards and wharves. The residential areas spread around these. The peninsula, named after Count Muravyov Amurski, founder of the Russian power in this area, is a fine green-belt with beaches, sanatoria and market-gardening. The run down this peninsula by the main line begins after the Ugol'naya ('Coalfield') station (for Trudovoye, 'the workplace') where the branch line to Nakhodka departs. All the little stations mark beach resorts – Sadgorod ('Garden City'), Okeanskaya, Sedanko, Sanatornaya, Chaika ('the Seagull'), etc, very crowded in summer when the people of Vladivostok count on a sea-bathing season of over a hundred days. There is also a Botanical Garden. At the exit to the Vladivostok railway station is a statue of Lenin inscribed with his own version of the 'possession of the east': 'Vladivostok is far away, but it's ours' (*'gorod-to nashenskii'*). The idol is emphasising the proposition in dialectical fashion by pointing away from the town towards the sea.

Nakhodka was formed out of a number of small settlements on 27 km of the shoreline of a magnificent rounded bay encircled by hills. Many foreign ships are to be seen there – an array of foreign flags never seen in the inland U.S.S.R. and equalled only at Odessa and in the Baltic. The population is increasing rapidly: 90,000 in 1964, nearly 100,000 in 1968. Housing and other facilities are developing accordingly, on the rising ground inland.

Vladivostok is certainly the finest city in the S.F.E. – many say, the finest in all Siberia. It is from the Soviet point of view by no means an expendable outpost at the end of the line – it is of high civic, industrial and logistical value, a main point in the national defences. In the 'cultural' aspect, besides the Academy of Sciences' Institutes of Fisheries Economics and Oceanography and other centres of higher education (polytechnic, fisheries and medical colleges, the Makarov Naval Academy) together with middle schools, etc., there are the Far Eastern University and three museums (the Arsen'iev Museum of Local Lore, the Pacific Fleet Historical Museum and the Museum of Fishery Economics and Oceanography). The local *Krasnoe Znamya* (Red Flag) was the first Bolshevik newspaper in the Far East. There is a printing works and publishing house.

The streets and buildings (many of six or nine storeys, modern residential districts constantly being added), parks, urban and suburban transport (trams, buses, trolleybuses, suburban electric train, taxis) are all of high quality by Soviet standards. The central Station Square is the terminal for all these. Nearby across the tracks is the Maritime Station, a recent structure of cement and glass. The First Sea Street leads from there to the Shore Street on the Amur bay, the west side of Vladivostok. In the other direction is the 25 October Street with the Far Eastern Shipping Office, residential buildings, the Writers' Union and shops on its left-hand side, on its right-hand side the Artists' Union and Fine Arts Foundation. On the Lenin Street corner is the Fisheries and Oceanographic Institute, which conducts research and expeditionary activities all over the Pacific and Arctic and maintains many riverine stations in all parts of Siberia. This building includes the Institute's museum.

On Lenin Street are the Golden Horn Hotel, the Gogol and Komsomol theatres, the Fisheries High School, a monument to heroes of the Revolution, the Ussuri cinema, the largest department store in the S.F.E., the General Post Office, the 'Red Flag' newspaper, Communist Party offices, the Naval Officers' Club and a park. On 1 May Street at the Lenin Street corner is the Academy of Sciences, further along 1 May Street are the Arsen'iev Museum and the Geographical Society with its fine library. By the Academy is the statue of the Partisan leader Sergei Lazo, inscribed: 'For this Russian soil on which I stand, we shall die rather than yield it to anyone.' There is also a memorial to a warship, near an art school. In this vicinity is the home berth of the Soviet research vessel *Vityaz'*, which carries its flag all over the world.

In the same area there are a Memorial Garden to Heroes of the Revolution, a wide view over the Golden Horn, a monument (1897) to the explorer Nevel'skoi, the oldest technical school in the S.F.E. and the Pacific Fleet Museum. A funicular rises to a point with a grand view of Russian Island (where there are large cold-storage plants) and to the wharves of the Egershel'd port-area to the west. Inland are the resort areas and sports facilities, on the coast are numerous beaches, boat and yacht clubs, etc., all easily accessible by public transport.

These particulars may suffice to give an impression of the quality of Vladivostok. There is no city anywhere, local patriots naturally say, like Vladivostok. Certainly it is a most Russian city. Lenin's word 'ours' and Lazo's 'die rather than yield it' ring true and firm today, at this eastern terminal of Russian confrontation with China.

INDUSTRY AND MINING

The Vladivostok sub-region is also a main industrial base. The Maritime Province – very predominantly this southern corner of it – produces nearly a third of the industrial output of the whole S.F.E. The industries evolved some time ago out of the needs of food-processing, freight-handling and ship-repairs. Since about 1942 the development has been considerable; in the leading sections, here as in Komsomolsk and Khabarovsk, technical levels are quite high. In the Seven-Year Plan (1959-65, abandoned in 1963) capital investment in the Vladivostok area was to have been increased 2·7 times; five years later, development on a considerable though lesser scale had been broadly achieved. For 1965-70 the more restrained but still high target of 73 per cent increase in industrial activity was set for this sub-region, plus larger provisions than before of housing, institutional and public health facilities.

The largest enterprises are the Dal'zavod (Far Eastern Factory) general engineering works in Vladivostok and the ship-repair yards in Nakhodka. There are smaller shipyards and floating docks at other coastal points. 'Metallist' is another group of factories including machine and instrument works. The machine-building industry makes conveyor-belts for handling coal or fish, mine-waggons and other pit equipment, pumps, metal fittings, girders, sorting gear and taps or valves. Most of these are used locally, some in the rest of the Province, but a few are exported to more distant parts of the Union. A new machinery plant in Vladivostok to produce gear for the fisheries and food-processing industry was to have been completed by 1971. In Artem (population 65,000) there are electro-mechanical shops serving the mines.

The heavy requirements of timber have to be served by bringing it not only from within the Maritime Province but from the Khabarovsk and even the Amur Provinces. Most of the processing is done in the Vladivostok area. The largest specialist unit is the Ocean Plywood Factory, whose products go to all parts of Russia. There is also the production of lead batteries and accumulators, casks, barrels and fish-boxes within the same combine. There are three garment factories in Vladivostok, one in Artem and one in Suchan. The population of

Suchan is 50,000. At Okeanskaya there is a large leather and shoe factory, which uses whaleskin as well as the hides of cattle. There is a glove and handbag factory in Suchan. The musical instrument works in Artem produces for a nationwide market: its 'Primor'ye' brand of pianos is well known. Food industries are naturally prominent: meat (Vladivostok, Nakhodka and Suchan), confectionery (Vladivostok and Suchan) and dairy, distillery, brewery and soft-drinks plants in Vladivostok, as well as flour-mills and bakeries.

In 1963 this sub-region produced about six million tons of coal, 85 per cent of the output of the Province. The mines of Artem (north-east of Vladivostok) and Tavrichanka (at the head of the Amur bay) produce brown coal, those of Suchan (north of Nakhodka) and the 'suburban' field near Vladivostok yield hard coal. The Artem basin produced 2·4 million tons in 1965, Tavrichanka 0·6, the Suchan basin 1·9. A new coal mine is planned at Shkotovo west of the Amur bay. Some of the old Artem pits are closing down, while new developments in other parts of the Province where extensive open-cut mining is in prospect tend also to reduce the *percentage* share of these southern fields in the total for the Province; nevertheless the absolute amount of coal production in the southern sub-region is still rising. The electric power needs are so pressing that local deposits formerly deemed uneconomic for mining are being reconsidered.

Suchan produces 900,000 tons a year of coking and boiler coal which goes to the cement factories, for export, to the fleet and other 'special' users; the other hard coal (1·1 million tons) and lignite (3·8 million tons) is used locally for the Suchan and Artem power stations, the largest in the S.F.E. These serve local needs and transmit electricity by power-lines to the Kavalerovo mining belt in the north-east and to Arsen'iev, Spassk, Lesozavodsk and Iman in the north. The main railway line is electrified from Vladivostok to Ussurisk.

FISHERIES, FOOD AND ELIXIRS

Far Eastern waters supply a great part of the Soviet Union's catch of fish (see Map 5). They also supply certain other marine products specially in demand among the Chinese, Koreans and other East Asians, which have therefore figured as profitable exports. These marine products are chiefly appreciated as tasty items of diet, but the Chinese and some of their neighbouring peoples also attribute to them medicinal – even magical – properties. This applies even more strongly to another product of the southern sub-region of the Maritime Province, also culti-vated there specially for export; namely the horns of a certain kind of deer, believed to be a wonder-working tonic drug. And most strongly to the root of the ginseng plant, which is cultivated and exported very profitably because the Chinese and Koreans think it cures almost all ills, moreover conferring virility and longevity. The Soviet Union is apparently willing to cater to superstitious beliefs, against payment in foreign exchange; but happily Soviet scientists (also the Maoist ones on their side) have in any case proved that, as with most ancient items of folk-medicine, there is a real pharmaceutical basis for the reputation of these products.

The fisheries of the whole Far Eastern Region of the U.S.S.R., largely based on Vladivostok, are primarily important in the food-supply of the Soviet Union. The ordinary 'western' types of farming in the southern Maritime Province are important for its own subsistence and that of the whole north-eastern U.S.S.R. beyond it. And there are in addition the special 'Oriental' items referred to in the last paragraph, which give exotic colour to the life of the Soviet Maritime Province, as well as adding to its means of livelihood. The Province, especially its southern part, may therefore be described as remarkable in dealing in fish, food and elixirs.

Among the shore-based activities, there are only a few scores of collective farms in the southern sub-region. In the older-settled rural areas in the river-valleys they are engaged in 'basic' farming, others are suburban and supply the markets of the newer towns with animal products, potatoes and vegetables. Of the total agricultural area, pastures and hayfields take the main part; of the sown area, fodder crops take the largest portion. Only lately, after some reclamation of land (both new and long neglected) on the higher slopes less liable to flooding, has there been any increase in the proportion of the area under the plough, which remains very small. Animal husbandry is pressed to concentrate on the production of meat and milk, suburban farming on vegetables. The southern sub-region supplies only 16 per cent of the Province's output of fresh milk, 16 per cent of the vegetables and 13 per cent of the meat; its consumption-ratios are a multiple of those percentages.

Most interesting are the exotics. The deer-horn is that of a special kind of deer. A kindred animal is found in Western Siberia in the Altai mountains (Barnaul) area, called the maral deer. Its horns, when still young and soft, contain a powerful rejuvenating tonic – good for the health in general, but supposedly aphrodisiac in particular – known and used from ancient times in Russian Siberia. The tonic essence is nowadays produced under commercial laboratory conditions and is called pantakrin. The West Siberians still esteem theirs the best, but the ancient Chinese and East Asian traditions, especially, consider the true, proper and best source is the similar 'noble spotted deer' (*Cervus dybovskii*) found only in the Sikhote Alin' mountains of the Maritime Province. The young 'velvet' horns of this species, at their crucial life-stage of sexual maturity, are known as *panti*, apparently a Chinese word.

The panti-deer is a timid little animal. Until recently it was common in a wild state in the southern Maritimes, but lately was becoming rapidly extinct. Before the Revolution it was bred commercially on a few farms near Vladivostok. Consumption in China was formerly an Imperial prerogative – a herd of these deer was kept in the Forbidden City of Peking – but after the Republican Revolution in 1911 a wider market developed. The old antlers are shed in springtime and the new horns which replace them contain the magic medicine. They have to be cut off at the right time, which usually means killing the animal.

The business was nationalised and extended by the Soviet Government. In 1963 there were ten Sovkhoz in the southern Maritimes with 25,000 head of panti deer. The horns are processed in Kiev and in Khabarovsk rather than locally in the Maritimes. The main breeding centres are near Cape Gamov on the western shore of the Amur bay, near Razdol'noe in the Nadezhinski district and along the frontier near Astrakhanka and due west of Ussurisk.

The other special product is ginseng, the 'man-root', mandrake root or 'root of life' in Oriental folklore. A particular centre for attempts to grow this as a crop is north of a line between Artem and Suchan. Cropping is not really the way; the plant resists efforts to subject it to plantation treatment. A popular nickname in this area for recalcitrant peasants who did not take whole-heartedly to Soviet collectivisation was in fact 'ginseng'. Left to its own devices it grows strongly, in single plants only, in damp shady ravines. Technically it is a plant of the *Araliaceæ*.

The roots are valuable for the Chinese market if they can be drawn intact from the ground. They are shaped like a nude human figure, 'male' or 'female'; if the details of the shape can be kept undamaged in the plucking (at the moment of which, just like the European mandrake-root, the plant is supposed to 'shriek') the value used to be higher in the Chinese market. Traditionally the matter also involves a number of other superstitious conditions, e.g. that the plucker should carry no metal object on his person. These requirements are not of course observed officially in the Soviet Union, where the gathering of this root is to a great extent systematised and considerable attention is paid to the utilisation of the ginseng root, powder or extract on modern pharmaceutical lines. Nevertheless some sort of shamanistic individualism still clings to this occupation. There are 'prospectors' for ginseng, determinedly lone workers, who disappear into the mountains for long periods far out of touch with the townsman's sort of 'Soviet reality'. They often find plants which are not yet ready for plucking; then they merely mark them out secretly for attention later when the plant is mature for gathering, or can 'stake a claim' to a plant they have discovered.

Dealings in panti and ginseng – or anything else – were a great feature of back-street life in Vladivostock before the Revolution, in places like the famous 'Millionka' arcades. Some of the principals in this one-time Alsatia (now puritanised in the new moral climate of the Soviet Union) led in those days what might today be called a 'jet-set' existence in fine villas in the direction of the Korean frontier (across which they quickly disappeared when the Red Army arrived). Yet some adventurist or individualist spirit, even if its more swashbuckling and reprehensible manifestations are now impossible, may still hang about the Farthest Soviet East in this connection.

The other exotics are much less romantic, being marine plants highly prized in the Chinese cuisine, also endowed in Chinese or Korean belief with various health-giving properties, but not so sensationally as the panti and the ginseng: sea-urchins or sea-cucumbers, trepang or bêche-de-mer, which are gathered by divers. Other minor items for the special Asian market are certain kinds of octopus and shrimps. There is also agar-agar which is used in the food industry and in laboratory work; and sea-kale.

THE NORTH-EASTERN MARITIMES

The remaining significant portion of the Maritime Province is a narrow coastal belt 40-150 km wide along 600 km of the Japan Sea north-east of Vladivostok and Nakhodka. The mountains covering this area (400-1200 metres) come right down to the coast, so the shoreline is steep and has hardly any good harbours. The only partial exceptions are the Ol'ga bay and such river-mouth places as Tetyukhe and Ternei. This area is designated as the Tetyukhe–Kavalerovo sub-region; it comprises the Ol'ga, Tetyukhe, Kavalerovo and Ternei districts.

Many small rivers run down from the Sikhote-Alin' range to the sea. A cold current sweeps along the coast. Transport between the valleys is only by sea or pack-trails overland, except for a single (270 km) motor road joining Tetyukhe Wharf (Pristan') and the town of Tetyukhe (about 30 km inland) with Kavalerovo, Novo–Mikhailovka and Varfolomeyevka, where at last it connects with the railway. The potential value of this area – little utilised as yet – is its wealth in tin and other light metals. The best-known deposits are around Tetyukhe; they consist mostly of galerite and sphalerite with a high proportion of lead and zinc. Tin ore is found around Kavalerovo. Near Ol'ga iron and manganese ores exist, not yet fully prospected. Tin mining developed in this area (Sinavcha, Lifudzin) during the War and subsequently expanded.

The mountains are forested, to the extent of 1·8 million ha or over 80 per cent of the total area – half of it coniferous, but much deteriorated, overgrown and damaged by fires in the long droughts. Even in summer the rain is cold in this mountainous coastal sub-region. The precipitation is 800 mm a year, 80 per cent of which is in the summer. The climate is cloudy and foggy, with extremes of temperature between summer and winter. Agriculture is therefore limited. This sub-region has 26 per cent of the area of the Province but only 6 per cent of its population, and none of the amenities of the south, nor any significant development prospect except for the mining centres. Each of the latter has some ore-grading plant; at Tetyukhe there is also a lead-foundry. Tetyukhe Pristan' is only a shallow-water port; loading has to be by lighters. Electric power was brought to the mining area from Suchan by power line only at the beginning of the 1960s. Some metal working has been carried on at Tetyukhe since 1911 but it is not on a large scale; the population of the town is 23,000. Tin, developed at Kavalerovo since 1941, appears more important at present. Kavalerova has a population of 14,000; its output all goes eastward to the railway. Tetyukhe Port handles only the lead which is locally smelted and the zinc concentrates of the Tetyukhe mines: the latter product is shipped all the way to European Russia. There are five fisheries Collectives on the coast, with two processing plants – at Kamenka and Nel'ma (the latter is in Khabarovsk Province, but works for the Maritime Province fishing fleets). However, the Collectives work far out in all the north-eastern fishing grounds.

About 60,000 cubic metres of timber are cut and worked for local needs in Tetyukhe and Kavalerovo. In the Ternei area the Far Eastern Fisheries Organisation Dal'ryba runs its own saw-mills and makes casks, boxes, etc. Only 3 per cent of the sub-region's area is usable for agriculture – of which hardly 10,000 ha is arable. The crops are extremely subject to fungus and dampness. More than half of the tiny sown area is under oats and wheat, a quarter under potatoes and vegetables, making very little contribution to the local needs for food, most of which has to be met by supplies from other parts of the Province. Most of the villages are in the river valleys; they are very small, with two or three hundred inhabitants, only three rural places having more than a thousand. In the northernmost part there are some indigenous Udegeitsy living in primitive simplicity by fishing, hunting and trapping.

The north-east of the Maritime Province is thus in stark contrast to the more comfortable and prosperous south and south-east. It belongs to the cold and empty outland; four vast Provinces which have still to be described before the survey in these pages is complete. The southern Maritimes, Vladivostok in particular, are the supply-base on which all these outlands greatly depend. Unless or until the whole dynamic of the development of Siberia – and therefore of the whole Soviet Union – can be powerfully changed by the emergence of a new, strong and resourceful 'heartland' in the great north of the continent, this gigantic periphery will remain in a condition of dependency, largely ultra-marginal and negative from the development point of view. The main present candidate among the northlands for some such more dynamic role is the vast, rich and already to some extent connected central part of the interior called Yakutia – which is the subject of the next chapter.[1]

CHAPTER 8

Yakutia: Main Hinterland

The last four chapters have traced the whole line of the frontier with China beyond Central Asia. There are two ways in which the border may be strengthened, from the Soviet point of view. One is to build it up with resources from the main bastions of Soviet strength in the western parts of the Union. The other way, concomitant rather than alternative, is to reinforce the border zone by developing strong hinterland positions to its northward. Now the Yakut Autonomous Soviet Socialist Republic is, if not a stronger and richer area than the north-eastern and Pacific territories, strategically more central in location and access. It is therefore certainly the main hinterland in the present perspective.

THE LIFE OF THE NORTHLAND

Yakutia is a huge area: 2 million sq. km, or one-seventh of the whole U.S.S.R., bounded by Irkutsk Province on the south-west, in the south by the Buryat Republic and Chita and Amur Provinces, in the east by Khabarovsk and Magadan Provinces. From north to south (74°N on the Arctic Ocean to 55°N at Nagorny north of Nyevyer in Amuria) and equally from west to east (105° to 163°E) it is some 2500 km across. All this is tundra or sub-tundra country with an arctic or sub-arctic climate. There are some slightly better-favoured agricultural areas on the middle reaches of the Lena river. It is almost uninhabited – one person per 6 sq. km on the average. It does not have a single railway, though the projected new northern Trans-Siberian is likely to pass such areas as Nagorny and Vitim. It has, however, one good road linking it with Nyevyer in Amuria, passing the city of Yakutsk and continuing to Magadan on the Okhotsk Sea. The Lena river, like all the

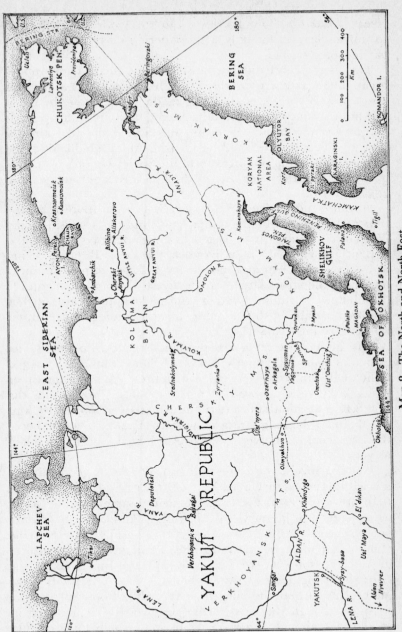

Map 8   The North and North-East

rivers of Yakutia, flows northward to the Arctic, which is open to full navigation for only a short period every year – but it carries some traffic.

The list of disadvantages must be continued. They appear great. But Yakutia is prodigiously rich in mineral and forest resources. Great efforts are being made to overcome, by novel techniques, the various disadvantages, and to develop agriculture by new means. The minerals are: diamonds (already very significantly exploited), gold (the Aldan goldfields alone have yielded about one-quarter of the Soviet Union's output of gold), tin, mica (70 per cent of the U.S.S.R.'s output), coking coal and iron.

Forestry and agriculture are localised, even more than the mineral deposits, but their total contribution is considerable. The cultivable area is restricted to some sheltered valleys; the agricultural emphasis is on livestock, the Yakut Republic being at least self-sufficient at a modest level of consumption in meat and milk, though in large part the livestock population consists of reindeer. Fishing, hunting and fur-trapping are further staples of rural life; the fur trade, like the mining, concentrates on items of high value.

The mineral reserves are prodigious: according to Soviet estimates 3,400 billion tons of coal, $1\frac{1}{2}$ billion tons of iron, 2,300 billion cubic metres of natural gas. In tin, gold, mica and other items Yakutia is believed to be the leading Province in the U.S.S.R. The Aldan mica deposits extend over 200,000 sq. km, the diamond-bearing strata of western Yakutia over 300,000, the Lena coal basin over 400,000. All these are hardly touched as yet.

The Province is the coldest part of Siberia. A good third of it is within the Arctic Circle. Yakutsk, the capital, is 20°C colder than other places in the U.S.S.R. at the same latitude (averaging – 43°C in January, 19°C in July). There are only 90 days without frost in the year. This is the world's most extreme climate; the range between the highest and lowest temperatures in Yakutia is 100°C. In June and July the sun is above the horizon for eighteen or twenty hours a day. The position far inland means that the climate is very dry. Consequently the summer, though short, is intense; crops are well matured in good years, though the growing period is only forty or fifty days in the north and eighty or ninety in the south-east and centre. This, however, is unreliable; there are sudden changes in temperature, and frosts may occur even in summer.

The inhabited places are covered with a strange icy mist in mid-winter – the condensed vapour from the dwellings. Even the Arctic has smog! The temperature is below – 40°C for 48 days in the year at Yakutsk, for 87 days at Verkhoyansk, the world's 'cold pole'. The snow cover is, however, slight and the rivers are frozen, facilitating transport by sledges and motor traffic. The severe conditions last from October to March. The soil is permafrosted deeply; for every kind of construction special techniques have to be used to secure the foundations. The Yakut Republic counts no less than 100,000 lakes and 12,000 rivers. Nine huge rivers (Lena, Aldan, Kolyma, Vilyui, Olyokma, Indigirka and three others) rank among the 37 'giant' rivers of the Soviet Union (those with an average annual flow exceeding 1000 cubic metres per second). The electric power potential of the Lena basin is reckoned at 20 million kW, the Indigirka at 4 million, the Yana at 3. Considerable industrial development is possible.

Meanwhile the rivers carry no less than 80 per cent of the goods traffic of the Republic. There are some 70,000 km of navigable river, of which about 15,000 are regularly used at present. Roadways open all the year round total 18,000 km. The population is concentrated on the river valleys, which have the meadowlands and the workable forests. The total forest area is 127 million ha (about 60 per cent of the taiga-covered portion of the Republic), of which 112 million consists of larch, 8 of conifers, less than two of birch, less than one of fir, only 35,000 ha of cedar. All the trees are, however, small; only 8 per cent are over 18 cm in diameter, 24 per cent are between 13 and 18, 19 per cent are between 3 and 12, so that nearly half the timber is negligible for forestry purposes. The average yield of timber is thus only 0·8 cubic metre per hectare – the lowest in Siberia – though there are some areas and types of timber in which the yield is far above this average.

Ploughed land totals 185,000 ha, meadow and pasture 4½ million. One-fifth of the territory, north of 68° latitude, is tundra with only stunted bushes and mosses, where reindeer feed. In the south, however, the Yakuts had developed settled agriculture and tillage before the Russians came; they are the only indigenous Siberians to have done so. In this spacious land, even the villages are widespread – the houses stand fifty to a hundred metres apart. Each may contain, however, a dozen or even twenty persons and the villages are small. Their operations are scattered: hunting and fishing over distances, using widely separated bits of pasturage. The larger towns and settlements are more 'Russian', on more modern lines.

POPULATION AND OCCUPATIONS

The whole population of the Republic (662,000 in 1968) has rapidly increased (488,000 in 1959 and 559,000 in 1962). The natural increase was about 10,000 a year in the mid-1960s, so there has been a considerable immigration of Russians. In 1962, 10 per cent of the population (then 289,000 persons) were Russians, 82 per cent Yakuts. By 1962 the Russians were almost as numerous as the Yakuts, each counting about 45 per cent. The Ukrainians are the next largest 'national' group (2·5 per cent), the others are the minor indigenous tribespeople. The migration is also internally to the towns. The population is now 58 per cent urban, against 47 per cent in 1962.

60 per cent of the working population is in mining, nearly 10 per cent in forestry, about 1 per cent in fishing. The Lena goldfields are famous. The Aldan fields began working in 1923; in the 1930s they produced a fifth or a quarter of the U.S.S.R.'s output of gold. This was then largely alluvial; more recently ore has begun to be the main source in the Aldan. Gold mining extended right out to near the Okhotsk coast beyond Yakutia (notably dredging in the Dzhugdzhur range inland of Aya, from 1932). In 1944 new alluvial workings started on the upper Indigirka (north-eastern Yakutia), where production later outstripped that of the Aldan fields. Tin is found mainly on the Indigirka and between it and the next big river to the west, the Yana. Tin ore is mined around Batagai east of Verkhoyansk and processed there into 60-75 per cent concentrates, alluvial tin is taken around Deputatski, 300 km further north-west. Much of this tin contains other precious metals. The famous diamond field is around Mirny in the far south-west of Yakutia;

this is the only source in the Soviet Union except a far poorer one in the Urals. Mica has been mined and quarried since 1941, south-east of Tommot in mid-southern Yakutia.

Only one-thirtieth of the timber-lands were exploited by 1961, but the output of lumber was then 3·6 million cubic metres; more than a half was, however, used locally for fire-wood, a main fuel in the Republic. Over half the output was on the Lena between Vitim and Olyokminsk, the best forest areas, though the Aldan and Indigirka are also important. The timber is mostly rafted along these rivers. Some is exported to Bodaibo north-east of the top of Lake Baikal, some to the treeless north of Magadan. Yakutsk and Peledui (near Vitim) are the main places producing prepared timbers, mainly for building pur-poses. The Republic produces annually about 47,000 cubic metres of sawn wood. Another large processing centre is de-veloping just above Yakutsk.

There are over a hundred coal deposits, the best of which are west of the Lena. In the extreme south is the largest deposit of coking coal east of Kuznetsk, with reserves believed to total 40 or 50 billion tons. Actual output in the whole Republic is over one million tons, principally along the Lena at Kangalassy and Sangar, but also on the Aldan and the Kolyma. Some coal is exported to Irkutsk Province for the gold and mica industries and some to northern Magadan. The total output of coal was planned to reach 1·6 million tons in 1965, of which the Lena basin would contribute 1·2, the north-east a mere 200,000-300,000 tons. The next priority was to develop mining at Chul'man in the far south-east, linked by road to Skovorodino on the Siberian railway in Amuria, which was until recently supplying mainly the local electric power stations. There are large resources of natural gas around the confluence of the Vilyui and the Lena.

The Republic's annual catch of fish is 6500 to 7500 tons, 70 per cent in the lower Lena and Kolyma; fishing under the ice in winter has recently been improved, and aeroplanes carry supplies to fishermen and bring back their catch, so that opera-tions in winter and at a distance are now possible. Some salt is mined (about 3000 tons a year) in the Vilyui basin, which is used for fish-preserving and may lead to development of a chemical industry at Olyokminsk.

SFE G

The generation of electricity is concentrated in a few main towns, the consumption being about 250 million kWh a year. All the plants are thermal, mostly using wood as well as coal or imported oil. Yakutsk and the Aldan mining area are the best equipped in this respect. The Indigirka goldfields get their power from Arkagala in Magadan. The diamond centre Mirny gets its power by high-voltage lines from Mukhtuya, an important transhipment point on the upper Lena near the border to its southward. It is planned to build a hydroelectric station on the Vilyui, serving this area especially. Others are in prospect on other rivers and at the fields of natural gas.

Light industries are little developed; some leather and clothing shops and the like, principally in Yakutsk. Repair shops naturally exist, not least for the river shipping. On the list of occupations there is one startlingly characteristic of contemporary Yakutia; in 1957, no less than 10 per cent of the employed population were engaged in geological prospecting.

The area in agricultural use was about 1½ million ha in 1960 – about ½ per cent of the total area. In the north there are Collectives for reindeer and fur-farming, some meat and dairy, some combining dairy and vegetable-growing activities. In other parts (notably the Aldan, Indigirka and Yana basins) State Farms do almost all the market-farming. There are 45 million ha of reindeer pastures in the Republic. Ploughland and hayfields are very scattered, all in small plots; 11 per cent of the kolkhoz units are less than one hectare, another 31 per cent between one and five hectares. In central Yakutia the raising of cattle and horses is the main and most efficient agricultural activity, followed by grain, vegetables and hunting. All the farmers must depend heavily on other occupations, such as lumbering, animal care and stevedoring, in winter. Hardy 'quick-fattening' types of cattle have been bred for the northern conditions. These are mostly small (300 kg live weight on the average) though economical in the consumption of hay (2·7 tons a year). Oxen are much used for haulage, sometimes for ploughing.

Yakutia is the northernmost horse-ranching area in the world. About 100,000 head are counted, mostly kept out of doors even in winter, finding their food under the snow; 20,000 are work-horses for cartage, which are stabled. They require much fodder in total though little per head – about one ton of hay a year for a riding horse, two and a half to three for a workhorse. The herds, especially, are cheap to maintain and are largely to provide horseflesh, which is widely consumed in Yakutia and is much cheaper than other meat. Meat consumption is two-thirds beef, 20 per cent horseflesh, 13 per cent reindeer and 5 per cent pork.

The numbers of cattle increased by one-third between 1940 and 1958, reindeer by a half, pigs more than doubled, but the number of horses declined about 20 per cent in that period. In the early 1960s there were altogether 356,000 cattle, 154,000 horses and 354,000 reindeer; the number of horses seems to have continued to decline. Sheep cannot be kept. 25,000-30,000 tons of meat are produced annually, 175,000 tons of milk; these are double the 1953 figures, but the population meanwhile nearly doubled. 70 per cent of the milk is used to make butter.

The main agricultural areas are, however, only the central part of the Republic and the Verkhoyansk lowlands, both of which are dry and frosty. On the rivers of these areas a few hundred dams or dikes have been set up for irrigation; especially at the river confluences, this gives high yields of grasses. Irrigation is important also for the watering of livestock. The cattle often go 2 or 3 km to drink. A main agricultural gain has been the extension of double-cropping in recent years, as more agricultural machinery and equipment come to hand. The average kolkhoz in Yakutia has about 40 ha of land farmed, of which 3·4 is ploughed. Central Yakutia had in the early 1960s 77,000 horsepower applied to agriculture, of which one-third was animal (horses and draft oxen), two-thirds machines. Cereal cultivation is entirely mechanised; animal husbandry much less so. In 1961 there were 3200 tractors and 350 combine-harvesters but nearly all applied to cereal cultivation – hay being mown almost entirely by hand.

Nearly all this is in the central part of the Republic – which recorded, in 1958, 88 per cent of the cattle, 80 per cent of the horses, 97 per cent of the sown area. Even 43 per cent of the income from the production of furs arose in the central area, leaving little for the outlying areas, except for the 57 per cent of the fur industry and 93 per cent of the reindeer, plus of course hunting and fishing. The reindeer provide food and

account for almost all the money income of the (largely indigenous) people in the remoter areas where they are the main
means of transport. In such areas only 20 per cent of the local
income is from agriculture. Apropos the extent of mineral prospecting and other resource-reconnaissances: every year well
over 10,000 reindeer are hired for such expeditions.

FOOD, TRADE AND TRANSPORT

The output of potatoes was less than a fifth of the Republic's
requirements in 1958, that of vegetables little more than a fifth,
the grain harvest less than half. The plan target for 1965 was
to raise the production of potatoes, especially, to the point of
self-sufficiency; but much of the rest would still have to be
imported. 250,000 ha of meadow land was to be improved by
the same date and irrigations work extended over 45,000 additional hectares, milk production to be raised to 300,000 tons,
meat to 50,000. Fur-farming was to be developed, especially in
the north. Generally in the U.S.S.R. the 1965 targets were not
met; or if met, only some years later.

One-fifth of the U.S.S.R.'s exports of furs emanate from
Yakutia: the valuable varieties are squirrel (especially in the
Verkhoyansk mountains, the south-west and Vilyui areas),
foxes (in the central and tundra areas), ermine (everywhere, but
especially in the middle Indigirka, Kolyma and Yana basins)
and musquash (an introduction into Yakutia, now quite at
home in the lakes of the Kolyma and lower Vilyui basins).
These account for 80 per cent of the value of all the furs
produced. But the yield fluctuates greatly, with marked swings
in the populations of the various animals from good years to
bad: in some years the output of white-hare pelts is 3 million,
in bad years it can fall well below 100,000. In 1958 all the
collective farms in Yakutia reported a total of 805,000 man-days
of labour expended on getting fur-bearing animals, i.e. 3 per
cent of their total expenditure of labour; but this brought in
14 per cent of their money income. Hunting is also, obviously,
for getting meat; in 1958 the 72 collective farms in the northern
part of Yakutia obtained 40 kg per household in this way.

Though the methods are still basically shooting and trapping, the breeding of animals in cages makes great advances. By 1959 it accounted for over half (54 per cent) of the total value of fur production in the Republic; by now the proportion is higher. In 1959 there were 15,000 silver foxes and 3000 blue foxes in fur-farms. This – together with the rising proportion marked 'urban' in the census, the efforts at irrigation and land reclamation, the formation of mining, lumbering and other centres – is another indication of how the population and the living pattern of Yakutia are becoming more settled. One or two generations ago, all was highly nomadic; the small population was highly mobile. Even Yakutsk, now quite a modern town of nearly 100,000 people, was a simple overgrown village. Even the 'settled' Yakutians of those days had summer residences different from their winter ones.

The poet Ryleyev, who was executed in 1826 as a Decembrist but had been secretary to the Russia-America Company, wrote:

> Monotonously the days pass
> For the dweller in wild Yakutsk,
> The year round. But once or twice
> Among the weary throng of convicts comes
> A squad of troops.

The outlook has vastly changed of late – although in Stalin's time this old pattern was grimly repeated, under far more horrible conditions than in the Tsars' days. Now there are hospitals, schools, a university in Yakutsk and all the other usual institutions – including of course the administrative and political network. Yakutia was energetically dealt with in Stalin's initial *Gleichschaltung* in the late 1920s and 1930s, when all the Yakutians were organised into Collectives. The war-time and post-war development brought rapid modernisation and comparative prosperity.

Everything depends, as everywhere in the Soviet Union, on problems of transport. Freight comes from other Provinces preponderantly by the Lena river. Another link is the Arctic sea route, connecting – scantily and laboriously, but increasingly – Yakutia and other northern areas with European Russia on the one side and the Pacific on the other. River transport is important within the Republic.

Roads serve the mining areas and the central vicinity of

Yakutsk; principally the good motor road right through south and south-east Yakutia from Amuria to Magadan, via Nyevyer on the Siberian railway, Nagorny, Aldan, Tommot, to Sysy-Basa on the Lena 80 km south of Yakutsk. There the huge river (which has nearly double the flow of water of the Volga, for instance, besides being about one-seventh longer) interposes a formidable unbridged barrier; but the road continues north-ward to Yakutsk on the left bank from Best'akh opposite Sysy-Basa, also on the right bank to a point opposite Yakutsk, where it swings east to Khanyga. Just before Khanyga the Aldan river presents another barrier, but the road continues across the Indigirka beyond Kuidasun (near Oimyakon) to Myaundzha in Magadan. At Myaundzha there is an important branch road northward to the mining area of Ust' Nera in Yakutia, but the main road passes south-eastward through Susuman, eventually reaching the port of Magadan.

Since the rivers are open only briefly over stretches and various localities are off the rivers, co-ordinated road transport is vital. Lorries are specially fitted for winter use with cater-pillar tracks, driving and sleeping compartments, etc. A pic-turesque sight is the local trapper's or prospector's mobile hut on a reindeer – or sometimes motorised – sledge camouflaged for stalking purposes. Some use is made of motor-sledges and other types of special vehicles on the winter roads ('*zimniki*'). Within the Arctic Circle, as elsewhere in the Polar regions, dog-teams are used, as well as reindeer. In 1957, 84 per cent of the freight was handled by trucks or lorries, less than 14 per cent by water; subsequently all transport has increased but the pro-portions remain about the same. The water distances being greater, however, if one calculates by ton-kilometres instead of by arrivals and despatches, the share of water-transport rises to about 90 per cent.

The Lena is by far the most important water-route; it took no less than 90 per cent of the water-borne freight in 1959 (which totalled for the whole Republic 1,773,000 tons – some 35 times the 1933 figure). The next largest carrier is probably the northern sea route, using Tiksi at the mouth of the Lena, developed in recent years. The traffic on the Yana, Indigirka and Kolyma is much less. The Aldan is used for freight from its mouth up to Tommot, the Vilyui up to Suntar, the Yana to

Verkhoyansk, the Indigirka to Khonuu, the Kolyma to Ust'
Srednikan in Magadan. There is very little shipping on the
Olenyok and the Anabar in the north-east. Downstream traffic
predominates on the Lena and the Kolyma, upstream on the
Yana, Vilyui, Aldan and Indigirka.

An enormous recent stimulus has been the new railway line
from Taishet on the Siberian artery some 600 km west of
Irkutsk, past the great electric power station at Bratsk to Ust'
Kut, the river port of Osetrevo on the upper Lena. This carried,
by the 1960s, about 80 per cent of the freight coming into the
Yakut Republic. Yakutian hinterland development is heavily
weighted at present in the direction of linkage – for import-
dependence especially – with the industrial construction proceeding around Irkutsk, Bratsk and the south of Eastern Siberia;
rather than with Amuria and Magadan, or the northern sea
route, each of which still plays a minor part. The northern sea
route is qualitatively important for the intake of key items of
machinery, etc., from European Russia (Archangel); but it
also connects the mouths of the other main rivers and the basins
of the Yana, Indigirka, Olenyok and Kolyma for the circulation
of products within the Republic, as well as the distribution of
arrivals from and exports to European Russia. Even the
arrivals from the south-west by the railway from Taishet are
distributed to some extent ultimately by the northern coastal
route.

Apparently the traffic on the northern sea route has recently
increased, reaching on the import side as much as one-seventh
of the intake of goods into Yakutia. On the export side the
picture is certainly different: westward traffic greatly predominates (in bulk especially). According to the higher estimates it
takes as much as a half of Yakutia's exports. The position really
is that the Arctic sea route is supplying largely the whole north
of Siberia along its whole length, with necessities of life as well
as the sinews of industrialisation from European Russia. Secondly it has a great role in more local (though still long-distance)
cabotage. In return it is carrying valuable materials, gold and
furs, to European Russia.

In all this Tiksi is but one of many way-stations, having only
part of this traffic. The northern sea-route is not only a question
of regular services; especially in the eastward traffic, for in that

direction much cargo-use is made of new ships being built in European Russia for delivery to Siberia. Between 1952 and 1960 Yakutia received 236 vessels in this way – having, like the rest of northern Siberia, no shipbuilding facilities of its own. This must form a large proportion of the shipping available for Yakutia's internal use, which probably did not continue to increase at the same rate in the 1960s – an estimated 300 vessels would probably suffice to carry all Yakutia's estimated one and a half million tons of waterborne traffic per year.

The highway from Amuria to Tommot carries over 300,000 tons a year. There is considerable road haulage to and from the tin-mining areas of the Yana and Indigirka, also the Mirny diamond area, for which figures are not available. Such transport uses – in a characteristic and historic way – not only roads and frozen riverbeds but the 'tract', i.e. broad trains over the frozen and lightly snow-covered countryside. Such a tract connects Mirny with Mukhtuya on the Lena; others are Yakutsk–Verkhoyansk in the north-east, Nyurba–Daldyn (east of Mirny) and from Deputatski to Kuiga on the Yana at 72°N latitude. Convoys of vehicles use these main routes. In March 1958, for example, the Mirny diamond centre was largely equipped (two years after its first opening) by the delivery of 500 tons of technical supplies carried by a column of over a hundred vehicles from the Trans-Siberian railway at Nyevyer via Yakutsk and Nyurba, 3300 km of road-distance.

The composition of the river cargoes reflects the economic development. About 1930 one-third consisted of cereals. The main components in 1957, the latest firm figures available, were timber (26 per cent), coal (26 per cent), oil and oil products (11 per cent), grain and flour (6 per cent), the rest being machinery, equipment, building materials and consumer goods (in that order) coming into Yakutia. The imports, however, total only about a quarter of the whole traffic by volume, three-quarters being the products of Yakutia (timber, coal and construction materials of mineral origin). Forty years ago, the proportions were in the opposite ratio; imports by river into Yakutia increased no less than twenty-five times between 1933 and 1960: especially timber (which nearly tripled), oil (more than doubled), coal (increased over 50 per cent). The main loading and unloading centres are Yakutsk, Tiksi at the Lena mouth, Zyryanka on the Kolyma and Nizhni Yansk on the lower Yana.

Naturally air transport has a great part to play, with many internal and external connections. By the 1960s nearly half the passenger traffic of Yakutia (46 per cent) was by air, a third (36 per cent) by river and nearly a fifth by road. The air freight carried was 33,000 tons in 1959; since then it has increased greatly, owing especially to use of helicopters.

The imports of Yakutia greatly exceed its exports; they are about three times as great. Imports rose from about 144,000 tons in 1948 to about 500,000 in 1958, and this trend continued thereafter. The exports in 1962 were in the order of 200,000 tons (Table 8.1).

Table 8.1   Exports of the Yakut Republic
(in 1962)

	to Irkutsk Province	to Magadan Province	to Amur Province (by rail via Nyevyer)	Total
Coal ('ooo) tons	75	40	–	115
Timber ('ooo cu. m.)	40	20	–	60
Miscellaneous ('ooo tons)	5	–	12	17

CENTRAL YAKUTSK

The district of the capital city Yakutsk comprises 10 per cent of the area of the Republic but has one-third of the population and more than a quarter of the output, both industrial and agricultural; practically all the products are, however, locally consumed. South of Yakutsk the terrain is mountainous taiga up to 1000 metres, bare at higher altitudes; north of Yakutsk between the Vilyui and Lena rivers there are vast expanses of swampy fields, south of that there is some steppe. The valley of the Lena is comparatively well wooded, with more arable and grassland, some black earth; but especially a slightly more moderate climate with a longer frost-free period makes this the centre of some agriculture. Olyokminsk, for example, has an average of 103 days without frost while Dzhikimde less than 200 km up the Olyokma river has only 70. There are some coal

SFE G 2

deposits not far north of Yakutsk – hard coal at Sangar, lignite at Kangalassa. Development extends from those places south-wards along the river to Pokrovsk.

Yakutsk itself (population 98,000 in 1968, 74,000 in 1959) has considerable educational and research activities: a branch of the U.S.S.R. Academy of Sciences including its Permafrost Research Institute, as well as a dozen polytechnical and labora-tory establishments. The specialisation throughout is in study and experiment on new techniques of living and working in Arctic and sub-Arctic conditions. The Yaroslavski Provincial Museum, founded by political exiles at the beginning of this century, is also notable.

The city's industrial development is modest; it employed not more than 4000 workers in the early 1960s, hardly one-twentieth of the population. It supplies mainly the needs of the city itself – in sawn wood, furniture, shoes, clothing including furs, bakeries, printing, fish-processing, etc., a few of these items going to the rest of the Yakut Republic, but none beyond it. Fuel has been one problem – firewood used to be largely used, brown coal now comes along the Lena from Kangalassa (40 km) inadequately supplying the small local electric plants and factories, but now there is natural gas from Tas-Tumus by pipeline.

Yakutsk is distinctly the transport centre, handling yearly some hundreds of thousands of tons of goods and tens of thou-sands of passengers. The Lena near Yakutsk is wide, shallow and filled with innumerable islands, through which the boats crossing to Bestyakh take a lengthy winding course. There is a graphic description by Goncharov (author of *Oblomov*, in his *Frigate Pallas* describing his journey to Japan about 1858) of how he spent a long time crossing one channel after another, finally asking 'But where's the Lena?', only to be told they had passed it long ago. A typically Siberian incident; it might be repeated on many rivers, including the Amur where the main-stream frontier is uncertain and Chinese and Russian patrols have fought. At the spring flood vessels come right up to Yakutsk, for the rest of the year the wharf is at Darkylakh 7 km away.

Yakutsk is rapidly modernising, especially its central part, but wooden Siberian single-storey houses, plank sidewalks,

roadways of wood-blocks – wood everywhere – are still characteristic. Because of the permafrost, all constructions are on
piles. All piping, central heating, etc., has to be specially clad,
building and maintenance costs are very high. There are no
cellars. Yakutsk's satellite townships are: Zhatai 18 km away (a
boat-repairing centre), Kangalassa (coal mining output 200,000
tons a year), Pokrovsk (population 6000, with a brickworks
accounting for 40 per cent of the output of bricks in the Republic), Bestyakh near Prokrovsk (a new cement works) and
Tabaga (a sawmill centre).

This old-settled district (Yakutsk dates to 1632) has some
well-established but small agriculture – covering 425,000 ha in
all, or 4 per cent of the area, virtually all pasture and hay land.
Dairy cattle are fairly numerous around the settlements, large
herds of horses are seen further out. Four or five thousand horses
are slaughtered every year for meat; the total production of all
kinds of meat is over 3000 tons a year, of milk 28,000 tons.
People in Yakutsk are much better provided in these items than
other north Siberians. Silver foxes are bred on farms in the
district. The sown area is 20,000 ha, half under cereals, more
than a third under fodder crops. The production of cereals,
vegetables and potatoes varies extremely with the weather
conditions, the crops are far from sufficient for local needs; in
recent years the one extreme, drought, has been combated
strongly by the extension of sprinkler-irrigation but the defeat
of the other, frost, remains one of those matters of the Great
Soviet Future which some Russians sarcastically refer to as
'science fiction'.

Further west at Olyokminsk agricultural conditions are better.
The temperature both at Yakutsk and Olyokminsk is above
12°C through May to September (though with risks of frost
even in that period), but Olyokminsk has more moisture (242
mm of precipitation against 192 for Yakutsk) and a good topsoil (25 cm depth with 16 per cent humus content). There 70
per cent of the sowings are grain, 23 per cent fodder crops; this
area has the Republic's highest per capita production of grain
(about 180 kg per annum) and potatoes (about 140), also doing
well for meat (70 per cent beef, only 15 per cent horseflesh, 10
per cent pork, 5 per cent reindeer). Squirrel furs are produced;
the squirrel population in some of the broad outlands is said to

be twenty or thirty animals per 1000 hectares; kolkhozes combine fur farming and herding reindeer (totalling in this sub-region some 8000 head).

At Olyokminsk some 250,000 cubic metres of lumber are worked a year, for shipment to Sangar and the polar north. Ship repairs are carried out there and another source of its livelihood is the mining of gypsum. Salt is widespread in this sub-region; in many places 'flowers' of salt crystals appear on the surface of the ground. The Olyokminsk deposit covers an area of over 7 sq. km and is said to contain 900 million tons of good salt in thick layers at depths down to 400 metres but fairly easy to mine, not yet significantly exploited. The area also promises oil; some petroliferous gas has been taken off in recent years. Another prospective plan has been the construction on the Lena at this point of a hydroelectric plant.

At the confluence of the Vilyui with the Lena both natural gas and coal have been found. The Sangar coalfield produces over 200,000 tons of coal a year (calorific value 7-800, ash 6 per cent, sulphur 0·3-0·6 per cent, moisture 5 per cent) Sangar has about 6000 inhabitants. Fishing is another feature; in this part of the Lena carp are a speciality (400 tons a year). The countryside is full of swamps and lakes. It is a great area for musquash. Cattle and horses are reared on the drier lands. The 400,000 ha of grassland in the area could support many more; at present not more than 8 per cent of this grassland is used for cutting hay. Though much of it is too damp (and frozen near the surface) to use fully, there is great room for expansion; collective farms some distance away send hay-gathering 'expeditions' into this area in dry weather.

The natural gas of the Tas-Tumus area began to be tapped in 1956 and has since 1967 been available through pipelines to Yakutsk and Bestyakh. Ultimately, it should reach as far as Amuria. The reserves are reckoned at 40 billion cubic metres. The various mineral possibilities raise expectations of the eventual development of a chemical industry in this sub-region.

THE NORTH-EASTERN LIMIT OF FARMING

More important agriculturally is the next sub-region to be considered – the area north of Yakutsk between the Lena and Amga rivers. This is the furthest north-east location in the Soviet Union in which any significant farming activity is carried on. It is only 3 per cent of Yakutia, but still a huge area – 100,000 sq. km. It has 14 per cent of the Republic's total population, 44 per cent of the sown area, 30 per cent of the cattle and horses. Its agriculture is also the best equipped, having for instance 40 per cent of the total number of tractors in the Republic; but industry is virtually nil. The main agricultural activity is in a very large number of scattered *alasy* – the local term for hollows or depressions in the karst landscape, where water is found and conditions are favourable. These contain 60 per cent of the 260,000 ha of hayfields in the sub-region. There are 360,000 ha of good pasture, much more that is inferior and infra-marginal at present.

On this the horses and cattle graze freely from May to October, the rest of the year they are stabled and fed on coarse fodder, silage being inadequate though steadily increasing. The annual hay crop is 300,000 tons. One third of the cattle are cows, about 8 per cent work-oxen, and nearly two-thirds calves. Annual production figures are approximately 4000 tons of beef, 50,000 of milk (over 7 tons per 100 ha of land in agricultural use). Most of the horses are herded out in the open, even through the winter; like reindeer, they find food under the snow. In this sub-region the annual abattoir count of horses killed for meat is 7000, representing a quarter of the total local meat-supply. Not all this horse-meat is for human consumption, however; it is cheap enough to be used also to feed the caged silver foxes in the local fur-farms, an activity much developed since 1948. Nevertheless hunting or trapping still predominates with 60 per cent of the local earnings from furs, against 40 per cent for the fur-farms. In good years hares are especially prolific and provide 10 or 15 per cent of the meat eaten locally.

Cereals are a notable contribution of this area – 80 per cent of the output and of the sown area. But the ploughing is on a great number of small strips in numerous scattered places – 17,000 bits of ploughed land averaging less than $3\frac{1}{2}$ ha each. Though collectivisation brought much consolidation – for example the Maiya (Kangalassa) district counted 1723 inhabited places in 1926 but had consolidated these into 209 by

1959, though the population had greatly increased – the natural conditions (and the traditions and outlook of the peasants) still compel a scattered pattern of tillage. To the occasionally serious crop-failures not only the vagaries of the climate but also errors of human judgement have often contributed. The small food base of Yakutia is improving but still precarious.

WESTERN YAKUTIA: THE SIBERIAN KIMBERLEY

This large sub-region (860,000 sq. km or 28 per cent of the Republic) contains 20 per cent of its population and sown area, 30 per cent of the horses and 30 per cent of the cattle, 15 per cent of the reindeer. It produces 38 per cent of the lumber and 25 per cent of the furs. It is rich in mineral reserves; with coal, cooking salt, Iceland spar, limestone and gypsum, as well as the famous diamonds. It is a plateau rising to 1000 metres. Its two main rivers, the Olenyok and Vilyui, are not navigable in this area. Frost and poor soil, marshiness and distance inhibit any notable cultivation of crops. 67 million ha of forest cover three-quarters of the sub-region, which has 40 per cent of the forested area of the Republic. 90 per cent is larch, 9 per cent pine; but nearly all, moreover all the best-quality wood, is on the Lena river near the southern border.

The 'pipes' of clay containing kimberlite – the diamond-bearing rock – are diverse and scattered in the basins of the Lesser Botuobuya river (a right-bank tributary of the Vilyui), the Daldyn (a left-bank tributary of the Markha), on the upper Muna far to the north-east, on the upper and middle Olenyok and in other places, i.e. in all parts of this sub-region except its south. The original working is at Mirny ('Peaceful') where there is a diamond-pipe called the Peace Pipe and some washings on the Irelyakh river; but the rich Aikhal pipe on the Markha some 300 km further north has added a large output, though the climate there is extremely unattractive. The Aikhal development consists of two kimberlite pipes, each larger than Mirny's; one (Aikhal) opened in 1964, the other (Udachny) in 1968.

Mirny sprang suddenly into existence in 1956. Numbers of people flocked there in a 'diamond rush' ahead of the formal planning decision. The population is now said to be 30,000; 5700 was recorded for 1959. The town consists largely of monotonous two-storey pre-fabricated blocks. There are cement and fibre-block plants on the outskirts. The diamond-handling plant is simply built of wood but well equipped. The cutting is largely done at Smolensk in European Russia. The diamonds are 80 per cent industrial, 20 per cent gemstones. About half the diamond workers are women. The people of Mirny live very well, receiving priority issues of all types of consumer goods made in the Soviet Union and consignments of fresh fruits and vegetables by air. A high proportion of the cars there are brand-new – for the reason just given, but also because cars do not last long. Even metal cracks in the $-40°$ to $-70°C$ winter temperatures and the engines must be warmed before they will fire. Life in Mirny is therefore very different from anywhere else in the outlands.

The sub-region also has much coal, mostly brown coal, along the Lena, other deposits being on the Olenyok and upper Vilyui. The best locations are around Nyurba on the Vilyui and Zhigansk on the Lena but these are not yet significantly worked. Yakutia's coal production was 1·4 million tons in 1965; half of this came from Kangalassy and Sangar. The main source of salt is Kempendyai about 100 km south of Nyurba, where there is an outcrop of about 70,000 tons of good salt; about 3000 tons a year are produced by simple drying and boiling processes. The activities are varied in this sub-region, including also furs, cartage, fishing. Mukhtuya (population in 1968 over 16,000; double that of 1959) is a main transport centre. The Lena valley in the south is the best forestry area; it exported 370,000 cubic metres of timber in 1960. At Peledui (population about 5000) there is considerable boat-building activity. In the south and centre are many cattle: in the north, reindeer. The sub-region has just over three-quarters of a million hectares in agricultural use, of which 412,000 for herding, 274,000 for hay, 41,000 ploughed. In the north there is of course no ploughing, in the central part only 2·3 per cent of the area is ploughed, in the south 4·5 per cent. The cattle population is about 118,000; horses at 40,000 are outnumbered by reindeer (44,000) but over 35,000 of the latter are in the northern part. In the extreme south on the Lena a third of kolkhoz income is from cattle, less than a quarter from planting; cartage and other side-occupations make up most of the rest. In the centre on the Vilyui the proportions are 48 per cent from cattle, 10 per cent from hunting, fishing, etc., 18 per cent from casual wage-earnings. There are four State Farms specially serving the plutocratic centres Mirny and Markha with meat, milk and vegetables. The sub-region produces a quarter of the Republic's furs.

North of Mirny a large hydroelectric plant began to be built in 1964 on the Vilyui just below the confluence of the Akhtaranda, the biggest construction ever planned in a permafrost zone, with a 550-metres dam 65 metres high, to provide power for south-western Yakutia, including the central heating of all buildings in Mirny.

MINING IN THE SOUTH

Southern Yakutia, an area of 242,000 sq. km or one-twelfth of the Republic's surface, has one-sixth of the total industrial output, in the form predominantly of minerals. The population is only 44,000 and all but 4000 are in settlements dependent almost entirely on the mining of gold, mica, quartz sands, iron and coal, facilitated by the presence of the road into Amuria. This is mountainous (to 2000 metres), cold (frost-free only 60 days in the year), wet (300 mm of annual precipitation in the northern part, 550 in the southern) and marshy. Yet the permafrost is patchy in this sub-region, construction is easier. Half the area is forested (135,000 sq. km) representing nearly two billion cubic metres of timber (1·3 of larch, 0·4 of pine).

In 1923 gold was discovered on the upper Aldan. The population rose from a handful to 13,000 in 1926 and 53,000 in 1959; but not all the gold mines were successful. Those that continue (which are very profitable) are highly mechanised, so the immigration later moderated and the population is now about 45,000, less than in 1959. The town of Aldan (13,000 inhabitants) arose from a small mining creek and was originally named Nezametny ('Inconspicuous'). The main yield of gold is from workings by hydraulic dredges moving around the Leninski and Lower Kuranakh fields, but they are now having to work deeper into the sands and the ore workings (Lebediny, 'Swan' mine, with a processing plant nearby also producing copper concentrate) have recently been further developed. Mica has also been mined and processed in this area, beginning in 1941 around Emeldzhak and Kuranakh, in 1948 at the Snezhny ('Snowy') mine on the middle Timpton river. The township of Tommot developed accordingly (population 7000; 5000 in 1959); Emeldzhak has 3100, Kankunski 3600, Nadyozhny ('Reliable') and El'kon are small places. 40 per cent of the mica is taken at the surface. Quartz sands are mined on the upper Timpton and Aldan rivers – at the vividly-named localities Kholodnoe ('Cold'), Severnoe ('Northern'), Pustynnoe ('Wilderness') and Khrustal'noe ('Crystal').

The area has twice the supply of electricity, per head of the population, that the rest of the Republic gets; from the Yakokutsk station near Aldan (7000 kW) and other small plants. The Ugol'ny ('Coal') mine not far from Chul'man, about 300 km away, provides their fuel. At present the Chul'man coal mine (output 108,000 tons in 1965) sustains a 20,000 kW electric plant, opened in 1963. Local timber processing (half a million cubic metres a year) and brickmaking (over two million a year) have developed especially in connection with the mining. So have market gardening and dairying: 75 per cent of the 1400 ha of sown area is devoted to simple vegetables and potatoes (67 ha and 465 ha respectively) – a scale of very modest local self-sufficiency. There are 2300 head of cattle, 22,000 reindeer. The latter are mainly for transport: killings for meat are about 100 a year. Pork is a local speciality, 25 per cent of the output of meat.

There are some 45 billion tons of coal and 2 billion of iron ore (perhaps half of it industrially likely), all of good quality, in southern Yakutia. Limestone and other useful materials are found in close conjunction. Only accessibility is required to make this a very large industrial base. For that, however, tremendous developments in transport are needed, such as a railway right through southern Yakutia from west to east, presumably part of the intended network of the northern Siberian railway.

YAKUTIA TO THE EASTWARD

The mountainous Yana and Kolyma area, of 870,000 sq. km

has 16 per cent of the Republic's population, on more than a third of its territory. It is distinguished for the mining of light metals (engaging 70 per cent of the population) and for the production of furs (one-third of the Republic's output). It has also one-third of the reindeer population. 45 per cent of its area is forested, all in the southern part in sheltered valleys, but the wood is of comparatively poor quality and the milling capacity is low. The population (mainly Russians) is as thin as one person per 100 sq. km on the upper Indigirka at the lowest, only 6·6 persons per 100 sq. km at the highest in the upper and middle Yana. Batagai is a township of about 7500 people, near tin mines, with a concentrating plant and an electric station. Verkhoyansk is a mere village of 1500, Deputatski (1800) depends on alluvial tin-workings; there are others in the upper Yana, gold on the upper Indigirka, served for transport by the Kolyma motor road from Magadan and for power by the Arkagal station just over the Magadan border. From the latter a 280-km line supplies Ust' Nera, a town of some 11,000 inhabitants.

The other development is on the Maya about 300 km south-east of Yakutsk, served by maintenance workshops at El'dikan (population over 3000) and Khandyga (5000). Near the latter are fields of good coal, on the navigable part of the Aldan, producing annually some 250,000 tons. Another coalfield (output 120,000 tons a year) is on the Zyryanka, also accessible by river transport. Zyryanka has about 4000 people and is the base for river-shipping on the Kolyma and the Indigirka. In the 1960s this area has developed its lumbering industry considerably.

One-third of the cattle and over 40 per cent of the horses of this sub-region are concentrated in the Verkhoyansk area. The sub-region produces 25 per cent of the Republic's output of furs. There is little agriculture or fishing. The principal development, mining, connects the sub-region as much with Magadan Province as with the rest of the Yakut A.S.S.R. In Yakutia, only its eastern part seems at all close to the Pacific Ocean, or to look eastwards at this stage in its development.

The farthest north of Yakutia requires only brief notice here. It has a quarter of the area of the Republic but only some 7 per cent of the population. Most of the fishing (90 per cent) is, however, done in the Arctic north. The land is low-lying. Reindeer account for 40 per cent of the money income and 70 per cent of the total output of the (largely indigenous) rural dwellers, who number only about 30,000. Furs account for 20-50 per cent of the income in various districts. The largest and most modernised centre is the Lena mouth port of Tiksi (population 7200), for the northern sea route. A local lignite field produced 1000,000 tons in 1965.

Meanwhile southern Yakutia presents a hinterland of some substance, especially for the western portion of the Soviet Far East. At the present stage of development it has little linkage with Khabarovsk Province, but some with Magadan, as will be seen in the next chapter. Yakutia's mica is now of special importance, being of the phlogopite type (magnesium mica) of special significance in advanced electrics, replacing 'Muscovite' (potassium) mica. The area provides examples of changes in resource patterns. Gold was once Yakutia's main contribution; Kolyma in Magadan largely replaced it in this respect in the 1930s. Tin is being significantly developed; the Ege Khaya mine near Verkhoyansk, operating since 1941, recently appeared depleted, but in the 1960s it began to produce indium and the Batagai concentrator is still very useful. The Deputatski lode in the far north of Yakutia has now become the tin-mining centre. The Yakut Republic is a diversely developing part of the vast northern hinterland.[1]

CHAPTER 9

Magadan: The Far North-East

THE Province of Magadan extends to the extreme eastern end
of Russia, within a few miles of Alaska, U.S.A. It is cold,
remote and largely mountainous; mostly between 600 and 1500
metres, a few places are over 2000 metres. The total area is just
under 1·2 million sq. km, the population only 340,000 in 1968.
Its main present wealth is in gold, followed by fisheries and
furs, some forestry, a little coal. As a hinterland in relation to
the main development of the S.F.E. along the axis of the Trans-
Siberian, it has as yet only a secondary role. Ultimately the
varied resources of this vast territory may become important;
but now and for a long time to come, distance and natural
difficulties force it to be for the most part only a potential
contributor to the process of development, except for its very
valuable contribution of gold.

This is where Russia and America meet, but fortunately not
in tension. The conjunction is only of the remotest and emptiest
parts of the two countries; rather the opposite of a confrontation,
for the United States and Russia are here 'back to back', with
very limited but quite neighbourly relations. To understand
the structure of the S.F.E., it may, however, be useful to apply
to Magadan the metaphor of a hinge. The long south Siberian
corridor ends at the Maritimes with a door on the Pacific
(Vladivostok). Development to the north of that corridor is
important, to strengthen the whole layout; and a main hinterland for that purpose would appear to be the great and rich
central-northern area of Yakutia.

The development at the south-eastern end of Yakutia noted
in the last few pages distinctly spills over into the western end
of Magadan Province, which pivots on the hinterland development of Yakutia. Magadan has little or no connection with
Khabarovsk, except indirectly through Yakutia and Amuria. It
has practically no overland connection with Kamchatka either;

but the eastern parts of Magadan relate fairly actively by sea to Kamchatka, Sakhalin and the Kuriles – the offshore domains of the Soviet Union in the North Pacific, described in the following chapters. Finally, northern and eastern Magadan has another 'hingeing' role, in that it is the terminal of the potentially important Northern Sea Route across the top of the Soviet Union: a cold and difficult route, but 'Mare Nostrum' from the Soviet point of view.

It is therefore useful to bear in mind that the development of the S.F.E. is in its grand lines pivoted on these connections: Yakutia–Transbaikalia, Yakutia–Amuria, Yakutia–Magadan, Magadan–Soviet Pacific Provinces and Magadan–Northern Sea Route; while not forgetting that the foundations of this whole construct, pending more massive development in the North than is yet in sight, remain very predominantly along the frontier with China in the south.

A good third of Magadan Province is within the Arctic Circle, the whole is permafrosted; all construction costs in the northlands are double or treble what they are outside the zone of permafrost. Huge expanses of the interior are uninhabited, empty in every respect. Considerable economic activity appears in the area between the western border of Kamchatka and the eastern border of Yakutia. There are four zones of development. One is around the middle reaches of the Lesser and Greater Anyui rivers (tributaries of the Kolyma near its mouth), centred on Bilibino. The second is around the northern port of Pevek. Further east there is a third area between Egvekinot at the head of the Anadyr bay and Iul'tun to its northward. The fourth development area is the lower Anadyr river valley, where recently oil and natural gas were discovered. Finally there is some development along the Bering coast facing Alaska.

Magadan much resembles its neighbour Alaska. Gains are evidently to be made there in the field of metal mining. The Province, besides being one of the world's largest goldfields, contains notably tin and wolfram. It has therefore been very energetically prospected, from the geological point of view especially, by the Soviets – and long before them, since the beginning of the present century. Perhaps Magadan has been studied, from the mineral point of view, even more intensively than Yakutia. Between 1932 and 1955 the State organisation

Dal'stroi allocated no less than 41 per cent of its total capital outlays to geological prospecting. That is, of its *capital* outlays; it spent little on the maintenance and equipment of its workers. For the name Dal'stroi (Far East Construction) is a euphemism for the abominable concentration camps of the Stalin period, which were especially notorious in this area. A large part of the capital and general outlays for this Province in the current plans still continues to be for geological and topographical prospecting and survey.

The population was only about 20,000 at the time of the Revolution, consisting largely of the various 'aboriginal' tribes (Chukchi, Eskimos, Evenki, Yukagirs, Chuvantsy, Koryaks, Orochi, Yakuts). In 1926 new gold discoveries were made on the Srednekan river, a tributary of the Kolyma, giving the first modern impetus. A major expedition in the Kolyma area followed in 1928-30 and thereafter exploration further north-east proceeded systematically, disclosing reserves of gold, tin, wolfram and coal. The upper Kolyma development gained speed from 1931, that of Chukotia (the easternmost part) later. In 1962 a fresh overall planning view was officially propounded in which Yakutia and Magadan were considered together as a North-Eastern Economic Region: an official volume with that title (*Severo-vostochny Ekonomicheskii Rayon*) was published in Magadan in 1965 giving details of the developments to that date.

Gold is by far the leading element in Magadan's development. The output is not disclosed, but forms some significant part of the total Soviet production. The amounts of tin and wolfram are also not known specifically, but are evidently less important. A still smaller share of the U.S.S.R. total is contributed by Magadan in fisheries and furs, although these products too are to some extent exported from Magadan to other Provinces and ultimately (not directly from Magadan) to other countries. The annual production of furs is stated as 50,000 roubles' worth from trapping and hunting, 100,000 from fur-farms. Agriculture is hardly developed at all; virtually the Province's entire requirements of meat, milk, vegetables and potatoes have to be imported from tremendous distances, though the indigenous people in the interior live largely on their reindeer, while around the mining settlements and townships there is a little market-gardening. Even in the latter areas the stress in recent years had been on fur-farming. Table 9.1 summarises the employment of the Province's very small work force.

Table 9.1   Occupations in Magadan Province
(Percentage of all workers employed, 1963)

Industry	38·8
Transport and communications	11·4
Construction and maintenance of buildings, etc.	9·2
Geological prospecting	8·1
Trade, catering (public provision of food) and distribution	8·2
Agriculture	4·8
Education, training, science, arts, public health, etc.	18·1
	100·0

Considerable parts of the first three items are really in the nature of the fourth, 'geological prospecting', since mining is so much the dominant activity.

THE PROVINCIAL CAPITAL

Although the gold-rush has recently developed in the eastern part of the Province also, the south-western area traversed by the motor highway (over 1000 km long in Magadan Province) is still the main one. Along the highway is a belt of gold-mining settlements beyond which the taiga stretches widely. The gold-fields further north-west on the Indigirka river are politically within the Yakut Republic but for practical purposes belong to this southern or Magadan–Kolyma sub-region of Magadan Province, as it is formally designated by Soviet geographers. Its two subdivisions are the upper Kolyma mining area and the Magadan coastal transport and fishing area. The least distance between the metal-bearing strata and the port of Magadan is about 400 km and this intervening strip is extremely undeveloped, being sharply mountainous with no agricultural possibilities except near the coast.

The coastal belt depending on the town of Magadan and its port Nagaevo contains one-third of the population of the whole Province; no less than 87 per cent of its population is urban.

The deep bay of Nagaevo provides the best harbour on the Okhotsk Sea. The port, established in 1933-6, is now well equipped with reinforced concrete quays and modern machinery; it is the main provider of all the needs of its hinterland and has an annual cargo turnover of 950,000 tons. Imports run at around 500,000-550,000 tons, of which 150,000 tons are hard coal (mainly from Sakhalin) and 80,000 tons timber (from the southern part of the S.F.E.). Practically all this coal and timber is used within the Magadan coastal area itself. Although this immediate area is quite thick taiga country, much of the local woodlands have already been severely cut, so a great deal of timber has to be shipped from distant places. It was planned, however, to develop the mining of lignite near the town of Magadan (the Lansk coalfield) by 1970, whereby the need to import coal might be diminished.

The air link with Magadan (reference is to the town of Magadan, unless Magadan Province is specified) is also important, connecting with Khabarovsk–Moscow, Yakutsk–Irkutsk–Krasnoyarsk, Petropavlovsk in Kamchatka, also by a northern route Tiksi–Noril'sk, as well as places within the Province. The highway from Magadan is well equipped to facilitate both goods and passenger traffic. From Nagaevo port there is an oil pipeline running along the road for 72 km to Palatka, which is the transport centre and the site of the Marchekanski machine shops and other installations performing ship repairs, also making boilers and other parts of ships.

Magadan itself produces fairly advanced mining equipment, trailers, winches, dust-filters. It performs basic repairs and refits of bulldozers, etc. It is a considerable centre of mining research and experiment, with a Gold and Rare Metals Research Institute, a fuel laboratory and the large Dal'stroi-proyekt (Far Eastern Constructional Planning) organisation, receiving research and repair commissions from other Provinces as well as from Magadan itself. It is interesting that official planning concentrates chiefly on this latter role for Magadan in the next period – i.e. research and general technical services, primarily of course for Magadan Province but also for other areas – the evaluation being that the scope of activity in the upper Kolyma gold-mining area, hence the role of Magadan in providing it with equipment, transport and services, is now at a maximum and will be 'stabilised' for some time to come.

Another activity is the building industry and the production of materials for it. The construction of a cement-grinding plant was begun in 1965. This was to bring clinker all the way from Spassk in the Maritime Province (2600 sea-kilometres from Vladivostok and another 270 km by rail from Spassk!) and to supply all the requirements of the sub-region and the Indigirka goldfields. In Magadan various ferro-concrete, mortar, brick, sand-block and the like items are already being produced; 72 km from the town is a glass factory producing window panes, bottles, etc. Considerable construction is to be seen in the town, at the rate of some tens of new stone buildings a year; it lies on gently hilly ground, the main Lenin Street has good three- to five-storey modern buildings and is tree-lined, but the surrounding hills show large areas bare of trees.

Light industry in Magadan includes a garment works, a shoe factory, confectionery, furniture, distillery, milling and baking. The tailoring and garment industry returns an annual output of 58,000 roubles a year. The footwear seems to be mainly of felt (*valenki*), 140,000 pairs a year being recorded as made of it. Other items are leather goods, including reindeer skin, and furs. The population of Magadan is rising rapidly; 78,000 was estimated in 1965, the 1968 figure was 85,000. Electric power is provided by a number of small stations in and around Magadan; a larger thermal station was under construction in 1966, but the power supply still remains inadequate.

Practically all the fishing is in this area. Local fisheries output averaged 15,000 tons a year in the period 1953-60. In the next period 1960-4 the catch was greatly increased, to an average of 80,000. This is the local-based activity only; if the catches of the fleets operating from the Maritime Province and Sakhalin off the Magadan coast are added, the total catch in these waters in 1964 was no less than 210,000 tons. There are seven Fisheries Combines in the Magadan area, on the Magadan (Taui), Yamsk and Gizhiginsk bays, providing just over half the catch, plus a number of kolkhozes on the coast which furnish just under half. This is almost entirely herring and salmon, the former increasing, the latter declining.

The mature herring are mostly taken within 120 miles (the official definitions still use miles in this respect, not kilometres) of the coast, chiefly in the bay off Nagaevo, but westward as far as the provincial border and eastward as far as Babushkin bay. This activity began in 1952, increased rapidly in 1962-4 and became the main kind of fishing in this sub-region. The younger herring are taken only in the Gizhiginsk bay and only in springtime; stocks are seriously declining. The planners expect to be restricted to a future output of only 15,000 tons a year in this category of young herring; but the catch of mature herring may be largely increased. The latter varies greatly from very good years when it may reach as much as two million tons to very bad ones when it may be only a few tens of thousands of tons. This is in contrast with the situation in Eastern Magadan, where the decline in fish stocks is much greater. Fish do not collaborate with the planned economy.

Salmon averaged 7000 tons in the middle 1960s, on a declining trend with fluctuations between 4500 and 11,000 in different years. The processing plants in this area handle some of the fish taken by the Maritime and Sakhalin fleets; until recently the offshore catch was mostly handled directly by the alongshore villages but now larger vessels are introduced, supplying local factory-type plants and leading to an increase in the export of fish to other provinces. Longer-range operations are extending, but in this sub-region the necessity is also improvement of processing, as the bulk of the fish is still heavily salted, little being canned, dried or smoked.

In this sub-region there are seven collective and five State farms, subsidiary farming units and an Agricultural Experiment Station. One of the State farms specialises in reindeer-keeping; this and the collectives are manned by indigenous people. Four of the State farms, also most of the subsidiary enterprises, are suburban producers for the towns. The rest are mainly for fishing, mixed with fur-farming, hunting, stockraising and potato and vegetable growing. The results for potatoes are almost negligible; vegetables can hardly be got to grow at all in this climate. The frost-free period of the year on the coast is 75 days. 90 per cent of the small crop of potatoes in the Province comes from the Magadan area, representing only about 80 per cent of that area's own requirements. The yield in 1959-63 averaged just over 8 tons per hectare per year. In vegetables, the Magadan area produces only 22 per cent of the Province's total and only

56 per cent of its own needs. Nevertheless it sends a large proportion of its output of both potatoes and vegetables to the upper Kolyma – chiefly the former, as the mining areas are increasingly producing vegetables for themselves – and imports large quantities from other Provinces of the S.F.E. The production of fresh milk is far below the local requirements.

Fur farming has been developed since 1952 with mink, blue fox and silver fox on both State and collective farms, which are cheaply fed on fish-waste and scraps, also on seal-meat, etc. Reindeer are an important means of livelihood in this area also (the reindeer population is about 80 per cent of the human population), though not so numerous as in Chukotia at the eastern end of the Province (where the numbers of reindeer are nearly nine times the number of human beings). The Magadan area accounts, however, for only 10 per cent of the total output of furs in the Province.

THE KOLYMA GOLDFIELDS

The upper Kolyma basin is probably the richest goldfield in the Soviet Union. Most of the workings are served by the main highway from Magadan into Yakutia, but the 'loop' track (*trassa*) cutting across the great bend in this highway between Atka and Debin is also to be noted – though it does not figure on many maps – as it serves the important Ten'kinski district (Ust' Omchug). This Kolyma sub-region contains no less than 41 per cent of the population of the whole Province, in a small fraction of its area: almost all in the mining settlements and transport posts, in deep valleys between steep mountains. These are largely forested with larch up to about 1200 metres (though the rise from the valleys to the adjacent heights is more usually about 400 metres). The valleys, though actually colder than the heights in winter, are sheltered from the strong winds which make the higher places very unpleasant. The work of keeping the road clear of snow every year requires a heroic effort.

Prospectors made the first gold-strike in 1926 on the Srednekan river. That was still in the NEP period when individual enterprise was allowed, but the State organisation *Soyuzzoloto* stepped in (1928) and operated the whole Kolyma field. By

1934 the Kolyma goldfields' output already exceeded that of the Aldan fields in Yakutia. From then until the death of Stalin, all these areas were worked largely by the wretched political prisoners. The construction of the highway in the 1930s gave an enormous stimulus. Output reached a maximum in 1940, but had fallen by 1956 to only about half.[1]

The great increase in the 1930s was due to the opening of many new workings: from 1928 to 1959, 1200 alluvial and 150 underground in this whole area (including the Indigirka gold-fields as well as the Kolyma). Notable among these are the extremely good alluvial centres of Malo-At-Churyaksk, Khaty-naksk, Chai-ur'insk, Omchak, Shturmovsk and Mal'd'yaksk. These were so prodigious that they furnished about two and a half times as much gold, in a quarter of a century, as the Bodaibo fields on the Lena in Yakutia.

Later, however, the richer alluvia were worked out, the gold content in the sands steadily fell. The range of working con-stantly extended into the mountains but diminishing returns were obvious, the average gold content sharply falling, espe-cially from 1951 to 1955. Ever since 1932 all gold-working had been very strictly a State monopoly. From 1957, however, in the turn away from Stalinism, personal prospecting was again permitted: 11 or 12 per cent of the output of gold in the last few years is recorded as provided by *starateli*, i.e. individual operators. In 1963 nineteen workings were functioning on the upper Kolyma; still very predominantly alluvial, though the ore-mining operations increased. The latter have throughout played only a very minor part; from the first opening of gold mining on the Kolyma to 1959 alluvial gold accounted for 97·4 per cent of the output, in 1963 still 94·8 per cent. This is because even the best underground workings, such as the Matrosov mine, provide ore with a low metal content; the poorer ones furnish very low-grade ore. Recently great efforts have been made to raise the technical level of extraction.

In terms of the amount of bedrock and sands processed, in former years at the height of the productivity underground material represented as much as 30 to 45 per cent; in 1960 it had fallen to 13 per cent, because bulldozers, mechanical shovellers and conveyor belts had been much more extensively brought into use to strip the top-layers of 'peat' (as the topsoil

is called locally) which contain gold-bearing sands, over the
areas of the older underground workings, i.e. more (and improved) surface working is being widely introduced over the
old shaft-workings. For in the old days all places with an overlay
of 'peat' more than four metres deep were worked by digging
below it. Nowadays the topsoil is worked from the surface to
depths of twelve metres by clearing it with bulldozers; methods
of thawing out the permafrost are also increasingly applied. By
1959, it was reported, 19 million cubic metres of earth had
been thus bulldozered off – already 85 per cent of the relevant
material of this kind. This might indicate that the limits of this
handling had been nearly reached; but the percentage may
relate to the surface area of only the old underground workings,
this technique being presumably greatly extensible in new areas.

Dredging remains much more important, in any case, than
topsoil processing. The Kolyma fields are well equipped nowadays with efficient mobile electric dredges, assembled locally;
these account for no less than 70 per cent of the output of gold.
The first dredges appeared on the Kolyma in 1950. By 1963
there were seventeen electric dredges at work, fitted with 210-
litre scoops. Six of these were working in the Susuman district
(on the Berelekh, Chai-Ur'e, Lesser At-Uryakh and Chel'ban
rivers), four on the Omchak river (Ten'kinsk district) and three
in the Yagodnoe district (on the Debin, Burkhal and Greater
At-Uryakh rivers). They provide the lowest-cost gold, though
they are extremely hampered by permafrost, so this method
will be concentrated on henceforward. Great attention is being
given to methods of thawing the ground. Though there is no
firm evidence as to the exact methods, it is stated that already
5 or 6 million cubic metres of earth or sandy mud are thawed
by mechanical means every year; and that as much as 40 per
cent of the output of gold from the Kolyma fields now comes
from that mass of defrosted material.

Hydraulic (slurry) methods are, however, officially stated to
be comparatively poorly developed or applied; because the
streams in flood are too swift or have too great a head of water,
but also because the local cost of electric power is extremely
high. The operation of dredges with chains of buckets and the
like is comparatively economical, but the application of heavy
power units to build up counter-pressure to the current and

the depth of water and to operate lifting gear is prohibitive. Nevertheless such appliances have come into quite wide use since 1961.

Another great difficulty is the seasonality of the operations. There is water for the dredges' proper operation and for hydraulic purposes generally only for 150 to 160 days a year (from the 15 or 20 May till the beginning of October). Indeed in that period there may be too much rather than too little water – though the dredges are usually working fifty or sixty days longer than that. One reason for all the working of topsoil and the continuance of underground working in cases where it is intrinsically less profitable is the availability of surplus labour in the rest of the year.

Some mines and workings have closed, but some new ones are constantly opening. Between 1932 and 1955, 69 alluvial workings and four mines were closed. The official line is that all these were replaced by new ventures, while output is in any case constantly raised by technical progress and rationalisation. The number of workings was 40 per cent greater in 1963 than in 1957. Some of the new ventures are dated by their names, e.g. Semiletka (Seven-Year Plan) and Sorok Let Oktyabr'ya (40th anniversary of the Revolution). Others bear place names, e.g. Burkand'ya and Adygalakh in Susuman district. The Kurchatov mine may be named after V. I. Kurchatov, the eminent scientist.

The 'shifting' or mobile operations naturally involve a different 'infrastructural' pattern of investment and organisation (with shanty-type removable dwellings, etc.) from the more permanent ones (with capital more literally 'fixed').

It is difficult to know what the balance between all these forces is, but clearly this is a very important and copious gold-mining area. A few of the oldest alluvial stretches, worked out in the early days of the Kolyma gold-rush, are being restarted with new dredges and new techniques. This movement is officially noted to be carrying the 'centre of gravity' of the fields towards the westward, from the upper Kolyma to the upper Indigirka. With the road connection to Aldan, the western Magadan gold industry is 'gravitating' towards the Lena and Yakutia. It was proposed in the 1960s to build a railway joining Khandyga (on the Aldan about 300 km east of Yakutsk) with

Kadykchan (in the Susuman district of Magadan Province) and these goldfields.

Equipment of existing ventures and provision for new ventures is rapidly accomplished; on the supply side, this industry is well organised. The provision of capital and labour, though not without serious difficulties, is relatively ahead of the availability of land in the economist's sense. That is to say, new deposits of gold are being eagerly sought in this area, because equipment could easily, rapidly and profitably be brought to work on them with quick returns. Hence the continuing pressure to make further prospecting the main outlay priority. The question is, what are the prospects of anything but diminishing returns from the factor land? Though the deposits are numerous, most of them have to be classified as small or medium, practically none are large. Some of the major alluvial deposits remain still not fully worked out; other deposits are buried under strata which have been frozen hard for thousands of years.

The technology available makes it most immediately advantageous now to rework first, by dredges and hydraulic plant, the dumps and residues in the older mining areas. For the development of new areas (which will be small and scattered, though numerous) it is now necessary to build up a 'complex' or network of more solid and permanent settlements and infrastructural facilities. This is being done; the settlements are being energetically modernised and consolidated. The main new 'frontiers' for this include as longer-term prospects the areas of the upper Omolon river, the basin of the Stolbovaya (a right-bank tributary of the Kolyma, where panning operations began in 1960) and the middle reaches of the Korkodon river; also the Taigonos peninsula far to the eastward.

There are other minerals in the area. Deposits of mercury remain untapped. Tin was formerly of some importance on the upper Kolyma. Between 1937 and 1957 forty small tin deposits (seventeen mines and thirteen alluvial workings) were used at various times but on a declining trend, all of them being closed by 1957. In the mid-1960s there was only one mine working, north-east of the gold belt at Omsukchan more than 400 km north-east of Magadan; it has a concentration plant and an electric power station, with a coal mine producing thirty or forty thousand tons of lignite a year. There are a score of small but rich deposits of tin in the Omsuchkan district, which is connected by a road from Gerba with the main Magadan highway, so that this activity may be revived in future.

Electric power is furnished by the Arkagala plant, the largest in the North-East (established 1955: 50,000 kW). This is fed by coal from a few mines 10-50 km distant, producing about a million tons a year of hard coal. Power lines of 110 and 35 kW almost 2000 km long carry this station's current to the whole of the Kolyma and Indigirka mining areas, but there is urgent need both to increase the capacity and to extend the grid. Another requirement is more repair and workshop capacity. The principal centres for this are Spornoe (automobile shops), Orokutan and Yagodnoe (general machine shops). The Orokutan installation includes the only open-hearth furnace in the North-East. All these were to be remodelled and reorganised on new bases of specialisation in the later 1960s.

Timber is a basic requirement for housing and the mines. Woods grow in very narrow strips along the rivers, providing poor quality material. Each hectare bears on the average 57 cubic metres ripe for cutting, but only 10 cubic metres of this is good lumber. The total annual output is less than 200,000 cubic metres and sharply declining, as the woodlands near the mines are exhausted. Timber costs a fantastic price on the local market – up to 40 roubles per cubic metre. Not surprisingly, it is being replaced by other building materials. Timber is fetched great distances, especially from the Indigirka basin; the average haul is 500 km. There is only one processing enterprise. The main utilisable reserves are on the upper Kulu (near the western border) and a number of other streams outlying the mining centres. The forests throughout Magadan Province are badly deteriorated, the problem of their regeneration has not been tackled. The Indigirka contains reserves which may provide the Kolyma until about 1980; thereafter timber may have to come from the Aldan and the Lena. Meanwhile the places producing cement blocks and the like, the brickworks at Arkagala and the limestone worked at Mylga are important. The Kolyma sub-region itself lacks suitable clay for bricks. The production of pressed blocks from slag materials is being developed locally. It is planned ultimately to set up a limestone-processing works on the upper Lyglytakh river with an annual capacity of about a hundred thousand tons.

Agriculture is weakly developed; only 40 per cent of the necessary vegetables and 15 or 20 per cent of the fresh milk are produced locally. Almost no potatoes are grown, they are killed by the frosts which occur even in summer. Some hardy types of cabbage do slightly better. The main villages are mining centres with populations between 500 and 1000. Under these, small offshoot mining and prospecting encampments of a temporary nature proliferate as the search for gold expands. Some last for ten or fifteen years and attain a population of 300 or more; at the other extreme some are mere bivouacs. The transport centres have larger populations – between two and five thousand. Such are Palatka, Atka, Myakit, Strelka, Berelyokh, Spornoe, Neksikan and the frankly named Transportny. In the agricultural aspect there are only some minor reindeer and dairy or vegetable collectives and State farms. The district administrative centres, performing also some or all of the economic functions, are of course the largest townships, ranging from Omsukchan with only 3500 inhabitants to Susuman with 12,000. Ust' Omchug, Yagodnoe and Seimchan have numbers between those figures. In this group may be included Orotukan, a repair centre for mining equipment. Most of these have modern two-storey stone buildings. Talaya is a sanatorium.

In sum, the whole Kolyma and Indigirka region is a rich goldfield, a main source of wealth for the Soviet Union, working under complex and strenuous conditions of development: from the Russian point of view, another possession that is by no means an expendable wasteland, but distinctly to be held and developed.

CHUKOTIA: THE FARTHEST EAST

The same applies, with increasing strength as time passes, to the rest of Magadan Province. Politically all this is designated as the Chukchi National Area (*Chukotski Natsional'ny Okrug*). It is an expanse of almost 738,000 sq. km, i.e. 61 per cent of Magadan Province (of which it is part) and about the same size as the state of Texas – some 60 per cent larger than its

American neighbour Alaska – but contains only 97,000 people (not much more than a third of the population of Alaska). The capital Anadyr has 6000 inhabitants. 75 per cent of the population is urban: that is to say, in urban-type or village settlements. This National District was designated as such in 1930, whereas Magadan achieved the status of a Province only in 1953. The Chukchi are not the only indigenous race, there are Evenki and Yakuts too, but altogether they are a minority. They are mainly in the eastern part facing Alaska, in the Chukotian peninsula and along the Anadyr coast. From the economic point of view especially, the whole area divides into the two following sub-regions.

THE CENTRAL NORTH OF MAGADAN PROVINCE

The area of the Chaun bay on the north coast of Magadan, the basin of the Greater and Lesser Anyui rivers and part of the Omolon basin constitute one economic sub-region. It contains 11 per cent of the population of Magadan Province; 85 per cent of its people are 'urban' dwellers. This is another area of mining development, on the age-old background of the reindeer, hunting and fishing economy of the bare tundra. The Chaun mining area has the tin mine of Krasnoarmeisk ('Red Army') served by the Val'kumei concentrating plant near Pevek; also the Komsomol goldfield, on the eastern side of Chaun bay, connected by a motor road with the port of Pevek. Around these are three reindeer-keeping and hunting and fishing collectives of indigenous folk, plus a State reindeer farm.

Tin was discovered in this locality in 1934-6 in quantities assuring ten years' operation of the Krasnoarmeisk workings and the Val'kumei plant which were opened in 1941. Before the ten years ran out another deposit was opened. Further finds were necessary if the operation was to be continued or extended, but these have probably been made by now. The Komsomol alluvial goldfield, about 100 km further to the south-east of Pevek in the basin of the Ichuveyem river, was opened in 1958 after five years' prospecting, showing a good future.

Pevek (population 10,000) is a well-equipped port on the Northern Sea Route, with a freight turnover of more than

200,000 tons a year, mostly coal and timber. The provision of coal to this sub-region is a great problem; it has to be brought from Zyryanka in Yakutia, from Ugol'naya (Anadyr) in eastern Magadan, from Sakhalin, sometimes even from the Maritime Province – chiefly to keep the power station going at Pevek, on which all the mining activities depend. It would obviously be most economical to use only Zyryanka as the source, although it is in the upper reaches of the Kolyma, so special efforts are made in that direction. The timber is mostly brought from even greater distances from places right up the Lena.

The difficulties of the Northern Sea Route are great. Even in the short open season masses of pack ice, frozen for many years, may obstruct the port of Pevek and ice may block the Aion Island at the north-western end of the Chaun bay. There is another 'ice-jam' place far to the west at Cape Chelyuskin, the northernmost point of the Siberian mainland, though similar difficulties may arise on any part of the route. The Lena mouth area is, however, comparatively free of blockage by ice.

The goldfield on the middle reaches of the Anyui river was opened in 1959. By 1964 three workings were in operation, named Bilibino (after a famous Soviet prospector), 'The 22nd Party Congress Field' and Aliskerovo; the last-mentioned had the first dredge to be operated in Chukotia, a second one should have been added by 1970 and the area extended. A rough summer road, later to be rendered usable all the year round, has been made from the Bilibino mine to a site near the mouth of the Kolyma (350 km away) which is to be developed as a new port. A motor road is also being made to Pevek and electricity is being supplied from that port. It is hoped to obtain wolfram and mercury as well as gold. Bilibino was founded in 1960 and its population reached 12,000 in 1967.

Much more striking developments were to follow between Chaun Bay and the mouth of the Kolyma. A port for the latter is to be developed at Nizhnie Kresty (this offensively non-Communist name, 'Crosses', being changed to Cherski in 1963). At Zeleny Mys a floating electric generator was moored in 1969, using coal from Zyryanka (output 150,000 tons a year). Before the end of the 1960s a power line was to join this with Pogyndan, Bilibino, Boronikha and Pevek. An airfield at Keperveyem on the little Anyui serves the Bilibino area, which is also connected to Zeleny Mys by a road-track, usable at least in winter. The next and most dramatic move was to erect an atomic power plant at Bilibino, to come into operation in 1970.

This sub-region accounts for 20 per cent of the Province's output of furs, mainly white fox. The sable became extinct in this area and attempts were made from 1953-5 to reintroduce it, with results not known. There is little fur-farming, mostly shooting and trapping.

The fisheries are hardly sufficient for local requirements, with a catch of two or three hundred tons a year; 'industrial' collective operations began only in the 1960s, at the mouth of the Chaun river. The indigenous people in these parts are still nomadic, though modernisation is beginning, with such inducements as offers to supply permanent dwellings, radio stations, etc., and furnish new modes of transport such as motor-sledges and helicopters.

ANADYR': PROSPECTS OF GOLD AND OIL

Finally there is the eastern sub-region of Chukotia, that of Anadyr'. This has developed as another highly promising goldfield. Four mining enterprises were working there in the mid-1960s: the Iul'tin combine, the Amguyem river goldfields, the Anadyr' goldfields and the Bering (Ugol'naya bay) coalmines. Yet they have not had much impact on the background of the life of the indigenous people with their reindeer, fishing and hunting. The interior places are extremely isolated, with little communication between them. In the few towns there has been in the last few years some influx of Russians, over-dramatised in some accounts as a new 'gold rush'; nevertheless it must be emphasised that this is another gold-bearing area of prime importance, likely to be the next to undergo powerful development.

The main communications are in fact by sea, and these are with other Provinces rather than within Chukotia itself. Anadyr and Bering to its southward are useful ports; Egvenikot north of Anadyr' takes more part in the Northern Sea Route traffic. Most of the activities are centred on Anadyr'. Along the coasts there are some sealing and other stations. Up the Anadyr' river there is one area slightly more favourable for agriculture, which has some willow trees and succeeds in producing a few vegetables and potatoes. The lower reaches, like all the lowlands of the whole Province, are frozen swamps.

The Amguyem mining area has two neighbouring enterprises, the Iul'tin tin and wolfram combine and the Polyarny ('Polar') goldfield. The former was built in 1959 north of the Kresta bay – a modern mechanised and even automated complex, including the mine, ore-enrichment plant and repair facilities. It has a motor road to the port of Egvenikot, receives current by a high-tension line from the Ozerny electric station near there, and has developed as a modern township with 3500 inhabitants. Egvenikot has 3800 and also features two- and three-storey houses built of slag-blocks. The Polar alluvial goldfields on the Amguyem river were opened in 1963. The coal mines at Beringovski supply all these places. Their timber has, however, to be brought all the way from the southern parts of the S.F.E. Water supply was a great problem in this cold and permafrosted region, only overcome at high cost. The Iul'tin plant is scaled and equipped far above the level justified by the local availability of raw materials; prospecting is being busily extended, especially to the westwards, in connection also with the long-term plan to build a motor highway across northern Magadan Province.

Development around Anadyr' is also a primary phase. Coal has been mined on the Ugol'ny bay ('coal bay') since 1941. This is still primarily for the bunkering of ships taking the Great Northern Sea Route (referred to with respect, in this part of the world, in capital letters). The output steadily rose, recording 300,000 tons in 1963. The reserves are plentiful, the quality good (calorific value 6200). To the original single pit a second larger one was being added in the mid-1960s. Beringovski (formerly called Ugol'ny) has developed similarly to the other townships mentioned above. It produced 200,000 tons of coal in 1965. Brown coal is also mined near Anadyr, on the scale of about 70,000 tons a year for local general consumption. However, oil and natural gas exist in the Anadyr' district, which may see swift development.

Although 70 per cent of the population of this sub-region is classed as urban, the old ways of rural life are somehow more strongly surviving than in other parts of the Province, though the indigenous population is very small (about 10,000, 80 per cent of them Chukchi). 65 per cent have been loosely collectivised. The collectives specialise in taking seals and other marine animals; there are centres for this in Provideniya bay (Plover, established in 1932) and Lavrentia bay (Pinakula, established 1948), but the output is heavily declining with the numbers of walrus and seals.

The Anadyr' fisheries combine was established in the 1930s with a cannery in Anadyr and another at Maino-Pylgino. The catch was in those early days a maximum of 28,700 tons in a good year, until 1944, when a serious decline began. This reached its nadir in 1953. It is attributed by the Soviets to over-fishing by the Japanese further out to sea. The catch is now only about 1000 to 1500 tons a year, hardly sufficing for purely local needs. A long period of conservation and restriction lies ahead, with catches limited to two or three thousand tons a year.

There are eight reindeer to every human inhabitant of this sub-region (cf. eleven in western Chukotia). There is some surplus of reindeer meat. The animals are enormously useful for transport, in which activity they generate 20 to 30 per cent of the money income of the outlanders. It is a curious sight to watch bags of mail being taken from the aeroplane which brought them from Europe, to be delivered 'locally' (over hundreds of kilometres) by reindeer sledges: though there is nowadays sometimes a helicopter in the offing waiting to take over.

This sub-region accounts for no less than 40 per cent of the output of furs in Magadan Province, mostly foxes. Fur-farming began only in the 1960s. Great efforts are made to induce the indigenous tribesmen to settle around such centres. Even the capital Anadyr is still small, with a population of 6000 – but this shows an increase of 1000 in the period 1965 to 1968. There are some urban facilities, including a technical school.

Hardly any activity exists on the Bering Strait facing Alaska, or on the remote north-eastern coast. Those areas are certainly quiet and empty. Uelen, facing a place called Wales in Alaska, the farthest eastern settlement in the Soviet Union – about 1500 km farther east than Petropavlovsk in Kamchatka and roughly 2500 km farther east than Vladivostok – is interesting chiefly

for the life of its indigenous people, who resemble the North
American Eskimos. Their artistic work in carving on bone is
highly appreciated.[2]

Chukotia is far from the tension of the Chinese frontier, but
it is a rich source of gold for the Soviet Union's investment in
economic and general development, and it is a place with a life
and spirit of its own. In the consciousness of the Soviet soldier
as he faces the angry Chinese, all this is part of the fatherland
and the way of life he is ready and able strongly to defend.

CHAPTER 10

Sakhalin:
The Island Beyond Japan

THE last two chapters described the northern hinterlands Yakutia and Magadan. A much more central position is held by the island Province of Sakhalin. First in the merely locational sense: the northern end of Sakhalin is close to the mainland, almost a peninsula, while the southern end is in full communication with Vladivostok. Secondly in its development: all the Provinces of the S.F.E. have resources to offer but Sakhalin has a very special one, namely oil, besides coking coal, natural gas, other minerals, timber, fish and furs. Finally in a longer-term view Sakhalin raises especially the question of the possible relation of development in the S.F.E. to the industrial and technological giant of Asia – Japan.

The sub-heading of this chapter borrows the title but not the substance of a novel by John Paris published many years ago. The author imagined an island lying beyond Japan where the customs, culture and mannerisms were even more Japanese than in the real Japan. The scene of this satire was the sub-tropical south, quite unlike Sakhalin. The southern half of Sakhalin was, however, occupied from 1905 to 1945 by the Japanese, during which time they did not achieve spectacular development of the territory. Basic development of Sakhalin was perhaps beyond Japan's capacity; at least it was beyond Japan's inclination to give this colony much priority.

Nor have the Russians developed Sakhalin very widely or deeply. They annexed the whole island in 1853, held the northern part of it ever since, lost the southern half (up to the 50th parallel) to Japan in 1905 after the Russo-Japanese war and recovered the latter at the end of World War Two in 1945. Incidentally the Japanese forces in Sakhalin offered a far more stubborn resistance to the Soviet Army in 1945 than did their units in Manchuria. Sakhalin, called in Japanese Karafuto, was, however, a much more integral question in that period for the Japanese than for the Soviets. In Japanese militarism and fascism there was a dispute as to strategy; the Army and Navy were divided as to whether Japan should strike southwards against the European and American possessions in the southern seas, or northwards against the Soviet Union as well as in China and Manchuria, the former policy finally prevailing.

In the changed post-war conditions the Japanese do not aspire to the recovery of southern Sakhalin (only of the Kurile islands), but the trade and development interests of the area in general and of Japan in particular obviously coincide so greatly that it is not possible much longer to envisage anything but an interconnected, multilateral and mutual pattern of trade and development in this whole area, involving especially Japan. Sakhalin is one of the thresholds beyond which Japan's contribution in trade, investment or expertise can – or must – henceforward spread. For all these reasons it may be useful to bear in mind, besides the intrinsic importance of Sakhalin to the Soviet Union's internal development planning, its implications for the new relationship which is maturing with Japan.

Sakhalin is the Soviet Union's largest island. 10,500 km from Moscow, it has an area of 76,500 sq. km, a narrow strip of land 950 km long from north to south. Politically and administratively the Province of Sakhalin includes also the Kurile islands, which have a total area of 10,600 sq. km. The Kuriles are briefly described in the next chapter as part of the outer Pacific fringe of the Soviet Union; the particulars in the present chapter relate to the island of Sakhalin itself, unless otherwise indicated. Sakhalin produces good oil and coal, fish and lumber, under difficult conditions. The coast has few indentations or good harbours. Conditions differ in the various parts of the island, communications are good only in the south; sea transport is especially important. The island is moderately mountainous, in two main ranges (eastern and western), the highest elevation being 1609 metres. The north is flatter and the two ranges are divided by the marshy valleys of the Tym' and Poronai rivers in the broader middle of the island.

RESOURCES

Forest or bush covers some 50,000 sq. km or 60 per cent of the total area, but roughly a quarter of this is sparse, poor, burnt or already cut. The run-down of the forests is especially marked in the south; the Russians accuse the Japanese of unscrupulous 'plundering' of resources in the area they occupied. The prospective timber cuts are largely in the northern and central parts, representing a potential supply of 400 million cubic metres, predominantly spruce, pine and larch, with some birch and willow.

The oil wells in the north have been important for many years, yielding a good-quality light crude which is piped to Komsomolsk on the mainland where the refinery distils high fractions of benzine and kerosene; the sulphur content is low. Natural gas was recently located in the same area and should soon be similarly handled by pipeline to the mainland. The south is, however, also potentially rich in oil and gas and both are being sounded, especially in the most promising area of the west coast to the southward: around Krasnogorsk (a port in Tomari district fifty kilometres from Il'insk station), Chekhov and Gornozavodsk in Nevel'sk district.

Coal is similarly widespread but on the west coast it is good for both coke and gas, low in sulphur content and high in calorific value. On the east coast there are lignites in the Poronaisk district at Vakhrushev, Makarov and Dolinsk. There is brown coal on the west coast also at Gornozavodsk. The overall reserves total 19 billion tons, of which $1\frac{1}{2}$ billion are coking coal. Other mineral resources are gold, manganese, chromium, iron, rare metals, graphite, limestone, marble and other building stones.

The Japanese installed a useful railway system (1,000 km) in the south, on the narrow Japanese gauge with their own types of equipment. The lines run from Aniva and Korsakov, the ports in the middle of the southern end of Sakhalin, through Yuzhno-Sakhalinsk and up the east coast to Poronaisk, thence inland through the middle of the island to Tymovskoe; and more shortly on the southern part of the west coast from Gornozavodsk to Il'insk with a less efficient cross-line between Kholmsk and Yuzhno-Sakhalinsk. In the north there is a

railway from Moskal'vo to Okha and down the east coast to
Katangli. This is a narrow-gauge line; the Japanese gauge is
smaller than the European, hence much smaller than the mainland Russian, but the North Sakhalin line is only a light railway.
The gap between the two lines is a mere 150 km but the terrain
is very difficult; work is proceeding gradually to link the two
systems.

The most notable oilfields are Tungor in the Okha district,
Okha itself, Nogliki, Ekhabi (just south of Okha) and Katangli.
The output is noted in Table 3.10 above. A little natural gas
was produced from 1952. Output was reported to have been
two and a half times as great in 1958 as in 1952, 1965 production is given as 1·8 times that of 1958, but exact figures are not
disclosed. The oil pipeline to Komsomolsk on the Amur was
laid during the war; a graphic description is given in the novel
by V. Azhayev, *Far from Moscow*. Oil is, however, carried by
ships as well as by the pipeline for processing up the Amur at
Komsomolsk and at Khabarovsk. The Sakhalin supply is extremely useful but is far from meeting the needs of the S.F.E.;
and it is a weakness that the oil has to be carried so far for
refining. Fuel, lubricants and even crude oil have still to be
brought into the S.F.E. from western Russia over prodigious
distances; there is now a pipeline reaching as far east as Irkutsk.
The Komsomolsk and Khabarovsk plants do not have the
required capacity for 'deep' or catalytic processing, re-synthesis,
etc., providing only the products of direct distillation which go
mainly for fuel for the open-hearth furnaces of Amurstal',
numerous electric power stations, etc.

The output of oil in Sakhalin was to have been doubled
between 1965 and 1970, the yield of gas to have been multiplied
by six. Construction was begun in 1965 of a second oil-pipeline
from Okha to Komsomolsk, completed in 1969; and the laying
of a gas-pipeline alongside these is planned. A major 'reconstruction' of the oil and gas industry of Sakhalin is intended.
The situation where crude oil is exported and all its derivatives
imported over vast distances is irrational and irksome. The
construction of a refinery in Sakhalin is one of the planning
imperatives; together with the production of oil in other parts
of the island besides the north. Interestingly the emphasis is on
the possibility of Sakhalin supplying oil to Magadan and

Kamchatka in particular; Khabarovsk and the southern mainland can more easily depend on Tyumen' and other fields of subsequent development in central Siberia. Notable also is an increasing emphasis on the possibility of export to foreign countries, primarily Japan. However, the difficulties are very great. The drills are having to go ever deeper in North Sakhalin. The cost of production is extremely high, in respect especially of the high wages paid and the distance over which all supplies have to be fetched. The costs of prospecting, opening up new wells, testing and experiment, besides normal maintenance in this blizzard-swept land, finally of providing dwelling and communal facilities, are all inordinately high.

Coal is a much older industry in Sakhalin than oil, having started as soon as Russia gained possession of Sakhalin in the middle nineteenth century. It now accounts for 10 per cent of the Province's gross product. Most of the mining is underground but not deep (down to 300 metres). The seams are of varying thickness (0·9 to 8 metres) and the bedrock is usually broken in its configuration, while all the mines are now old; so the production conditions are not good. The largest mines do not yield more than 400,000 tons a year; moreover they do so at high cost, particularly because the mines consist typically of several disconnected pits. However the coal is of good quality, low in ash content, gaseous and long-burning. The output of coking coal is about one and a half million tons altogether, other coals 3·2 million tons. The costs in coal mining, as in all other branches of industry in Sakhalin, are the highest anywhere in the S.F.E. Cost levels in the mining of lignite coal at the Lermontov open cut at Vakhrushev (output 0·7 million tons in 1965) are significantly cheaper than at the underground pits.

There are dressing plants at four places which handle about a third of the whole output, achieving a reduction in the ash content to between 12 and 9 per cent. Between 1946 and 1961 the total annual output of coal rose from 2·4 to 4·3 million tons, but then remained static for the next five or six years. Besides catering for local needs the Sakhalin coal is sent to Kamchatka and Magadan and there are limited occasional exports to foreign countries. Major development of the hard coal industry of Sakhalin is not envisaged; partly for the reasons already indicated, also because of the turnover of shipping, hitherto the main consumer, to oil fuel. The possibilities of exporting coking coal and other high-grade coal are, however, very much in mind; for which, as in the case of oil, the conditions are the extension of mining into some new areas, the reorganisation, technical re-equipment and rationalisation of the industry and last but not least the reduction of costs. Meanwhile lignite production is to be raised (though this depends on the same conditions) to supply the Province's own fuel needs, principally for its electric plants.

Also substantially established (thanks originally to the Japanese) and experienced (if obsolescent) is the paper and pulp industry. It accounts for one-sixth of the Province's gross product, with an output of various kinds of paper (204,000 tons in 1963, 213,000 in 1965, or about 8 per cent of the whole production of the U.S.S.R.), cardboard, cellulose, ethyl alcohol, etc. Between 1952 and 1963 the production of pulp and paper increased 150 per cent. In 1965, besides the 213,000 tons of paper, there was an output of 271,000 tons of cellulose or pulp and 26,000 tons of cardboard. This was exported to many parts of the Soviet Union and to some extent abroad. The plants are all in the south: at Poronaisk, Makarov, Dolinsk, Kholmsk, Chekhov, Uglegorsk and Tomari. Some of these are on navigable rivers, down which their lumber is easily floated; but the upstream forests were severely cut (by the Japanese previously, the Russians insist). The mills are acutely short of material, which comes largely from the north of the island; so the development of lumbering in the central part is an important question.

The regeneration of forestry generally is a major issue in Sakhalin. This industry accounts for another 6 per cent of the gross product of Sakhalin. It supplies pitprops, cooperage and building material to the good markets within the Province of the mining, fishing and construction industries, besides the paper industry. Exports ran in the 1950s at around 3·3 or 3·4 million cubic metres a year, which is distinctly less than in 1945 or in the pre-war period (exports in 1936 were 5·6 million, but that was in excess of the natural growth in the year). The forests are recuperating, especially in the central part of the island; but the next assault is being prepared there, with the construction of the railway between Pobedino and Nysh. Meanwhile the restoration of the timber-stock in the south is being energetically pursued; but this will be a long process. At the same time suggestions are being made for rationalisation by redistributing the plant capacity. In this industry also, wages and other costs are high, the problem is complicated.

Sakhalin's fisheries secure one-fifth of the S.F.E.'s total catch. Until recently the activity was mainly in nearby waters; two-thirds of the catch was herring, the rest cod, flatfish, salmon and sea-perch. Offshore in the south-east of the island crabs and marine plants (principally sea kale) were taken. Sealing is a minor occupation. In recent years the offshore activities have greatly declined, owing chiefly to the reductions in the numbers of herring and salmon; while 'expeditionary' fishing has greatly increased, penetrating widely into the Japan, Okhotsk and Bering Seas and the Pacific Ocean, so that it now accounts for three-quarters of the catch. The equipment of the industry has been modernised accordingly; most of the landings are from large fishing and transporting vessels.

In 1961 there were six fish combines and three fish-processing plants on the coasts of Sakhalin, three processing plants and two whaling bases in the Kuriles. The headquarters of the Sakhalin Trawler Fleet Administration is in Nevel'sk, that of the Ocean Fishing and Marine Animals Fleet in Kholmsk. These two organisations handle between them 70 per cent of Sakhalin's catch, also process some of the catches brought in by fleets based in the Maritime Province or elsewhere. Their installations include canneries, refrigeration plant, fish-oil and meal factories, together with wharfing and repair facilities. There are also twenty-four fish-breeding stations in Sakhalin, working hard to restock the seas and rivers with salmon. However, the general transformation of the industry to the basis of operation by 'floating factories' reduces the function of the shore-bases and especially the smaller ports; there is already a considerable concentration of processing in Vladivostok and Nakhodka.

CONDITIONS

The Province's building and consumer-goods industries are

hardly significant; in these categories procurements are very largely from the mainland. Such industries may develop to some extent, if they can compete in cost with mainland produce, when the transport network is developed as intended. Besides the central railway, the creation of a trunk route or routes throughout the island is envisaged. The provision of a cross-line from Il'insk at the narrowest part of the island to Arsentievka is a current project, a line from Nogliki to Al'ba another. Moreover a railway link with the mainland is not a distant prospect. Two alternative train-ferry routes have been studied and experimental crossings made; one is across the narrowest part of the strait between Pogibi and Lazarev, the other between Kholmsk and Sovietskaya Gavan'. Meanwhile there are considerable air and sea connections with the mainland.

The agricultural conditions are poor and difficult: there is the pattern now familiar to the reader, of an output of potatoes, vegetables, eggs and meat broadly inadequate even for local needs. The sown area in 1964 totalled only 31,000 ha, half of which was under potatoes, 10 per cent under vegetables, the rest for fodder roots and grasses. Cattle numbered nearly 46,000 head, of which 25,000 were cows. The milk-yield per cow was about 2400 kg a year; the Province was fairly self-sufficient in milk. Pigs numbered 82,000, poultry about 1·2 million. There are reindeer in the north, but only in small numbers (about 14,000 head in 1964). The market gardens around the towns seem more efficient than those in the remoter parts of the mainland and will continue to be a main source of food. There are some fur-farms, which serve local needs and export mink.

The population totalled 110,000 in 1940. At that time the Japanese, in possession of the south, treated Sakhalin largely as a seasonal habitat, comparatively large numbers of them coming to work there only in the summer. They were mostly repatriated immediately after the war, though a number spent years of imprisonment in Siberia. The population rose by 1959 to 649,400 – much higher than it was in the 'Japanese period', but then declined between 1959 and 1965 to 611,000. Many emigrated, seeing better opportunities on the mainland. 80 per cent of the people are urban and a large proportion are in industrial and transport employment. Industry in Sakhalin had meanwhile been mechanised and rationalised, in response to the high costs and wage rates and to some of the constraints noted above. In 1968 the population was given as 639,000. These figures relate to the whole Province, including the Kuriles – which contained 14,400 people in 1959.

The density in Sakhalin Province is thus 7·2 persons per square kilometre; in the S.F.E. only the Maritime Province has a higher overall density. The urbanised areas in the south have a much higher ratio, around 20 persons to the square kilometre; but in the rural areas of the south the figure is still low, at about 5. The central part of the island has an overall density of less than 5 and a rural density little over 2; in the north the urban density is also 5 but the rural figure sinks to less than 1. The Kuriles return a density of 2.

Russians greatly predominate, with about 80 per cent of the population in 1959, followed by Ukrainians over 7 per cent, White Russians 2 per cent, Tartars 2 per cent and Mordvinians nearly 2 per cent. The indigenous 'northern peoples' were given as only 2500 altogether – mostly the nomadic Nivkhi who counted 1798, plus 349 Evenki and 190 Nanaitsy. These are reindeer-keepers and hunters in the north.

Four clearly marked internal regions are distinguished within the island: the south, the west, the centre and the north.

DEVELOPMENT IN THE SOUTH

The south contains the administrative districts of Aniva, Tomari, Makarov, Korsakov, Nevel'sk and Dolinsk, besides the Provincial capital Yuzhno-Sakhalinsk. This is the area of considerable development inherited from the Japanese. The climate, especially in the western part of this sub-region, is somewhat milder than in the rest of the island; the winters are snowy (to a depth over one metre in places) but the ports in the area of Kholmsk are not ice-bound. The summers are comparatively long, moist and warm; a precipitation of 600 to 800 mm is evenly divided throughout the seasons. The peaty soil is marshy under the surface. Most of the area is mountainous, extensively wooded with spruce, pine and broad-leaved trees. There is good pasturage only in the river valleys. The transport links with the mainland (Vladivostok, Nakhodka and Vanino) are good, with regular services to and from Kholmsk, Nevel'sk and Korsakov, to which a full train-ferry between Kholmsk and Vanino (Sovietskaya Gavan') should be added.

Agriculture is – in purely relative terms – comparatively well favoured in the south by the warmer climate. The farmed area is only about 60,000 ha, but this is about half the total for the whole island. The sown area is 12,000 ha, just under 40 per cent of the island's total; it is mainly under potatoes (6500 ha) and vegetables (1500). Some areas (especially the Tomari plain) are comparatively good for livestock; most of the island's cattle population, which is only in the order of 10,000, is in this sub-region. Priority is however given to extending the market-garden and poultry types of production; especially by land-drainage, involving the abandonment of some of the uneconomic pasturage rather than an expansion of grazing. The target is the usual modest one of 'supplying the needs of the local population in vegetables, potatoes, meat and milk products'.

Fisheries are, however, a major activity, in which there is much more than local self-sufficiency. The southern sub-region accounts for no less than 70 per cent of the output of fisheries products in the whole Province. There are processing plants in Kholmsk, Chekhov, Korsakov, Starodubovski (Dolinsk) and other places. In manufacturing industries – partly the provision of shipping and general repair and maintenance workshops and the like for fishing and transport – the southern sub-region has a relatively prominent position, accounting for more than half the manufacturing output of the Province.

Apart from metal-working, particularly the ship-repairs and fisheries equipment, there are service industries or light industries, food and building materials, in which the southern sub-region furnishes some 60 per cent of the Province's small gross product, from the towns of Yuzhno-Sakhalinsk, Kholmsk, Nevel'sk, Korsakov and Dolinsk, where these activities will continue to grow. The reconstruction and extension of the ship-repair facilities was planned for the later 1960s, with distinct 'overspill' effects on manufacturing generally. These facilities are in Kholmsk and Nevel'sk to a lesser extent (where it is, in Soviet parlance, on the level of 'factories' or single-plant organisation) and on a slightly larger scale at Korsakov.

The outstanding industry is, however, pulp and paper; 70 per cent of the Province's output in this branch of industry is in the southern sub-region. The largest combine is at Dolinsk, lesser ones at Makarov, Kholmsk, Chekhov and Tomari. There is a carton and box factory at Korsakov. All these are fairly substantial works, profitable in some lines of production; but they face difficulties on two sides. One acute embarrassment is the shortage of good material for paper-making, the supply of which is less than the installed capacity. On the other hand the plants have worked to some extent on making boxes, vats, etc., for the fishing industry; with the exhaustion of off-shore fish-stocks and the turnover of the fishing industry to pelagic and 'floating cannery' or refrigerator-ship operations, also to giving more attention to shellfish and marine plants, this demand is abating. Moreover the supply of wood may be inadequate, even in such lower-grade materials; despite the fact that the southern sub-region yields about a quarter of the Province's output of timber, the stock is somewhat deteriorated, the quality rather low. Some plants face closure for this reason. The power supply has been unsatisfactory, but a new electric station at Yuzhno-Sakhalinsk will greatly improve the situation.

Of the nineteen major towns in Sakhalin, with a total population of 350,000, ten are in southern Sakhalin, with a population of 250,000. The largest is Yuzhno-Sakhalinsk (South Sakhalin), the administrative and cultural centre since 1945, when the Soviets made it the capital of the whole Province; previously, when the Russians had only the northern part, their administration was at Alexandrovsk on the west coast. It had a population of 93,000 in 1968, showing a slight increase over the preceding few years. It is connected by rail with Kholmsk (87 km), hence with the west-coast line; and is on the east-coast railway southward to Korsakov (39 km with a branch line to Aniva) and northward all the way to Poronaisk and Tymov-skoe. There are some roads following the course of these railways.

Yuzhno-Sakhalinsk has locomotive and waggon repair shops, machine shops, a factory making rubber and leather footwear, another for furniture, a building materials plant, a brewery and a distillery. The town stands on level ground in the valley of the Susui river under hills of the same name. Soviet-style modernisation did not proceed rapidly, in its physical aspects, in the first two post-war decades; but stone buildings on wide streets now predominate over the little old Japanese houses. Curiously, in the outward and immediately visible aspect, South Sakhalin is still reminiscent, especially architecturally, of parts of Taipei or Seoul, former provincial cities in other one-time Japanese colonies, rather than of Russia. A Russian from Sakhalin arriving at Hakodate in Hokkaido remarked that Hakodate looked more Russian than Sakhalin – because it had a large old Russian church on its skyline. Among the buildings in Yuzhno-Sakhalinsk are the Science Research institute of the Siberian Branch of the Academy of Sciences of the U.S.S.R. (A local witticism some years ago was that this name was longer than the building itself, but that was not literally true and the work has greatly advanced since then.) There is also an Institute of Education and the appropriate array of middle and junior schools.

The other towns are less significant in size and in industrial output, but have developed in various ways of which they are reasonably proud. The second centre is Korsakov, the port on the Aniva bay; population 34,300, occupied in ship repairs and fisheries. Nevel'sk may perhaps be given third place. It has a population of 21,000 engaged in similar activities. The port does not freeze in winter and is the base for the trawler fleet. Kholmsk to the north of Nevel'sk has a larger population (37,400) and is another major ice-free port, the base for the seiner and sealing fleets, with ship-repair facilities also for the shipping to the mainland. Kholmsk has a paper-pulp mill, a ferro-concrete plant and a cannery. The wharves are equipped with mobile cranes.

The remaining towns, smaller in population, are mainly based on the wood-pulp industry. One of these is Chekhov, named after the great Russian writer. In his day Sakhalin was being developed as a Tsarist penal colony, under heinous conditions touching the liberal conscience in Russia and beyond. This matter lay deep in the heart of Anton Pavlovich Chekhov and, just before he was reaching the high flow of his career, he ful-filled a long-standing intention by setting off on his own account to travel all across Siberia to Sakhalin, to observe and report on the conditions there. At that time he had published, of his major works, only the *Motley Stories* and the play *Ivanov*. This journey was made in 1890; it is described in Chekhov's book *The Island of Sakhalin*, not easily available in translation. This travelogue is most interesting as a mixture of his dry-point descriptive style on the one hand, replete with his characteristic power of observing and conveying personality; and on the other of the attempt to produce a systematic report in the style of a Blue Book or Fabian tract, the result of which has been described as a treatise in medical ethnography. This aspect of Chekhov's life has been too little considered; he returned from Sakhalin with his health impaired; and went on, in an accelerated maturity, to produce his first success *The Sea Gull* (1896), thereafter *Uncle Vanya*, *The Three Sisters*, *The Cherry Orchard* and the rest.

The contemporary town of Chekhov on the Gulf of Tartary, with a population of 9000 (sometimes referred to, after the writer's own pen-name and nickname, as Chekhonte) has for its most distinguishing feature a wood-pulp factory. In the near-by village of Baikovo there is a fisheries combine. Tomari further north on the same railway is a similar place, with a population of 9500. Its paper-pulp factory is better supplied than most others with raw materials from local sources which reach it directly by water. Timber is worked at the village settlement of Il'insk at the northern end of this railway.

Dolinsk on the other side of the island, with a population of 15,100, has more variegated activities; it has a machine shop and nearby are the mines of hard coal at Bykovo and the fish-processing plant at Starodubskoe. Makarov further up the east coast (population 12,600) has another paper-pulp factory, also comparatively well supplied from two forestry combines in the vicinity and has a production of building materials; more importantly perhaps, Makarov is a centre of hard coal production from the mines of Vakhrushev and Gorny.

COAL AND TIMBER IN THE WEST

The western sub-region comprises the administrative districts of Uglegorsk and Alexandrovsk, in the western mountain range, which runs at heights of seven to nine hundred metres and is rich in minerals. The slopes are forested with spruce and pine up to seven or eight hundred metres above sea level, though bare at higher points. The coastline is steep or even precipitous, offering little accommodation to ships, though broken by numerous rivers and streams. This sub-region has one-eighth of the area of the island, with 20 per cent of its population (i.e. 125,000 people) of whom 75 per cent are classed as urban. Its products are hard coal, lumber and paper pulp. The coal includes the particularly valuable coking coal, but the position of the industry as a whole is complicated. Magadan Province used to be the principal consumer of coal mined in this and other parts of Sakhalin, but that and other Provinces are now developing cheaper supplies locally. A revision or restructuring of the mining in Sakhalin is called for, with a new emphasis on the development and export of the coking coal of the western sub-region.

This sub-region furnishes more than one-sixth of the gross industrial product of the Province. The main contributor to this has been coal, but neither its share nor its absolute amount has been growing – because the mining is carried on at high cost. The sub-region is well covered with forest and accounts, in terms of *worked* timber, for 40 per cent of the Province's output; this is the industry with the best prospects of immediate development, especially with the impending completion of the railway between Pobedino and Nysh.

The most important town is Alexandrovsk, the former capital of the Province, on the coast south of the northern end of the western mountain range. The mountains on the east and south-east protect the town from the winds from that direction, though it is very open on the north and north-west. Ships are loaded and unloaded in the offing, open to cold winds and winter ice. The population is 21,400. Building materials are produced and there are some service industries. There are coal mines in the area, at the villages of Mgachi, Oktyabr'ski, Arkovo and Khoe. Khoe also has considerable forestry. Tel'novski, Lopatino and Shaktersk ('Miner's Town') similarly have both coal and lumber. The usual minor agricultural activity has developed around these townships. The entire sown area is a little over 7000 ha, mainly under potatoes and vegetables, but there are another 13,000 ha suitable for agriculture, which it is hoped to use to raise the current output of potatoes, vegetables and fodder by 200 or 250 per cent. There is little else to relate concerning the western sub-region.

THE UNDEVELOPED CENTRE

The administrative districts of Poronai, Smirnykh and Tymovskoe in the great triangular valley of the Poronai river are designated as the central sub-region. The influence of the sea is screened by mountains on both sides so the climate is more extreme than in any other part of the island; the winters are colder, the summers warmer, it is windy and foggy. The podzol soil is marshy. The uplands are covered with firs and pines on their higher slopes, with larch lower down.

This inhospitable area represents one-third of the island's surface but is very lightly populated, with 86,000 people or 14 per cent of the Province's total; and there is in this sub-region a reversal of the usual situation of a predominance of 'urban' population, as 60 per cent of the inhabitants live in villages or rural locations. The agricultural area is considerable, at 30,000 ha, of which no less than 9000 is tilled, 7500 sown, 3600 under potatoes, 500 under vegetables. This is one of the areas in which it is hoped to achieve moderate extension of agriculture in the nearer future. The actual contributions of this sub-region to Sakhalin's gross product are 40 per cent of the forestry output, 20 per cent of the paper-pulp, but in overall industrial terms only 10 per cent. This is, however, the area most likely to benefit from the new railway which will traverse it from south to north. Meanwhile it has the one significant town of Poronai (population 22,900), lying on the existing railway on the shores of a bay which is perhaps appropriately named Terpenie – i.e. 'Patience' or 'Endurance' – though Poronai has already a cement factory, as well as the paper-pulp mill and fisheries combines.

THE NORTHERN OILFIELDS

Last but not least there is the northern sub-region, still somewhat separate, comprising the administrative districts of Nogliki and Okha. This is separated from the mainland only by a narrow and shallow channel – so unimpressive that the early explorers did not perceive it and did not think Sakhalin was an island. The climate of this northern oilfield area is severe, with long cold winters, strong winds or blizzards, short and chilly summers. The swampy soil is poor in everything but oil. This is mostly flat country sparsely overgrown with larch, but bushes and lichens are more characteristic of its tundra quality.

It has a little more than a quarter of the area of the island, but a population of only about 60,000 (10 per cent of the Province's total) of whom 44,000 are in townships or town-like settlements connected with the oil industry. New prospecting is continued energetically, as the need to reduce the high cost of production is urgent. The work is not very adequately served by the narrow-gauge railway, which connects the main town Okha with the port of Moskal'vo on the north-east coast and the east coast to Nogliki. There is also a road from Tymovskoe to Okha, looping westwards to visit also the minor port of Pogibi on the narrow strait. The pipeline and shipping connections with the mainland, the development and problems of the natural gas and oil industries, have been noted above.

The agriculture, forestry and fishing in this part of the island are of merely local significance. 1500 ha are devoted to potatoes and vegetables but these and other foodstuffs are largely imported. There are small numbers of dairy cattle. Okha is a town of 29,700 people serving the oil industry with repair shops and building works – but is not well supplied with amenities or consumer goods. Some stress is laid on extending its attractions in these respects, as well as building a refinery and pressing on with the technical regeneration of the oil and gas industry.

Considering Sakhalin generally, it may be permissible to close on a more subjective note. The different parts of this Province are more diverse, in both ambience and spirit, than is the case in any other of the Soviet Far Eastern Provinces – or anywhere in Russia, indeed almost anywhere else in the world. A full unitary concept of planning for the Province as a whole has even yet not strongly emerged, in the face of formidable natural barriers. The north is bound up with fuel; natural gas is now additionally in prospect. Whereas the south shows still the pattern more general to the S.F.E.: lumber, minerals (though gold is less plentiful than in other areas) with fish and some furs, but agriculture capable only of providing a parlous subsistence. The west straddles, it may be said, between these two positions – in the fuel sector with its coking coal, but having forests and the rest. The centre is grossly underdeveloped and awaits better connections with the north, south and west.

The whole southern half – and the Kurile Islands which belong administratively to it – were taken over from the Japanese. The stamp of their previous development and infrastructure (railways, the now obsolescent pulp mills, much of the housing) this area still bears. Around the foundations, some Japanese aura still clings. In the whole of Siberia (though this cannot be said of Central Asia in the last century, or the Baltic and other areas more recently) there is no other territory which the Russians have taken over (as anything but an economic and social void) from actual foreign occupants. The Soviet adaptation has not in this case been brilliant.

According to a local witticism, if you say Sakhalin, the echo still answers in Japanese: Karafuto. In fact, in Sakhalin Japan lies hardly below the horizon. Such is still more the case in the Kuriles, which Japan did not renounce in the peace treaty with the Soviet Union, tending to regard their occupation as transitional, like that of Okinawa by the Americans. Politics apart, the natural complementarity of these areas – Sakhalin in particular, the whole S.F.E. to some extent – is with Japan as well as with the Soviet fatherland. Open and multilateral relations must, on natural economic grounds if no other, in the not distant future be restored, for the Maritimes and Sakhalin especially. The Japanese for their part are looking – fortunately now for business not power – in all directions beyond their own shores. One of those directions, of distinct though not predominant interest to them, is the northward. The now internationally sophisticated Soviet Union, on the other side of the Japan Sea, is naturally and substantially interested in the whole Asian Pacific; and must look to Japan and beyond.[1]

A general agreement was signed with Japan in July 1968, after protracted preliminary negotiations, for Soviet–Japanese collaboration in the development of the S.F.E. (and possibly further westwards in Siberia). It was envisaged that Japanese equipment and expertise would be drawn on to facilitate port, shipping, lumber, mining and communications development in the S.F.E. The Japanese would receive in return various products of the S.F.E. and Siberia. There were a number of continuing difficulties in the scheme, both technical and financial (especially, at first, concerning the rate of interest). At the end of 1970 the matter was still in process; reactions and discussions vary from the extremely cautious to the highly imaginative. The initial agreement of 1968 specified that Japan would export machinery and equipment worth $130 million and consumer goods worth $30 million over five years, and import 8·8 million cu. m. of Siberian timber. Subsequently a wide range of speculations developed, including ideas of Japanese assistance in extending the oil pipeline from Irkutsk to the Pacific, developing coal mining at Chul'man, natural gas and other resources.[2]

CHAPTER 11

Kamchatka and The Kuriles: Pacific Screen

THE ISLES OF MIST

THE great peninsula of Kamchatka is about 1500 km long, the chain of the Kurile Islands extends nearly 1200 km further south, enclosing to the Soviet Union the enormous sea of Okhotsk. The Kuriles, taken from Japan after the war and extending at their southern end to within a few miles of Japan's northernmost island of Hokkaido, number over a score of islands and islets, of which ten have a significant area (over 200 sq. km each). The Greater Kuriles are notably Shumshu, Atlasova, Paramushir, Onekotan, Shiashkotan, Ketoi, Simushir, Urup, Iturup and Kunashir; of the Lesser Kuriles, the only significant one is Shikotan.

The name Kurile means 'smoky'. These islands have many volcanoes, rising from smooth lower slopes and some coastal plains, while their cloudy and foggy climate also evokes the description 'smoky'. From the volcanoes and hot springs some sulphur is gathered. From the sea large numbers of fish and seals are taken, especially during their migration seasons. The population (about 2 persons per square kilometre) is less than 15,000, two-thirds of which is in the numerous small settlements, working almost entirely in the fisheries.

The Soviets divide the islands into three administrative districts – which are in Sakhalin Province, though treated here with Kamchatka – namely the North Kuriles (with a village so named, Severo-Kuril'sk, population 4400, on Paramushir), Kuril'sk (again with a village so named on Urup, of 1600 inhabitants) and the South Kuriles (similarly with a village so named, Yuzhno-Kuril'sk, of 3900 people, on the island of Kunashir). On Shikotan there is a crab-canning factory (at a

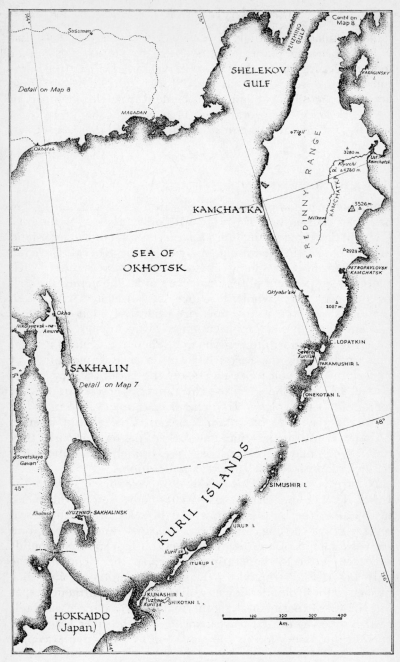

Map 9   Kamchatka and the Kuriles

village named accordingly Krabozavodsk). Severo-Kuril'sk has
a fish-processing plant; Yuzhno-Kuril'sk another, also other
food-processing and a brickworks. Podgorny village on Paramushir processes whales, as does Skalisty on Simushir. These
activities are all very slight, as is evident from the smallness of
the work force. The total sown area was 485 ha in 1965, of
which 39 were under potatoes and 122 under other vegetables.

THE GREAT PENINSULA

Kamchatka is comparatively huge, an area of 472,000 sq. km
or 15 per cent of the S.F.E.; but with only 129,000 inhabitants.
Kamchatka Province includes a large expanse of the mainland
at the root of the peninsula, designated the Koryak National
Area, also the Karagin, Komandor and other islands, which
represent 40 per cent of the Province's area, the peninsula itself
60 per cent. The whole Province is, however, virtually an
island, as overland connections are practically non-existent.

Kamchatka is very mountainous (to over 2000 m., ranges
lowering in the north to 300-600 m.). There is a Central Range;
then, paralleling the east coast an Eastern Range of lower
mountains and volcanoes marks off the central valley of the
Kamchatka river between the two ranges. The very impressive
high point is the volcano Klyuchevskaya Sopka (4750 m.). The
mainland part also has mighty ranges. Coastal and riverine
lowlands constitute less than one-third of the territory, and they
are largely marshy. Transport is extremely difficult; rural
Kamchatkans lead lives of extreme isolation.

Nature is violent. This is the only volcanic region of the
U.S.S.R. The peninsula has twenty-eight active volcanoes,
nearly all in the Eastern Range. Earthquakes are frequent and
severe, often causing tidal waves (*tsunami*) and necessitating
special methods of building construction. Hot springs abound;
they are usable for generating power. In the vicinity of the
only big city, Petropavlovsk-Kamchatski, not only are they
harnessed for urban heating as well as medical treatment in spas
but the first experimental geothermal electric station was built
in the 1960s at the Pauzhetsk springs on the river Ozernaya.
It went into operation in 1965, at 5000 kW. Another was pro-

jected at the Bolshie Banni springs with a capacity of 25,000
kW, moreover a steam heating project at Paratunka hot springs
was to serve an area of 60,000 sq. m., of which 10,000 would
constitute a hydroponic farm.

Mineral developments are also slight and experimental.
Some of the tufa and pumice near Petropavlovsk (deposits of
one billion cu. m.) are used for building. Coal, brown coal and
lignite exist in large quantities, prospected more on the west
coast (Podkager, Tigil' and Krutogorovsk) than on the east
(Korf), though actual mining is as yet only in the latter area.
Kamchatka has also the largest reserves in the U.S.S.R. of peat,
in fact exceeding all the others (White Russia, the Baltic and
Ukraine) put together, with deposits estimated at eight billion
tons; and this is mainly in the east Kamchatka depression convenient to Petropavlovsk. Petropavlovsk really has all the
situational advantages. Mercury, molybdenum and copper are
interesting possibilities. Gold began to be worked in 1964.
There is some oil along the east coast.

40 per cent of the surface of the Province is forest, representing a stock of one billion cubic metres; but much of this is
sparse-leaved upland birch not very usable as timber, and its
removal would endanger the water- and soil-holding properties
of the land. Usable conifers represent a total of 168 million
cu. m.; but again it must be said that this resource cannot easily
be greatly exploited. 80 per cent of it is larch and it is massed
in the valley of the Kamchatka river, the only area with conifers apart from some on the Penzhina river in the mainland
part of the Province; mass cutting would be deleterious. The
inhabitants of the forest regions rely greatly on the berries
(bilberries, blueberries, etc.) and mushrooms which abound
locally.

Pasture land utilisable for cattle totals 305,000 ha, a tiny
proportion of the area; and even this resource is of poor quality,
the yield of fodder-grass per hectare being 1500 to 2000 kg.
Kamchatka is truly reindeer country, having 34 million ha of
reindeer pastures, supporting herds of 180,000 head. Fisheries
are the main food base, yielding a million tons a year of fish
and crab.

The climate of Kamchatka is certainly far from gentle. It is
only slightly warmer and softer than that of Magadan. Strong

winds are frequent on the coasts and in the north; heavy snow-storms rule the winter, cloud and rain the summer. There is virtually no transport except by water, including some con-siderable rivers: the Kamchatka (619 km), the Penzhina and the Talovka.

Underpopulation and labour shortage are the other severe constraints. Before the Revolution the population was insigni-ficant in numbers and consisted almost entirely of indigenous tribes (Chukchi, Koryaks, Evenki, Itel'men). Though the in-corporation with Russia dates far back (to the end of the seventeenth century; Petropavlovsk was founded in 1740) the infiltration of Cossacks, traders and deportees was extremely slow and small. Peasants from Russia had a hard time in Kamchatka; they 'became Kamchadals', i.e. fell back to primi-tive levels and aboriginal ways of life.

In 1897, in the then boundaries, there were only 8400 people, in 1911 only 11,000; in 1923 (the late date at which Soviet power was finally secured in this remote peninsula 12,000 km from Moscow) even less (10,500). Soviet colonisation policy was, however, immediately vigorous; the 1927 population was double that of 1923, in 1939 it reached 132,700, in the early 1960s figures over 200,000 were given. In recent years the population declined.

Another cheerless aspect of Kamchatkan life is the heavy preponderance in this frontier area, unlike other parts of Russia, of males over females – except in Petropavlovsk and the surrounding Yelizovo district. Even in that metropolitan area there is a density of only three persons to the square kilometre; the average for the whole Province is only 0·5, while at the lowest (in Penzhino district) the figure is only 0·03. The popu-lation is found almost solely on the coasts and along the Kamchatka river. 80 per cent are Russians, the Ukrainians follow with 7 per cent, others from the mainland also figure, leaving the autotochthonous tribal peoples an insignificant and disappearing element, only 4 per cent of the total, most of whom are in the Koryak area in the north. Some of the last-mentioned elements are, however, nomadic and the above figures exclude migrant and temporary workers who come seasonally or on contracts.

95 per cent of the value of Kamchatka's exports (to the rest

of the Soviet Union, none go to foreign countries directly) consists of fisheries products, almost all the rest of furs. Agriculture
represents only 10 per cent of output in the Province, practically
all for local subsistence. The distribution of the small total work
force and its output is given in Table 11.1, which clearly
emphasises the preponderance of the fisheries, also the great
amount of repair work and fuel required by the severe climatic
conditions and the isolation of the Province.

Table 11.1   Industries of Kamchatka
(1963; percentages)

	Workers (numbers)	Output (value)
Fish	53	60
Other food	4	8
Repair and mechanical	11	9
Forestry and timber	10	5
Production of building materials	5	5
Others	6	5
	100	100

FISHERIES

Table 11.2 shows the Kamchatka fisheries concentrating especially on herring in the Olyutor bay in the extreme north-east
and on flatfish, the latter mainly in the Bering sea, northern
Kuriles and western Kamchatka.

Table 11.2   Fisheries, Kamchatka Province
(catch, in million metric tons, 1963)

	Bering Sea	Olyutor bay	N. Kuriles and W. Kamchatka	Eastern Kamchatka	Total
Herring	0·2	11·4	0·3	–	11·9
Plaice, flounder	5·2	–	4·3	1·5	11·0
Cod	–	–	1·3	1·1	2·5
Sea perch	0·4	–	–	0	0·4
Others	–	–	2·1	2·4	4·6
Total	5·9	11·4	8·0	5·1	30·4

It is unlikely that the plan for 1970 could be fulfilled. The
decline of salmon stocks has been serious. Other catches fluc-
tuate greatly from year to year. However, expansion has been
great in the past and future catches may be large, even if they
cannot continue expanding.

Fishing is the only aspect in which Kamchatka can claim to
be the leading Province in the U.S.S.R., having over 10 per
cent of the national catch and over one-third of that of the
S.F.E. – if account is taken of fish lifted around Kamchatka by
vessels from the Maritimes and Sakhalin. These fisheries engage
six 'floating bases' (cannery or factory vessels), about a hundred
trawlers, tens of seiners and hundreds of small boats. In 1963
there were seventeen State-enterprise groups, twenty-three
fisheries kolkhozes and two herring-processing bases (the last-
mentioned operating only seasonally).

The kolkhozes operate only coastally, up to twenty miles
offshore. They deliver their catch, which is only 10 per cent of
the total, to the processing plants; only the kolkhozes of the
Koryak National Area had managed, by the mid 1960s, to
establish a processing plant of their own. The trawlers deliver
mostly to the floating bases, only partly processing the fish
themselves. The plants ashore take a minor part – only 17 per
cent of the trawlers' catch in 1963. They work mainly in winter.
In the 1960s the trawler fleet opened up rich new grounds for
flatfish, perch and herring around the Pribylov islands and from
there to Alaska, so that recently this area has accounted for
one quarter of Kamchatka's catch. In the spring and autumn
herring seasons the Russian trawlers are busy in the Okhotsk
and Bering waters.

The State trawler fleet accounts for 40 per cent of the total
catch, the collectives for nearly 50 per cent, the big ships
('combines') for the remaining 12 per cent. Processing is increasingly concentrated in the 'floating bases', the trawlers
delivering to them and processing less themselves.

This modern industry was started in the late 1920s as a
seasonal activity of migrant workers. By the early 1930s about
fifteen up to date units had been established with canning and
salting plant for salmon, herring and crab. Cod fishing began
to develop at that time, herring from 1940; perch and flatfish
much more recently, but it is these which seem now to have the

best prospects. The progress has been very uneven. As already emphasised, salmon have greatly declined: 20,000-40,000 metric tons in the late 1920s, 60,000-80,000 in bad years and 90,000 to 150,000 in good years during 1941-57, but by the end of the 1950s the figure was down to between 20,000 and 50,000.

There is a curious feature: the bad years seem historically to have been those with uneven-numbered dates, the good years the even ones (1942, etc.). There was heavy mortality among the generations of humpbacked salmon in the even years of the last two decades. There is no space here to follow either the scientific or the lay discussions of the phenomenon. Local jesters noted that planning was inaugurated in the Soviet Union in an even year (1928) . . . but the decline is not to be taken lightly. The yield of cod also reached a maximum (14,300 metric tons); in this case in 1947, subsequently falling to between 7,000 and 10,000. The scientific evidence accepted by the Soviet authorities is that the yield of other kinds of fish is now somewhere near its maximum.

Thirty years ago or more, salmon varieties were a main part of the catch. It is to be remembered that they are caught in the rivers as well as in the open sea. Long ago, and up to about 1955, they were landed and handled to a great extent on the west coast of Kamchatka; but by 1962 the east coast was handling about 80 per cent of the total. Now that increasing returns seem to be associated especially with the flatfish and herring stocks of the north eastern waters of Kamchatka and of the Bering sea, the shift is accentuated.

Concentration of the processing activities explains the reduction in the number of plants from 32 in 1951 to 17 in 1963; and the policy was to continue this until there would be only half a dozen. Another aspect of rationalisation which is stressed is that the concentration on these plants and on the floating bases will even out the working throughout the year. In 1941, for example, a mere 2 per cent of the output was in winter (the first and fourth quarters of the year); by 1963 this proportion had been raised to 30 per cent. A third aspect is the improvement of processing techniques. As late as 1955, only 10 per cent of all the production consisted of frozen, semi- or medium-salted fish; by 1964, 65 per cent. By 1964 full-salted fish, once a high proportion, was less than 10 per cent. The proportion of less fully salted is, however, still high; much more refrigeration capacity is required.

The canning industry formerly specialised in salmon and crab; recently canned flatfish has been added. Fish-meal for fodder was increasingly produced at the main plants – at Petropavlovsk, Ust' Kamchatka, Ozernovski and Oktyabr'ski – output rising from 70 metric tons in 1953 to 500 in 1963, but the equipment is now old and continued increase depends on the fuller utilisation of waste products on board the vessels. There are no reports of significant use for fertiliser. The highest-priced product, caviar, is now scarce. In the first half of the 1960s annual output fluctuated between 300 and 2400 metric tons a year, thereafter it fell sharply. The Ust' Kamchatka, Petropavlovsk and Ozernovski plants have transferred this capacity to making vitaminised cod-liver oil. Kamchatka fisheries yielded altogether little profit till the end of the 1950s, when their modernisation began. They returned a profit of 44 million roubles in 1963; a level of prosperity which may not be greatly increased in future if the average quality of the fish stocks continues to deteriorate.

INLAND ACTIVITIES

The production of food other than fish is slight in Kamchatka. Potatoes, vegetables, dairying, forestry, on relatively modest scales, rich furs and many reindeer in the north, have long been the list of activities on the land, though poultry-keeping and fur-farming began to feature about 1954. Cattle increased in numbers by about 26 per cent between 1954 and 1963, pigs by 47 per cent, but reindeer only 3 per cent. The numbers of cattle and pigs are, however, still pitifully small (Table 11.3). The fisheries kolkhozes are conducting much reindeer and poultry-keeping, also fur-farming.

The Province provides all its own potatoes, but only 30 per cent of its needs in meat, 50 per cent in vegetables and eggs, 65 per cent in unskimmed milk; the rest must be imported from vast distances. Present long-term targets are to raise the cultivated area to 45,000 ha (more than double 1963), the cattle population to 27,000 (only about a 10 per cent increase), poultry to 430,000 (about double). The total cultivable area is, however, given as only about 200,000 ha; to take this up, many times the present population would be required, plus the corresponding 'infrastructural' provisions in housing and other basic amenities, while all types of construction are even more difficult and expensive in Kamchatka than in other parts of the Region. In 1956-65, 436 million roubles of capital investment was devoted to this Province; large State Building Trusts operate, but their work is less mechanised than in other Far Eastern Provinces and they fail to meet the needs of the scattered settlements.

Kamchatka supplies only fish and furs to the rest of the Soviet Union; it imports annually in return (at about the following quantities) coal (over 400,000 tons), timber (200,000 cu. m.), oil, cement, salt, cereals, meat and consumer goods. For every ton of cargo outwards from Kamchatka – which consists almost solely of fish – over six tons of other loads come inwards. Total inward freights are 1·3 million tons a year, half of which is coal from Sakhalin and Suchan and timber from the Maritimes and Khabarovsk.

This account makes Kamchatka seem like a poor dependent outpost of the Soviet Union. Its shortages make it seem like a land that God has overlooked, man has barely reached. However, if Kamchatka has been historically a 'frontier of desperation', it has also been one of high adventure; against the gloomy aspects must be set considerable potentials for the future. The landscape is spectacular, pleasant localities do exist, the resources are as impressive as the obstacles to their exploitation. It is therefore worth examining the terrain in more detail.

THE METROPOLITAN SOUTH-EAST

The southern half of Kamchatka is the more populated and developed part. The south-east coast must be considered first, especially Petropavlovsk and the Yelizovo district, occupying a splendid 20-km-wide space on hills on Avachinsk bay with three rivers. The Province's only motor road links the town of Petropavlovsk with Nachika to the westward, thence north to Mil'kovo with branch roads to Yelizovo, Paratunka and

Table 11.3 Agrarian activities in Kamchatka (mid-1960s)

	State Reindeer Farms	Other State Farms	Fisheries Collectives	Other Collective Farms	Other State and Co-operative	Private plots, private sector	Total
Numbers of units	5	18	20	6	–	–	49
Cultivated area: ('000 ha)							
Potatoes	–	2	–	0	2	–	4
Vegetables	–	1	–	0	0	–	1
Fodder crops	–	14	0	0	1	–	16
Total	–	17	0	0	4	–	22
Livestock: ('000 head)							
Cattle	0	15	1	1	4	4	25
Pigs	–	4	0	0	4	7	15
Horses	0	1	0	1	2	0	4
Poultry	1	163	29	3	30	8	234
Reindeer	67	–	39	48	–	16	171
Mink and foxes	–	19	6	1	–	–	26

other places, continuing to Kozyrevsk and Ust' Kamchatka.

The Provincial capital Petropavlovsk-Kamchatsky has 45 per cent of this sub-region's population, the surrounding district another 21 per cent; together they contribute half the industrial output of Kamchatka. Half the sea-freight is handled at Petropavlovsk, which is also a main fisheries centre. Both the town's fishing harbour and its main port, in the fine sheltered bay, have modern equipment. The cargo wharfs handle over a million tons a year; but the fishing port handles only 10–15 per cent of the fish of Kamchatka, the rest being taken to other processing and distribution points, though most of the vessels do not omit to call at this pleasant port even if they do not unload much there. Organisationally, in any case, this is the main base of the fishing fleets. Some splendid passenger ships maintain regular connections with Vladivostok. The airport, too, is modern and well served, though often baffled by bad and swiftly changing weather. Soviet planners consider the life and transport of Kamchatka are much too greatly concentrated on Petropavlovsk; they wish to have other centres developed, but it is not easy to see alternatives.

The Trawler and Refrigerator-ship Administration located in Petropavlovsk employs no less than 15 per cent of the work force of the Province and has more than 150 vessels, which furnish 45 per cent of Kamchatka's fish-catch, or 50 per cent of all its food production. 35 per cent of its catch is herring, 20 per cent flatfish, 30 per cent perch, 14 per cent cod. Ship-repair facilities are correspondingly adequate, but there is no ship-building.

The population of Petropavlovsk trebled between 1939 and 1959; from 1959 to 1965 it increased 40 per cent. In 1959 it held 54 per cent of the population of Kamchatka, 66 per cent in 1965. Building activity increased accordingly; Petropavlovsk's dwelling space increased 50 per cent between 1959 and 1963. There are many three-storey and some four-storey buildings. Andesite and volcanic tufa are used as materials. The building enterprises are small, but are unified in two large combines. Minor activities such as bakeries increase in proportion, but depend on imported supplies.

Even agriculturally, Petropavlovsk looms large in the Province; 60 per cent of the tiny cultivated area is in this sub-region, 44 per cent of the cattle, 9 of the 23 State farms, also an Agricultural Experiment Station. Most of this activity is in the sheltered valleys of the Avachi and Plotnikov rivers. Output per head of local population was, in 1963, 145 kg of potatoes, 62 of vegetables (cabbage, etc.). The former represents local sufficiency, the latter a heavy deficit. Similarly, only 56 per cent of the fresh milk is produced locally.

An oil-fuelled electric power plant of 70,000 kW capacity was under construction in the mid-1960s, besides the Banni geothermal plant already mentioned (the planned capacity of which was 25,000 kW for 1968, together with a pipeline delivery of heat to Petropavlovsk). There are Institutes of Fisheries and Vulcanology, Commercial, Technical, Fishery- and Sea-schools – in short, many of the facilities of a good town.

Not far away, around the Kronoki Lake (where a large hydroelectric station may ultimately be built), is a wonderful scenic area with geysers, waterfalls and a huge volcano. On the adjoining coast is a large fish-processing plant.

The Komandor Islands, though about 600 km out to the north-east, are functionally related to Petropavlovsk. These islands, populated only by about 300 Aleuts and 500 people of other races, have a 'Sea Beasts Enterprise' conserving the (now few and valuable) fur-seals which resort there in summer, also some foxes, for the restricted marketing of their pelts.

THE CENTRAL BASIN

The second sub-region is the central Kamchatka valley (administrative districts of Mil'kovo and Ust' Kamchatka). This is the main forest area with a significant proportion of larch, birches, poplar and conifers. It has been worked since 1930 in the middle reaches of the Kamchatka river, from the mouth of the Kimitin to Krasny Yar. The area has reserves of 193 million cu. m., of which 98 million is coniferous. Three-quarters of the coniferous is larch, one-quarter spruce. The possible output is nearly one million cu. m. a year, mainly larch. The old centre was Klyuchi, now Atlasovo and Kozyrevsk are more significant; together they gave 470,000 cu. m. in 1960, but only about 300,000 in 1963. Almost all of this is rafted down the

Kamchatka river; the rafts run to as large as 1000-1200 cu. m. each in springtime, but only 300-400 in autumn. There is, however, much other timber floating loose, damaging fisheries; the river bed is strewn with sunken logs.

The industry needs much reorganisation and investment. Further, the quality of the wood was never high and is falling, since the best stands have been exhausted. In the southern parts of the Region, woodlands will regrow in about seventy years, but in the severe conditions of Kamchatka restoration would take at least two centuries.

The mills at Klyuchi process about 120,000 cu. m. a year into barrels and boxes for the fisheries, also some furniture, etc.; and ship these, the location being accessible to 1000-ton vessels.

There are six State farms in this valley; four produce vegetables and milk, one raises livestock and the sixth is a fur-farm. It is notable that these have replaced a number of the former Collective farms which seem to have been hardly viable; i.e. the State may in effect be subsidising much of the agricultural effort. The best local yields per hectare are given as ten tons for potatoes and twenty for cabbages. The valley is hardly more than self-sufficient in potatoes; it produces only 52 per cent of its requirements of cabbages. Yet it has 24 per cent of the sown area of the whole Province. It has the same proportion of the cattle population, but produces enough milk for itself. The higher parts of the valley have transport difficulties; the Mill'-kovo area often sends its light rural produce to Petropavlovsk, only 100 km distant, by air.

The area around the mouth of the Kamchatka river accounts for between a quarter and a half (in different years) of the east coast's salmon catch, among other fish. Two canneries in this area account for 15-20 per cent of the Province's output of tinned goods, but the work is seasonal and the capacity half-utilised. A quarter of a million tons of cargoes pass through the port of Ust' Kamchatka every year. The exports are almost solely (120,000 tons) the products of forestry, the only other item being about 3000 tons of vegetables. The imports are largely coal, followed by various consumer goods. The river is the distribution channel; it is navigable from mid-May to the end of October. There are regular boat services, notably a passenger-launch service from Ust' Kamchatka to Kozyrevsk;

the road has to make wide deviations to avoid marshy tracts in all this area.

The port of Ust' Kamchatsk is, however, heavily tidal and is blocked by sandbars, the approach being at most four or five fathoms deep; while the shore is swampy, lacking good sites. Nevertheless a new woodworking plant was planned there in the late 1960s to use smaller timbers for making boxes for the fishing industry, of which there continues to be a serious shortage.

THE ROUGH SOUTH-WEST

The third sub-region in the order of importance is the south-west. It comprises the administrative districts of Ust' Bolsher-etsk, Sobolevo and Bystrinksi (Esso). This sub-region has 18 per cent of the population of the Province, including some indigenous Evenki, very thinly spread; there are only two con-siderable settlements, Ozernovski and Oktyabr'ski, with 5000 persons in each, and nine with populations between one and two thousand. In 1963 there were eight fisheries factories served by seven Collectives, obviously on a small scale, especially as 30 per cent of the total output came from the private sector of small isolated operators. This was the first main fishing area to be developed in Kamchatka but is now the one with the greatest problems.

In the spring-to-summer spawning period its rivers are full of young salmon, easily taken – or they used to be so. In the first half of the 1950s, 70-90 per cent of the local catch consisted of salmon; but then the sudden and serious decline set in. In the first years of the 1960s salmon declined to 15-25 per cent of the total local catch; the proportions are now plaice 48 per cent, cod 15 per cent, herring 11 per cent. In 1953 this sub-region still accounted for three-quarters of the salmon catch of the whole Province, in 1963 only one-third. Though in the latter year it still gave high yields of other kinds of fish, stocks of some of these seem to be depleted.

The whole activity is highly seasonal, chiefly because of the fish-migration. The weather is foggy or cloudy, though this coast is very little ice-bound; but the fierce equinoctial gales cut it off from the rest of the world in October-November and March-April, smash dwellings, gear and installations and erode the shoreline, while this sub-region has no man-made ports giving refuge from these onslaughts of Nature; its coastline is one of long straight sandy beaches. Fishing is by small boats using lagoons. The whole hinterland is generally marshy. Only at Ust' Bolsheretsk is there – thanks to a harbour bar – entry for vessels drawing up to about two and a half fathoms. In autumn ships have been known to beat up and down this coast for weeks unable to enter even Bolsheretsk, finally having to return to Petropavlovsk. Roads are lacking, though one may eventually connect Ozernovski (a less marshy area) with Petropavlovsk.

Electricity is limited and dear. The new Pauzhetsk plant (5000 kW) can only supply the local needs of the Ozernovski workshops, but there is some coal near Krutogorovo where an electric plant might eventually be set up to supply both Petropavlovsk and the whole south-west.

The coast is so bleak that it is almost treeless for at least 5 km inland. Agriculture is correspondingly feeble; the sub-region produces 80 per cent of its requirements of milk, but only 26 per cent of the vegetables it needs.

THE NORTH-EASTERN TUNDRA

If the south-west is such a cheerless quarter, the vast north-east is an even rougher and more primitive zone. It consists of the Tigil' and Penzhino districts of the huge Koryak National Area. This sub-region represents no less than 42 per cent of the area of Kamchatka Province, but has only 5 per cent of the population. There are trees only in the south of this tract, except for some river banks and localities in the north. The climate is extreme. The adjacent waters are icy, navigable only in summer. Fishing is very limited; except that in the area between the mouths of the Icha and Kairyuzovo rivers on the west there are crabs – in greater masses, it is said, than anywhere else in the world. Some 70 per cent of the crab-catch of the S.F.E. comes from this area of the Penzhinsk-Shelikov gulf.

45 per cent of the population are of the indigenous tribes,

preponderantly (70 per cent) Koryaks; 61 per cent of the
Koryaks live in this part of their National Area. Itel'meny represent 20 per cent, Evenki 8 per cent, Chukchi 2 per cent.
These are scattered widely in tiny settlements or nomadic
groups; the capital of this National Area, Palana, is a mere
village of 2000 people, the only other place with over 1000 is
Tigil' (1500). Collective herds of reindeer – 60 per cent of them
in the basins of the Penzhina and Talovka rivers, an area of
over 9 million ha – are the basic subsistence activity, though
some potatoes, fish and milk are produced.

In monetary terms (reindeer meat being cheap – 25-35
kopecks, or about 10-17½ p., per kilogramme – and in surplus,
but not in export demand) furs are very much the greatest
business. The north-west provides 26 per cent of the Province's
furs. The trapping and hunting are necessarily the work of
individuals, but the skins are traded through Collectives.

OUTWARDS TO THE PACIFIC

The fifth and last economic sub-region is the north-east, which
comprises the Karaginsk (Ossora) and Olyutorsk (Tilichiki)
districts of the Koryak National domain, a mountainous and
inclement area. The sea – the only means of transport – is icy
from late November to late May. The north-east has 23 per
cent of Kamchatka's area but only 8 per cent of its population.

Russian settlement is recent, following the opening of the
fishing industry, and almost entirely along the coast in settlements such as Ossora and Il'pyrski, no larger than 3500 persons.
Yet the Russians represent 83 per cent of the population (cf.
73 per cent in the Koryak National Area as a whole). The 17
per cent of aboriginal stock are 62 per cent Koryaks, 32 per
cent Chukchi, 5 per cent Evenki. This is now the key area for
fish-migrations: the Olyutor bay is the main area where the
deep-sea herring come to spawn in May and feed in August to
November; other kinds of fish at other times. Vessels from
Sakhalin and the Maritimes come to take these, as well as the
local boats. Herring now predominates (82 per cent of the
catch, in the mid-1960s).

As in the north-west, reindeer ranging over vast inland pasturages are a staple of life for the indigenous population; this sub-region has one-third of all the reindeer in the Province. Otherwise the self-sufficiency ratios are even lower than elsewhere: 80 per cent in respect of potatoes, but only 6 per cent in vegetables, 60 per cent in meat and 40 per cent in fresh milk.

Notable, however, is the fact that the only mining of coal in Kamchatka occurs in this area, where it has been worked since 1929. This is brown coal worked by open cutting right on the shore of Korf bay near Medvezhka. Reserves are reportedly some tens of millions of tons; current output is only in the order of 10,000 tons a year, though in some years 15,000-20,000 has been reached. This would seem to promise a good source of supply for the whole north-east; yet it fails to develop greatly, as the construction of handling facilities would be costly in the difficult local conditions and the work force remains limited. So the east coast still imports coal from Sakhalin; there are still no port works in Korf bay. The only other mineral is a confirmed deposit of mercury 300 km inland from the same bay, the development of which depends not only on port works but also on the construction of a road.

With this outline of the life and problems of Kamchatka, the review of the various localities of the S.F.E. is concluded. Kamchatka is evidently a difficult area for development. It offers fewer prizes in resources, presents fiercer trials and more severe obstacles than most areas. Beyond the favoured southeast coast and the central valley, the interior and the eastern and western coasts are largely inaccessible to each other, except for some air links.

It is mainly fishing – and strategic interest – that draws the Russians to concern themselves with Kamchatka and the waters around and beyond it. Kamchatka is the part of the S.F.E. which has least traffic (economically, at any rate) with other parts of the Region – and with the centre in European Russia. Specialising in fisheries, facing largely east and north, it is rather the outer Pacific screen of the S.F.E. The thrust of the Soviet fishing industry right out into the Pacific, especially into Alaskan waters, brings the U.S.S.R. into contacts with the United States. In the more immediate vicinity, the Kuriles and Southern Sakhalin are not merely practically contiguous to

Japan, they are territories recently within the Japanese Empire.
Moreover these areas and Kamchatka itself could reasonably
be considered to be within the natural economic orbit of Japan;
with objective possibilities, whatever the political demarcations,
of development in some sort of co-operation with Japan. The
sun may rise next for the S.F.E. from Japan, if it has just set
for the time being, over China.[1]

CHAPTER 12

Summary and Conclusions

THE Soviet Far East, containing resources not inferior to those of North America, is the richest of the world's remaining development areas. For that reason alone, the Soviet (or any other Russian) State would never cede it; even if immediately unprofitable, it would subsidise the S.F.E. at present for the sake of future gain. Meanwhile it is not unprofitable in itself. It yields much of the gold that places the U.S.S.R. third among the gold-mining nations and high among the gold-holding ones; furs, timber and minerals other than gold. Among the latter are not only the diamonds of Yakutia and the minerals which are now older-fashioned (iron, tin, copper, tungsten, lead, zinc, etc.) but others of vital importance in modern electronics, nuclear power and weaponry, space research and astronautics (mica, lithium, tantalum, rubidium, etc.) which are bringing a new wave of development to the S.F.E.

The Region is not, however, to be considered by itself; it is an integral and vital part of the great Eurasian pan-Russian construct, which has extended magisterially eastwards, moving its industrial and strategic centre of gravity towards Central Asia and Eastern Siberia – though continuing to centralise control in Moscow. The Major Economic Regions of Eastern and Western Siberia now contain substantial industrial bases, for the functioning and defence of which the preservation and development of the S.F.E. is essential. Geopolitically there is what might be called a watershed in Western Siberia, whence power may flow either east or west (or both).

Does Russia choose to be a Western or an Asian power? (It is still Russia: even in Soviet parlance, all Siberia and much of European Russia constitute a single *Russian* Republic, the R.S.F.S.R.) From old history, reinforced by the latter-day position of the Soviet Union as the homeland and springboard of the Communist World Revolution, the answer comes clearly that Russia will be both European and Asian and will require a Pacific seaboard as essentially as the United States does. This used to be stated in terms especially of the desire for an ice-free port. That expression smacks, however, of a bygone age of steamboat hegemony. It is no longer a question of Vladivostok as a single main base, a Singapore holding both the Asian and Indian oceans in fee. Today it is a problem of great networks and vast systems; the whole north-western quadrant of the Pacific is involved and the whole of Siberia behind it, with its mines, oilfields, metallurgy, electricity, pipelines, land and sea routes, airways, workers, scientists and all else that it contains.

To use the Marxistic formulation, on these conditions of production and relations of production a huge interacting superstructure of ideology has evolved. The matter is highly charged with subjectivity. The Russians are a white race, with a European language, a basically Western culture. (Classical Marxism is Europocentric too. The Founder had no time at all for 'Asian despotisms' where not even the preconditions for the modern class-struggle existed; in which he included Russia as well as China and India, much as the Soviets now regard Middle Africa.)[1] Chairman Mao has broken out of this intellectual constraint, forged in the Rhineland and the British Museum a century ago: establishing the equivalent (in this sphere) of an Asian Protestantism, he has set up China as the alternative homeland of Liberation, a different model.

The S.F.E. is vitally necessary to China, too, for all the reasons mentioned in the above lines; 'China' could at many points be substituted for 'Russia'. China, like Siberia, is a land with no natural frontiers of an absolute kind, except perhaps the sea. The subjectivity of the matter is far more intense for China. The Chinese claim they once possessed much of the S.F.E. and were forced or tricked out of it; it is an actual *irridenta*, to them. The Soviets helped Communist China in its early days (or made a very effective pretence of so doing), then 'withdrew the dishes in the middle of the meal' (this expression of the Peking Government ingenuously reveals, incidentally, that the providers of the feast and deciders of the menu were the Russians).[2] More basically, however, China's is a cultural nationalism; the superior civilisation of the 'Central Country', as they call themselves, has ebbed and flowed through tens of centuries, alternately resisting, overcoming and assimilating the surrounding barbarians.[3] Last but not least, this cultural energumen is now driven by a tremendous physiological force – sheer massive overpopulation, on a scale the human race has hardly experienced before (or even, perhaps, the animal or insect kingdoms). 800,000,000 people are crowded in China, increasing every year by the whole population of Canada. China must have – in a word, even if it is an unsatisfactory and evil word – *Lebensraum*. Expansion is barred (along peaceful as well as violent paths) in all other directions, but to the northward the ground looks comparatively empty and open.

The conflict is already overt; blood has been shed,[4] most of the Soviet forces are now on the Asian frontier. War in some form between Russia and China seems probable. Again, this is not just a bilateral problem. There are three Super-Powers in the world – or two, with one pending – the Soviet Union, the United States and China. The role of the United States may still be decisive, and that of the lesser powers and the third world influential, though European unification is coming too late and too clumsily, in all probability, to play the part it should. There are more pieces on the chessboard than is sometimes seen; a prime instance is Japan, recently advanced enough, industrially, technically and otherwise, to have been transformed from an isolated pawn into a new queen. The substantial moves towards Soviet–Japanese co-operation in Siberian development[5] are a tremendous portent; as large a test-case, of a new spirit and practice of Soviet openness to the rest of the world economy and polity, as the issues of Germany or of disarmament. Any further Soviet relaxations (e.g. in disarmament talks) will be keenly noted – as will any further Soviet ruthlessness (as in Hungary or Czechoslovakia, or in arming Egyptians or others).

It is not the function of this book to write what is called, in the latest jargon, a 'scenario' of the possible Sino-Soviet war, but to describe one side of the battleground, the Russian side of the river. Readers will assess for themselves the rise of Chinese and Russian nuclear weaponry, the likelihood of Moscow, given its ostensible present superiority, being tempted to strike first through the stratosphere over the heads of the masses and the red books. China's *industrial* capacity would surely be thus largely eliminated; it is a small fraction of the U.S.S.R.'s and much more localised, exposed to the seaward as well as the landward. Basic in any case might be a multitudinous influx of Chinese guerrillas and squatters. It is doubtful whether this could really be a mass success. The conditions are too bitter for newcomers – even those so inured to hardship as the Chinese. The environment can only be mastered – as the Soviets are beginning to do – by applying advanced modern technology (electricity, heavy machinery and long-distance logistics). Which the Chinese do not sufficiently have: witness the grass growing in major projects started by the Russians in China, which the Chinese were unable to complete.

The nodes of development in the S.F.E. are scattered, but fairly substantial – as the foregoing pages may have shown. In 1945, at the nadir of the war's end, 750,000 Soviet troops were quite efficiently moved from Europe to the S.F.E., whence a competent three-pronged drive was mounted to seize Manchuria. The two main thrusts were from the Chita area to Mukden and Changchun and from the Vladivostok area to Kirin and Mukden, the subsidiary one from Khabarovsk to Harbin. Unexpected problems, such as drought, were well overcome; there was refuelling from the air, various other modern logistical and tactical feats. The Japanese opposition was certainly weak; but the whole operation was poles – and technological ages – apart from the Tsarist one in Manchuria forty years earlier.[6] The Soviets have little doubt that they could repeat this success, also bring to bear the rocketry and sea-power they have developed in the subsequent quarter of a century. The Chinese, too, have performed military feats in Korea and the Himalayas. All these matters, including how to deal with guerrillas (who are an old and effective tradition in Russia, as well as China), have certainly been fully weighed by the Soviet command and people, and local preparations made.

Amalrik (1970) reckons that such a war will disintegrate the Soviet Union through the internal strains it will generate. These, especially the Ukrainian and other nationalisms, and the transport problem, would certainly be great. The Siberian railway – the extreme dependence on which has been shown above – is certainly a very vulnerable lifeline. But it is already well stocked and garrisoned; and Soviet concern must be to keep the fighting south of it. Mongolia is a good ally – standing to gain more by defeating China than (for example) Poland gained from Germany. The S.F.E. population is very predominantly Great Russian; the aborigines are (alas) no more considerable than the Red Indians of North America. There will be no upsurge of separation in the S.F.E. Amalrik may underestimate, in any case, the ability of Moscow to cope with even the strongest nationalisms (e.g. the Ukrainians, or the Czechs); witness the depressed state of Georgia since it lost the protection of Stalin. There was once a Siberian nation – the Far Eastern Republic, 1920-22 – but it sided with Moscow. And there is a distinct Siberian patriotism – but it is a Great Russian one.

The S.F.E. is strong, at least on a garrison basis – able enough to stand a siege, able also to strike into China. Some of the Russian minorities in Europe initially welcomed the Germans in 1941. Resistance grew later, as Nazi bestiality was fully demonstrated. The Chinese would encounter not even the initial welcome. The West might help Russia – even if it helped both, the Soviet Union could use materials from the rest of the world, because of its modern industry, which works on western specifications, far better than China could. The present writer is therefore sceptical of assessments giving China any close priority in basic strength, underlying the bluffs and manœuvres of the present stage. Certainly the S.F.E. is also weak, in many fundamental respects – widely illustrated in this book: the heavy dependence on long-distance supplies, the tenuous transport links and infrastructural facilities, the heavy burdens of repair and maintenance, the inefficiencies of planning, the remoteness from Moscow.

On whose side is time? China has achieved much. So have Irkutsk and Chita and Khabarovsk and Vladivostok – behind which stands European and Siberian Russia, with material strength approaching America's. The technological gap widens, however, and the Soviet Union is on the 'have' side of it. It can reach the moon and the stars; it can reach the vitals of China. Whereas, in Siberia, China can reach the tundra. Soviet Russia has fifty years, Old Russia centuries, of local experience and progress. The anticipated war could bring prolonged chaos or disruption; at best for China, little likelihood of a clear solution.

Japan is most immediately interested, and is a big factor. When all is said and done, Japan adds more to its industrial capacity, in a few years, than the whole industrial capacity of China. Japan is negotiating with the S.F.E. a systematic relationship of economic development, such as it cannot even approach with Mainland China (though it does with Taiwan), while Peking treats the Japanese (like all others) as suspect barbarians.

The economic development of Siberia is still in 'low gear', but is gathering speed; many growth points have developed in the last few years, a more substantive basis is emerging. There is confidence in Siberia, less weariness than in Moscow. The S.F.E. feels itself on the threshold of the future; at least, its prison days are over, the prospects are broadly positive. One of the last doors in the world is being unlocked; one of the last and greatest undeveloped areas opened. European Russia and Siberia have seen much progress: the S.F.E. is capable of more. It is one of the world's key areas.[7]

Notes

INTRODUCTION

1. Salisbury, 1969.
2. *The Far East and Australasia*, 1969 ff.
3. Press and radio, 24-25 April 1970.
4. Mao Tse-tung, *Selected Works*, IV 21-2; *Peking Review*, no. 36, 6 Sep 1963, p. 10, gives an account of Mao's blunt speech, which persons present state is a 'toned-down' version.
5. P. T. Etherton and H. H. Tiltman, *Manchuria: the Cockpit of Asia* (1932); O. Lattimore, *Manchuria, Cradle of Conflict* (New York, 1932).

CHAPTER I

1. D'yakonov *et al.*, 1966, p. 10.
2. Ibid., pp. 10-20.
3. Ibid.
4. *Gudok*, 12 Aug 1966.
5. J. Ericson, in *Royal United Services Institution Journal*, Sep 1970, p. 28.
6. *Economist*, 14 Oct 1970, p. 16.
7. Reuter, 24 Mar 1965.

CHAPTER 2

1. *Pravda*, 6 Sep 1969.
2. Academy of Sciences, *The West Siberian Economic Region* (1967).
3. *Sovietskaya Rossiya*, 16 Feb 1969.
4. *Literaturnaya Gazeta*, 10 Mar 1966.
5. *Komsomolskaya Pravda*, 21 June 1969.
6. R. Ivanov, in *Problems of Economics*, no. 4 (1969).
7. *Fourth Session, Geographical Society of the U.S.S.R.* (Leningrad, 1964) pp. 37-9.
8. *Ekonomicheskaya Gazeta*, no. 2 (1963).
9. *Komsomolskaya Pravda*, 16 Nov 1962.
10. *Izvestia*, 27 Sep 1963; *Komsomolskaya Pravda*, 17 and 19 June 1969.
11. *Bulletin of Siberian Branch*, no. 11 (1967) p. 9.
12. *Literaturnaya Gazeta*, 17 May 1967, pp. 12-13.
13. L. Turgeon, 1969, p. 203; T. Shabad, in *New York Times*, 21 Apr 1964.

14. *Komsomolskaya Pravda*, 6 Apr 1968.
15. *Kommunist*, no. 10 (1963).
16. *Krasnoye Znamya*, 28 Mar 1965.
17. *Sovietskaya Rossiya*, 9 Jan 1968.
18. Ibid., 16 June 1969.
19. *Izvestia*, 6 Feb 1968.
20. See *Komsomolskaya Pravda, passim*, May-Oct 1962.
21. *Sovietskaya Rossiya*, 9 Jan, 26 Sep, 16 Oct 1968.
22. *Pravda*, 24 July 1969.
23. *Komsomolskaya Pravda*, 20 July 1969; 'Our Far East', in *Agitator*, no. 3 (1969) pp. 56-8.

CHAPTER 3

1. Howe, 1968.
2. *Ekonomicheskaya Gazeta*, 19 Oct 1963.
3. *Sovietskaya Rossiya*, 22 Oct 1968.
4. *Komsomolskaya Pravda*, 19 Jan 1969.
5. *Sovietskaya Rossiya*, 26 Sep 1968.
6. Ibid., 13 June 1969.
7. Ibid., 2 Nov 1968.
8. Ibid., 20 June 1970.
9. A. A. Tsymek, *Forest-Economy Regions of the Far East* (Khabarovsk, 1969).
10. *Komsomolskaya Pravda*, 4 Nov 1969.
11. *Pravda*, 16 Feb 1969.

CHAPTER 4

1. *The Far East and Australasia*, 1969 ff.
2. Krotov *et al.*, 1963; Pokshishevski and Vorob'yov, 1968; Heller, 1932; Portisch, 1969.

CHAPTER 5

1. D'yakonov *et al.*, 1966; Pokshishevski and Vorob'yov, 1968; Heller, 1932; Portisch, 1969; St George, 1970; Shabad, 1969.

CHAPTERS 6 AND 7

1. See works cited for Chapter 5.

CHAPTER 8

1. Krotov *et al.*, 1963, and works cited for Chapter 5.

CHAPTER 9

1. D'yakonov *et al.*, 1966; St George, 1970; Shabad, 1969, p. 273.
2. See works cited for Chapters 5-7.

CHAPTER 10

1. See works cited for Chapters 5-7.
2. *Mainichi* (Tokyo), 30 July 1968; Kirby, in *The Far East and Australasia* (1969) p. 903; R. Guillain, *Japanese Challenge* (1969); Connolly, 1970.

CHAPTER 11

1. See works cited for Chapters 5-7.

CHAPTER 12

1. K. Wittfogel, *Oriental Despotism* (New York, 1957).
2. N.C.N.A., Peking, 20 Feb 1964.
3. Kirby, 1954.
4. Kirby, in *The Far East and Australasia* (1970) pp. 988-91, summarises the border conflicts; B. Heaton, in *Far Eastern Economic Review* (Hong Kong) no. 38, 19 Sep 1970, summarises latest Mongolian situation.
5. Connolly, 1970.
6. J. J. Hagerty, 'The Soviet Share in the War against Japan', *Bulletin of the Institute for Study of the U.S.S.R.* (Munich), xvii 9 (Sep 1970) 5.
7. Kirby, 1971, gives another summation.

Bibliography

THE following lists main references, with brief annotations indicating the character of each work. It is divided between works in Russian and those in other languages. The literature in Russian is extensive; in other languages material specifically on the S.F.E. – apart from brief references in more general treatments of the U.S.S.R. or 'Siberia' at large – is scanty. Many of the works cited themselves contain extensive bibliographies, which are therefore not repeated here. Place of publication is Moscow for works in Russian, London for works in English, unless otherwise specified. Most Soviet writings are 'collective', sometimes anonymous but usually with 'responsible editor(s)' named; hence the listings below as '(eds)' or 'et al.'.

IN RUSSIAN

A. D. DANILOV and B. I. ANDREYEV (eds), *Economic Regions of the U.S.S.R.*, 2nd ed. (1969). Most useful recent Soviet 'college text'; all Regions of the U.S.S.R. are concisely described.

F. V. D'YAKONOV *et al.*, *The [Soviet] Far East: An Economic-Geographical Characterisation* [*Kharakteristika*] (1966). Basic reference, Academy of Sciences of the U.S.S.R., Institute of Geography. Encyclopaedic in its coverage, to its date, though not in sequentiality, information being dispersed in the various sections of this collective work (with no index, though an excellent bibliography). See Krotov, below.

V. A. KROTOV *et al.*, *Eastern Siberia: An Economic-Geographical Characterisation* (1963). Same comments as for F. V. D'yakonov *et al.*, above. Covers (880 pages) the Buryat and Yakut Republics and Chita Province as well as areas further west, whereas D'yakonov *et al.* deal (in 494 pages) specifically with the S.F.E. Planning Region, from the Amur Province eastwards.

E. P. ORLOV and R. I. SHNIPER, *The Economic Reform and Territorial Planning* (1969). Useful discussion of implications of the current reform (introduction of 'profit' criteria) for regional planning, including indicative references to the S.F.E.

V. V. POKSHISHEVSKI and V. V. VOROB'YOV, *Moscow–Vladivostok: A Guide to the Railway* (1968). An excellent pocket-sized guide for the traveller on the Trans-Siberian, with succinct notes on all parts of the route. V. V. Pokshishevski is an eminent geographer of Siberia.

V. E. POPOV, *Economic Problems of Siberia* (1968).

BIBLIOGRAPHY 259

IN ENGLISH AND GERMAN

A. AMAL'RIK, *Will the Soviet Union Survive until 1984?* (1970). Important concise expression of unofficial critical views within the Soviet Union, with glosses by some Western contributors.

A. CHEKHOV, *The Island: a Journey to Sakhalin*, trans. by Luba and Michael Trepak; introduction by Robert Payne (New York, 1967).

J. P. COLE, *Geography of the U.S.S.R.* (1970). Concise, clear, convenient paperback.

V. CONNOLLY, *Beyond the Urals: Economic Development in Soviet Asia* (1967). Excellent analysis: the basic general reference in English. Covers Siberia and Central Asia, less specifically the S.F.E. Full bibliography.

V. CONNOLLY, 'Soviet–Japan Economic Cooperation in Siberia', in *Pacific Community* (Tokyo) II 1 (Oct 1970). Valuable summary of the background and prospects of the agreement with Japan.

R. CONQUEST, *The Great Terror* (1968).

The Far East and Australasia (1969 ff.). Useful encyclopaedic yearbook of the whole area indicated in the title. The 1969 issue included sections on 'Mongolia' by C. BAWDEN (p. 829), 'Soviet Central Asia' by G. E. WHEELER (p. 883), 'The Soviet Far East' and 'Eastern Siberia' by E. S. KIRBY (pp. 892, 896). The 1970 issue included the same sections by the same authors, updated, on pp. 915, 969, 988.

O. HELLER, *Wladi Wostok! Der Kampf um den Fernen Osten* (Berlin, 1932). Interesting vivid reportage by a European 'fellow-traveller', *c.* 1931.

D. I. HITCHCOCK JR, 'Joint Development of Siberia: Decision-making in Japanese – Soviet Relations' *Asian Survey*, XI (Mar 1971) pp. 279-300.

C. M. HOWE, *The Soviet Union* (1968). Basic contemporary geography.

E. S. KIRBY, *Introduction to the Economic History of China* (1954). Study of the dynamics of Chinese society, culture and ideology, with reference to the borderlands and relations with barbarians.

E. S. KIRBY, *Economic Development in East Asia* (1967). General survey of the whole ECAFE area, the economic background and prospects.

E. S. KIRBY, 'The Soviet Far East: A Broad View', in *International Affairs*, XLVII 1 (Jan 1971). A summary article, reassessing perspectives.

W. KOLARZ, *The Peoples of the Soviet Far East* (1954; reprinted New York, 1969). A useful account of the races and their relations, from the ethnographical and current-affairs points of view.

W. H. PARKER, *An Historical Geography of Russia* (1968). A basic work, penetratingly interpretative.

H. PORTISCH, *Also sah ich Sibirien* (Vienna, 1969). Excellent reportage.

G. ST GEORGE, *Siberia: The New Frontier* (1970). Good vivid recent reportage; closely sympathetic to the official Soviet interpretation and viewpoint.

H. E. SALISBURY, *The Coming War between Russia and China* (1969). High-level journalism, based on much local experience and travel.

T. J. SHABAD, *Basic Industrial Resources of the U.S.S.R.* (New York, 1970). A clear, expert and thorough study of the resource pattern of the whole Soviet Union, with special reference to fuels, power, minerals and industrialisation.

J. J. STEPHAN, *Sakhalin: a History* (1971).

E. THIEL, *The Soviet Far East: A Survey of its Physical and Economic Geography* (New York, 1957). Translation of German work of 1954; excellent study, details now out of date.

L. TURGEON, *The Contrasting Economies* (New York, 1969). A good comparative study of the Soviet and other economic systems.

Index

Map References for Places follow the page references. An italic number (*6*, *7*, *8* or *9*) shows which main map is concerned; the small letters following it show in which general area to look (*nw*, *ne*, *sw*, *se* or *c* (centre)). e.g. Zyryanka, the last entry, appears as *8 sw*; meaning it will be found in the south-western part of Map 8 (p. 109).

Academy of Sciences, U.S.S.R., 2, 18, 21, 154, 158, 182
Africa, xiv, 33, 77
Agriculture, xviii, (electricity in) 5, 16, 56 seq., 87, 90, 93 seq., 98 seq., 107 seq., 121 seq., 139-40, 148, 174, 185, 187, 195, 205, 209, 219, 221, 225-6, 240
Aikhal, 186, *6 nw*
Air forces, 14
Airlines, 37, 102-3, 181, 196, 210, 241
Aks'enovo, *6 se*
Alaska (U.S.A.), 1, 6, 73, 205-6, 210, *5*
Aldan (river, area, town, goldfields), 3, 4, 170, 172, 188-9, 200, *6 ne*, *7 nw*
Aleutian Islands (U.S.A.), 73
Alexandrovsk, 72, 225, *7 e*
Aliskerovo, 207, *8 ne*
Aluminium, 46-7, 98
Amal'rik, A., 252
Amazar river, town, 84, *6 se*
Ambarchik, *8 n*
Amenities, 19, 23 seq., 31, 239
America, North, xiii
America, South, xiv
Amga river, *6 ne*, *7 nw*
Amur (river, district, province), Amuria (area), xv, xvii, xviii, 3, 4, 9, 10, 16, 24, 32, 36, 40, 55, 58, 61, 64, 69, 71, 72, 73, Ch. 5, 181, *3*, *6 e*, *7 s*

Anadyr' (river, area, town, coalfield), 4, 9, 37, 207, 208 seq., *8 e*
Angara river, Angarsk, *6 sw*
Aniva, 214, 220, *7 se*
Anyui river (Great, Little), Anyuisk (town), 207, *8 ne*
Arable, 57, 90, 94, 100
Arctic, Northern Sea Route, 33, 177-8, 179-80, 191, 193, 207, 209
Argun' (river and district), xv, 83 seq., 89, 93 seq., *6 se*
Arkagala, 27, 40, 190, 204, *8 sw*
Arms, army, armed forces, xvii, 12-14, 17, 23, 212, 252
Arsen'iev, 144
Artem, 39, 160, *7 s*
Aswan Dam (Egypt), 105
Atomic power, *see* nuclear
Australia, xiv
Autarchy, 6
Ayan, *7 ne*
Ayon Island, 207, *8 ne*

Baikal (Lake), Baikalia (area), 9, 27, 46, *6 se*
Balei, 86, 88, 94, *6 se*
Batagai, 190, 191, *8 w*
Beet, 59, 61
Belogorsk, 27, 34, 52, 109, *7 sw*
Bering (Sea, Strait), Beringovski (town), 17, 75, 208 seq., 235, *5*, *8 ne*
Bestyakh, 182, *6 ne*

Bikin (town, river, coalfield), 26, 39,
116-17, 127, 143 seq., *7 s*
Bilibino, 44, 193, 207-8, *8 ne*
Bira, 121, 123, *7 sw*
Birobidzhan, 37, 57, 121, *7 sw*
Blagoveshchensk, 36, 37, 40, 54, 109
seq., *7 sw*
Bogorodskoye, 37, 72, *7 se*
Bomnak, 37, *7 nw*
Borzya (river, town and area), 82
seq., 88, *6 se*
Bosphorus, Oriental, *see* Golden
Horn (Vladivostok)
Bridges, *see* Civil Engineering
Building (industry, materials), 3, 8,
24, 34, 36, 46, 87, marble 91, 98
seq., 117, 123, 142, 195, 197, 204-
5, 218-19, 232, 235
Bukachacha, 83, 84, 86, 88, *6 se*
Bureaucracy (*see also* Planning), 6,
8, 16, 17, 69
Bureya (river, area, town), *3, 4,
7 sw*
Buryat Republic, Buryat (Mongols,
people), xviii, 13, 79 seq., 120,
6 sw

Canada, xiii, xiv, 1, 2
Canning, canneries, 74, 77, 145
Cape Town, 6
Capital, *see* Investment
Capitalism, capitalists, 2
Cement, 24, 25, 26, 29-31, 36, 151,
197, 239
Central Asia(ns), xiii, xv, xvii, 29-
30, *1 sw*
Centralisation, *see* Bureaucracy
Cereals, 29, 34, 35, 56-7, 59 seq., 86,
94 seq., 108 seq., 139-40, 145, 148,
183, 185
Character, of people, 5, 6, 8, 11-12,
84-5, 89-90, 159, 183, 186, 193,
211, 253
Chaun Bay, 206-8, *8 ne*
Chekhov (town), 217, 221, 223 seq.,
7 se
Chekhov, A. P., 10, 223-4
Chegdomyn, 129, *7 sw*

Chemicals, 55, 173, 184
Chernigovka, 151, *7 sw*
Chernyshevsk, 86, *6 se*
Cherski, 207, *8 n*
Chikoi (river, area), 87, *6 sw*
China, Chinese, xiv-xviii, 1, 2, 6,
12-14, 16, 31, 36, 40, 46, 54, 80,
84 seq., 101, 140, 153, 248, Ch.
12, *1 s, 2 sw, 4, 7 sw*
Chita (city, province), xviii, 3, 20,
46, 80 seq., 91 seq., *6 s*
Chukotia, Chukchi (peninsula; peo-
ple), Chukotsk, 3, 35, 47, 120,
205-6, 210, *8 ne*
Chul'man, 173, 189, 229, *6 e*
Chumikan, 37, *7 ne*
Civil engineering, 3, 9
Civil War, xvii, 12, 80, 84, 124, 146,
151
Climate, 3, 4, 5, 10, 27, 83, 105, 134,
138, 147, 170, 181, 183, 187, 220,
226-7, 233, 244, 246
Coal, 30-1, 33-5, 38 seq., 84, 86 seq.,
97, 108 seq., 116 seq., 135, 138,
144 seq., 154, 161, 173, 180-2,
184, 187, 190, 196, 204, 207, 209,
214 seq., 233, 239, 247
Collectivisation, Collective and
State Farms, Co-operatives, 11,
16, 56, 57, 66, 74, 152 seq., 185,
198, 199, 240
Comecon, 13
Communism, xiv
Concentration camps, *see* Prisons,
Stalin
Construction, construction industry,
see Building
Consumer goods, 28, 35, 53-4, 85,
125, 160-1, 187, 197, 218-19, 239
Copper, 47, 86
Costs, 3, 5, 27, 33, 216, 219
Cuba, 36, 54, 61
Culture; cultural aspects or facili-
ties, 85, 125, 158, 211
Czechs, Czechoslovakia, 253

Dairy produce, 54, 86
Dams, 3, 106, 175

Darasun, 85 seq., *6 s*
Deer, deerhorn (*panti*), 154, 162
Denmark, 15
Deputatski, 190-1, *8 nw*
Development, xiii, 1-2, 6, 22, Ch. 3
Diamonds, 45, 170, 172-3, 186 seq.
Distance(s), 1, 2, 5, 6, 8, 27, 59, 64, 253
Dolinsk, 72, 214, 217, 220 seq., *7 se*
Dosatui, 82, 85, 93, *6 se*
Drought, 4, 148, 166
Dygdal, *6 ne*
Dzhalinda, 106, *6 se, 7 nw*

Earthquakes, 5, 84, 232
Eastern Siberia, 29-30, 44, 57, *1 c*
Education, 16, 153-4, 158, 195, 210
Egypt, *see* Aswan Dam
Eire, 16
El'ban, *7 se*
El'dikan, 190, *8 sw*
Electricity (*see also* Hydroelectric), 5, 9, (tidal) 10, 40, 44, 92, 93, 101, 171, 174, 189, 190, 197, 201, 204, 232-3, 245
Emel'dzhak, *6 ne*
Environment, 2-3
Erosion, 8
European Russia, xvii, 1, 6, 29-31, 33, 57

Fertilisers, 9, 62, 129
Finland, 1, 15
Fish, fisheries, xviii, 9, 10, 24, 26, 30-1, 33, 49, 50, 64, 71 seq., 132 seq., 162 seq., 173, 190, 197 seq., 208, 210, 218, 221, 235 seq., 239 seq.
Floods, 3-4, 5, 9, 40, 100 seq., 146 seq.
Fluorspar, fluorite, 46, 88, 89, 93, 154
Fodder, 57, 59, 61, 94, 107 seq., 122 seq., 175, 240
Food, 25, 50, 54, 107, 122 seq., 138-40, 176 seq., 219, 235
Forced labour (*see also* Prisons), 10, 177

Forests, forestry, 1, 3, 8, 70-1, 83, 92, 104, 129, 133 seq., 165-6, 186, 204, 214, 217, 225-6, 233, 235, 242 seq.
Freight, 32, 34, 125, 156, 177-8, 180, 239
Frontier(s), xv-xvii, 11, 12-13, 17, 80 seq. (Ch. 4), Ch. 5, Ch. 6, Ch. 7, 182, 192, 210, 239, 247-8
Fruit, 36, 91, 139, 144, 233
Fuel, 38
Furs, 63-4, 83, 86, 144, 175 seq., 179, 183-4, 190, 194-5, 199, 208, 210, 240, 246

Gazimurski Zavod, 89, 93, *6 se*
Georgia, 253
Ginseng, 154, 164 seq.
Gold (goldfields, gold-mining), 44, 45, 47, 86 seq., 94 seq., 101, 170, 179, 194-5, 199 seq., 206, 207, 208 seq.
Golden Horn (Vladivostok), 154-5
Guerrillas, 12, 252
Gusino-ozersk, *6 sw*

Hawaii, 6
Hay, *see* Fodder
Heating, 3, 5, 67, 183, 188
Hot springs, *see* Spas
Housing, 21, 25, 26, 239, 241
Hsinkiang (China), xv-xvi, 12.
Hydroelectric power, 9, 38, 96, 98, 112, 188, 242

Ice (*see also* Permafrost), 3, 4-5, 10, 27, 102 seq., 109, 130, 132, 156, 207, 220, 223, 244, 246
Il'pyrski, *8 se*
Iman, 141 seq., *7 sw*
Incentives, 19 seq., 23, 208
Indigenous peoples, 16, 82, 95, 116, 128, 132, 166, 176, 194, 198, 206, 208, 210-11, 220, 234, 244-6, 253. *See also* Buryat, Chukchi, Koryak
Indigirka (river, goldfields), 47, 171-2, 178, *8 sw-nw*
Indium, 191

Industries, industrialisation, xiii, 1, 5, 46, 48, 50, 94-5, 101 seq., 119, 125 seq., 130, 160, 179, 189, 195, 219, 221, 235

Inventories, 2

Investment, 21, 24, 49, 160, 194, 203, 239

Irkutsk (city, province), 1, 27, 181, *1 s, 6 sw*

Iron, 29, 34, 45, 85, 87, 98, 105, 117, 165

Islam, xv

Isolation, 5, 6, 8, 10, 134, 189, 232, 239, 253

Israel, 16

Iturup Island, 230, *9 s*

Izvestkovskaya (station), 34, 123, *7 sw*

Japan, Japanese, xiii, xvii, 1, 2, 6, 16, 32, 36, 79, 84, 155, 210, Ch. 10, 228-9, 248, Ch. 12

Jewish Autonomous Area, xviii, 16, 57, 114 seq., 120 seq., *7 sw*

Kamchatka (peninsula, province), xviii, 3, 4, 5, 10, 25-6, 28, 33, 35, 39, 55, 59, 61-2, 64, 71, 72, 73, Ch. 11, *9 ne*

Kamenskoe, 37, *8 se*

Kangalassy, 173, 187, *6 ne*

Karaginski Island, 73, 232, *8 se*

Karymskoe, 85, *6 se*

Katangli, 215, *7 ese*

Kavalerovo, 36, *7 s*

Kazakhstan, *1 sw*

Kempendyai, 187, *6 ne*

Khabarovsk (city, province), xvii, xviii, 3, 4, 5, 16, 25, 34-6, 37, 48, 52, 54, 55, 59, 61, 67, 68, 72, Ch. 6, 124 seq., *3, 7 ese*

Khandyga, 190, 202, *6 ne, 7n, 8 sw*

Khanka, Lake, 9, 57, 58, 59, 60, 61, 64, 145 seq., *77 sw*

Khapcheranga, 83, 85 seq., *6 s*

Kharanor, 82, 84 seq., *6 se*

Khasan, 155, *7 sw*

Khilok (river, area), 88, *6 sw*

Khingan (mountains), 40, *7 sw*

Kholmsk, 214, 217, 218, 220 seq., *7 se, 9 sw*

Khor, 127, *7 c, s*

Kirensk, *6 sw*

Kirovsk, *7 sw*

Klyuchi, 242-3, *9 ne*

Kolkhoz, *see* Collectivisation

Kolyma (river, goldfields), 4, 9, 10, 40, 178, 199 seq., *8 csn*

Komandor Islands, 73, 232, 242, *8 se*

Komsomol'sk (Chukotia), 206, *8 ne*

Komsomolsk (-on-the-Amur), 9, 35, 36, 37, 45, 48, 54, 72, 128 seq., *3, 7 se*

Korea, Koreans, xv, 13, 36, 60

Korf, 247, *8 se*

Korsakov (S. Sakhalin), 72, 214, 220 seq.

Koryak (people), National District, xviii, 58, 64, 120, 245 seq., *8 se*

Krasnoarmeisk (Chukotia), 206, *8 ne*

Kunashir Island, 230, *9 sw*

Kuriles (Islands), 3, 4, 5, 23, 72, 73, 76, 213, 220, Ch. 11, *9 sw*

Kuzbas, *see* Kuznetsk

Kuznetsk (Basin, coalfield) (East Siberia), 41-2, 45, 46, 87

Labour and manpower, 16-19, 21-2, 25, 50-1, 56, 76-7, 118, 195, 234

Lakes, 5, 8

Lavrentiya, *8 ne*

Lazarev, 219, *7 e*

Lead, 86, 165

Lebanon, 16

Lena (river), Lensk (town), 168-70 seq., 178, 182, *6 sw-ne-n, 7 nw*

Leninskoe, 113, *7 sw*

Lesopil'noe, 114, *7 sw*

Lesozavodsk, 142, 146, *7 se*

Libya, 16

Livestock, 62 seq., 86, 90, 108 seq., 122 seq., 139, 170, 174, 185, 190, 219, 238, 240

Location of industries, 2, 48, 50-1

Lorries, *see* Motor vehicles
Luchegorsk, 26, 39, 50, 117, *7 s*
Lumber, see Timber

Machinery, 29, 36, 48, 50 seq., 85, 91, 110, 124, 130, 153, 160, 180, 196, 229
Magadan (city, province), 22, 25, 28, 33, 35, 36, 37, 39, 55, 59, 71, 73, 181, 190, Ch. 9, *8 s, ne, 9 ne*
Magdagachi, 34, *7 w*
Maize, 139, 148-9
Makarov, 214, 217, 220 seq., *7 se*
Management, 8
Manchuria (China), xv, xvii, 16, 153, 213, 252, *7 sw*
Manganese, 165
Manpower, *see* Labour
Manzovka, 152, *7 sw*
Mao Tse-tung, Maoism, xv-xvi, 14, 80, 109-10, 255
Maritime Province (The Maritimes) xviii, 3, 4, 5, 16, 26, 28, 36, 37, 39, 54, 55, 59, 61, 68, 71, 72, 73, 76, Ch. 7, *7 s, se*
Markha river, 186, *6 nw*
Marshes, 3, 5, 8, 9, 66, Ch. 5
Maya river, 116, *7 n*
Meat, 28, 57, 87, 90-1, 175, 183, 185, 210, 238-9
Mechanisation, 5, 27, 60-1, 110, 152, 175, 185, 200 seq., 218-19, 239
Mercury, 46, 247
Metals, 31, 33, 36, 46, 82, 89, 144
Mica, 46, 173, 191
Migration, mobility of people, 11, 18-20, 23, 25, 172, 177, 205, 219
Military, *see* Army
Milk, 56, 90, 219, 245
Mil'kovo, 37, 242, *9 ne*
Minerals, mining, 1, 3, 46, 82 seq., 94 seq., 130 seq., 188 seq., 193 seq., 206, 233
Mirny, 186-7, *6 ne*
Missiles, xvi, 12, 14, 46
Mogocha, 86 seq., *6 se*
Mogzon, *6 sw*
Molybdenum, 46, 86, 88, 96

Mongolia, Mongols, xv, 12-13, 79 seq., *1 s, 6 s*
Moscow, 6, 37
Moskal'vo (N. Sakhalin), 36, 214
Motor vehicles, 32, 36-7, 52, 180, 204
Mountains, 8, 12, 91, 132, 232
Muslims, *see* Islam, Central Asia
Myakit, *8 s*

Nakhodka, 3, 28, 36, 72, 155, *3 s, 7 s*
Natural conditions, *see* Environment
Natural gas, 38, 40, 173, 184, 209, 214 seq., 229
Navigation, 10, 32, 133, 147, 244
Navy, naval, 2, 14, 146
Nel'kan, 37, *7 ne*
Nel'ma, *7 se*
Nerchinsk, 86, *6 se*
Nerchinski Zavod, 89, 93, *6 se*
Nevel'sk, 72, 76, 218, 220 seq., *7 se*
New Economic Policy (N.E.P.), 2, 199
New Zealand, 16
Nikolaevsk (-on-the-Amur), 37, 54, 133, *7 e*
Nogliki (N. Sakhalin), 37, 215, 219, 226
Norway, 16
Novo-Kievka, Novokievsk, 37, *7 w*
Nuclear power, xvi, 44, 46, 208
Nuclear weapons, 12, 14, 251
Nyevyer, 105 seq., 181, *6 se, 7 nw*
Nyurba, 187, *6 nw*

Oats, *see* Cereals
Obluch'e, 23, *7 sw*
Oil, oilfields, 27, 29, 33, 35, 36, 38, 40 seq., 180, 209, 214 seq., 227 seq., 239
Oilseeds, 61
Oimyakhun, *8 sw*
Okha, 37, 214, 227, *7 e, 9 sw*
Okhotsk (town, sea, area), 3, 4, 10, 37, 62, 73, 134 seq. *7 ne, 8 s, 9 nw*
Oktyabrski, 37, 74, 238, 244, *9 e*
Olekma (river), Olekminsk (town) (Olyokma), 173, 181, 183 seq., *6 ne*

Ol'ga, 7 s
Olov'yannaya, 88, 6 se
Olyutor Gulf, 73, 235, 8 se
Omchak, 201, 8 sw
Omolon river, 203, 8 c
Onekotan Island, 230, 9 se
Onon river, 82, 92, 6 se
Orotukan, 204-5, 8 s
Osetrovo, 179, 6 sw
Ozernaya, 8 sw

Pacific Ocean, xiii, 2
Palana, 37, 246, 8 se
Palatka, 196, 8 s
Paper, pulp, 9, 104, 128, 129, 143, 217 seq.
Pasture, 57-9, 83, 87, 90 seq., 233
Patriotism, see Character
Penzhino, Penzhinsk Gulf, 10, 245, 8 se, 9 ne
Permafrost, 3, 83, 106 seq., 182, 183, 193, 201
Pests, 5, 152
Petropavlovsk (Kamchatka), 25, 37, 72, 73, 233, 238 seq., 9 e
Petrovsk, 45, 87, 6 se
Pevek, 206-7, 8 n
Pipelines, 32, 43, 44, 129, 196, 215, 229, 7 e
Planning, plans, xvii, 6, 7, 8, 11, 25-6, 28, 50-1, 66 seq., 76, 160, 187, 194, 196, 227, 253
Ploughing, ploughland, see Arable
Pobedino, 217, 7 se
Pogibi, 219, 7 e
Pogranichny, 7 sw
Politics, political apparatus, 16-17, 70
Pollution, 9, 171
Population, 10-11, 13, Ch. 2 (p. 15), 64, 80, 82, 87, 103, 126, 132, 140, 157, 172, 190, 194-5, 197, 205-6, 219-20, 232-3
Poronaisk, 72, 214, 217, 226, 7 se
Ports, 27-8, 48
Potatoes, xviii, 56-7, 59, 61 seq., 91, 139, 183, 198, 205, 219, 238, 240
Poultry, eggs, 56, 63, 219, 238, 240

Power (industrial), 4
Priargun'sk, 82, 86, 89, 6 se
Prices, 2
Prisons, prisoners, 10, 12, 22, 47, 86, 194
Privileges, see Incentives
Providenia, 8 ne

Radar, 10
Raichikhinsk, 31, 34-5, 39, 84, 97 seq., 110-11, 7 sw
Railways, 1, 8, 28, 32, 82 seq., 93, 104 seq., 115 seq., 202, 214-15, 219
Regions, regionalisation, xviii, 7 (Map 1), 8, 80, 194, 1.
Reindeer, 57, 58, 62-3, 87, 175, 194, 210, 240, 246-7
Repairs and maintenance, 8, 55, 196, 204, 221, 235, 253
Resources, xiv, 5-6, 249
Revolution, xvii, 12
Rice, 59 seq., 68 seq., 147 seq., 151 seq.
Rivers, 3-4, 5, 8, 9, 32, 36, 83, 102 seq., 171, 178
Roads, 36-7, 85 seq., 104, 117, 145, 165, 171, 173, 177-8, 180, 208, 209, 222, 239, 244
Rockets, see Missiles
Russian Soviet Federated Socialist Republic (R.S.F.S.R.), 6

Sakhalin (island, province), xviii, 3, 5, 8, 10, 16, 28, 33, 35, 36, 39, 40, 43-4, 55, 59, 61-2, 71, 72, 73, 76, 207, Ch. 10, 7 se, 9 sw
Salt, 36, 135, 173, 187, 198, 239
Sangor, 173, 184, 187, 6 ne, 8 w
Secrecy, 31, 45, 47, 96, 110, 121, 124, 127, 129, 137, 194
Selemdzha river, 39, 3 n, 7 cw
Severo-Kuril'sk, 230-2, 9 se
Shakhtersk, 37, 225, 7 se
Shelekhov Gulf, 10, 73, 8 se
Sherlovaya Gora, 89, 6 se
Shikotan Island, 230, 9 sw
Shilka (river, town and district), 82 seq., 94 seq., 6 se

Shimanovsk, 37, 103 seq., 7 e
Ships, shipping, 10, 25, 28, 32, 33, 36, 53, 86, 133, 155 seq., 184, 190, 216, 225
Siberia, xiii-xiv, xvii-xviii, 2, 253
Sikhote-Alin' range, 32, 144, 7 se
Silver, 86
Simushir Island, 230, 9 se
Singapore, 6
Skovorodino, 36, 103, 173, 6 e, 7 w
Sofiisk, 37, 7 c
Soils, 5, 8, 9, 126, 147, 183, 220
Sovietskaya Gavan', 27, 33, 35, 72, 114, 133 seq., 219, 7 se, 9 sw
Soya bean, 54, 57, 59 seq., 65, 108 seq., 149
Spas, 5, 145
Spassk, 26, 34, 151, 7 s
Spornoe, 204-5, 8 sw
Srednekolymsk, 8 nw
Sredni Urgal', 37, 116, 129, 135, 7 se
Sretensk (river and district), 83 seq., 6 se
Stalin, J. V., 10, 120, 177, 194, 253
Steel, 27, 45, 87
Storms, 4
Strategy, strategic considerations, xiii, xvi-xvii, 5, 12-14, 89-90, 114, 213, 247, Ch. 12
Suchan, 39, 160, 7 s
Suez (Canal), 33
Sugar, 36, 54, 61
Sungari river, 113, 7 sw
Susuman, 201-3, 205, 8 sw, 9 nw
Svobodny, 36, 37, 52, 103 seq., 7 sw
Swamps, see Marshes
Sysybasa, 6 ne, 8 sw

Taiga (forest), 5, 196
Taigonos, 203, 8 se
Tantalum, 93
Tartar Gulf, 73, 7 se
Tea, 84
Television, 26, 109
Temperament of people, see Character
Temperatures, 3, 61

Ternei, 166, 7 se
Tetyukhe, 32, 36, 72, 165-6, 7 se
Tides, tidal waves, 5, 10, 232
Tigil', 233, 245, 8 se, 9 ne
Tiksi, 178-9, 8 nw
Timber, lumber, 5, 25, 30-2, 34, 112, 127 seq., 138, 141 seq., 160, 173, 180-1, 196, 204, 207, 224 seq., 229, 239
Tin, 23, 45, 88-9, 130, 145, 165 seq., 190-1, 206
Titanium, 85
Tommot (river, town), 173, 178, 180, 6 ne
Trade, domestic, 16, 27 seq., 176, 181, 196
Trade, foreign, 31 seq., 36, 133, 137, 156, 216
Trans-Baikal(ia), xv, Ch. 4
Transport, 3, 16, 27 seq.
Trans-Siberian Railway (existing), 1, 33, 57
Trans-Siberian Railway (second, projected, northern), 96, 129, 135, 168, 189
Troitskoye, 37, 72, 129, 7 se
Trucks (lorries), see Motor vehicles
Tundra, 1, 5, 168
Tungsten, 46, 89 seq., 146
Turii Rog, 151, 7 sw
Turkestan (Chinese), see Hsinkiang
Tygda, 103, 7 w
Tymovskoe, 214, 7 se
Tyndinsk, 6 se
Tyumen' (W. Siberia), 21, 43, 216

Uda river, 7 c
Udokan, 47, 86, 96, 6 se
Uelen, 1, 210-11, 8 ne
Uglegorsk, 217, 7 se
Ukraine, Ukrainians, 16, 82, 101, 116, 172, 220, 252-3
Ulan Ude, 80, 87, 6 sw
Umal'ta, 37, 7 c
United States, see also Alaska (America, North), 8, 192
Ural (Mountains, Region), xvii, 29-30, 1 w

Urbanisation, 10-11, 80, 82, 101, 115-16, 121, 126, 150, 172, 195, 206, 209
Urgal', see Sredni Urgal'
Urup Island, 230, *9 se*
Ussuri (river, area), xv, 58, 64, 140-6, *3 s*, *7 sw*
Ussuriisk (town), 34, 55, 153-4, *7 sw*
Ust' Kamchatka, 37, 73, 76, 238, 242 seq., *9 ne*
Ust' Kut, 179, *6 sw*
Ust' Maya, *8 sw*
Ust' Nyera, 190, *8 sw*
Ust' Omchug, 205, *8 sw*
Usugli, 88, *6 se*

Vakhrushevo (E. Sakhalin), 39, 214, 216 seq.
Vanino, 35, 36, 114, 132, 134, *7 se*
Varfolomeyevka, 32, 36, 143, 152, *7 se*
Vegetables, xviii, 59, 61 seq., 91, 139, 145, 198-9, 205, 240, 245
Verkhoyansk, 179, 190-1, *8 w*
Vershino-Darasunski, 88, *6 se*
Vershino-Shakhtaminski, 88, 94, *6 se*
Vietnam, 13, 36
Vilyui (river), Vilyuisk (town), 178, *6 nw*
Vitim (river), Vitimsk (town), 96, *6 c, sw*
Vladivostok, xvii, 1, 3, 25, 34, 35, 36, 72, 138, 154 seq., *1 se*, *3*, *7 s*
Volcanoes, volcanic, 5, 232 seq.
Vyazemsk, 128, *7 c, s*

Wages, 23-5, 77

War (Second World), xiii, xvii, 11, 59
Water (supply; conservancy; water-works), 4, 93, 175, 202
Waterways, 3
Western Siberia, 29-30, 57, *1c*
Whales, whaling, xviii, 74, 156, 218
Wheat, see Cereals
White Russia(ns), Byelorussia(ns), 16, 220
Wind(s), 4, 10, 225, 233, 244
Wolfram, see Tungsten

Yagodnoe, 201, 204-5, *8 sw*
Yakut Republic, Yakutia; Yakuts (people), viii, 36, 45, 120, Ch. 8, *6 n, 8 w*
Yakutsk, 182-3, *1 ne, 6 ne, 7 nw*
Yana river, 178, *8 nw*
Yasny, *7 nw*
Yerofei Pavlovich, 105, *6 se*
Youth, young people, 11, 20, 22, 26, 70, 77, 129
Yuzhno-Kuril'sk, 230-2, *9 sw*
Yuzhno-Sakhalinsk (S. Sakhalin), 8, 37, 54, 214, 220. seq, *7 se, 9 sw*

Zakamensk, 46, 80, *6 sw*
Zambia (Africa), 16
Zavitinsk, 110, *7 sw*
Zeya, river, 9, 58, *3 nw, 4, 7 w*
Zeya (town), 37, 40, 106, *7 nw*
Zeya-Bureya area, 8, 9, 54, 57, 58, 59, 64, 100, 103, *4, 7 sw*
Zinc, 165
Zlatoust', *7 c*
Zyryanka, 181, 190, 207, *8 sw*